Critical Issues in K–12 Service-Learning

CASE STUDIES AND REFLECTIONS

Edited by Gita Gulati-Partee and William R. Finger

PUBLISHED BY THE NATIONAL SOCIETY FOR EXPERIENTIAL EDUCATION

with support from
the Corporation for National Service
the DeWitt Wallace-Reader's Digest Fund
The Hitachi Foundation

Gita Gulati-Partee and William R. Finger.
Critical Issues in K–12 Service-Learning: Case Studies and Reflections.
Raleigh, North Carolina: National Society for Experiential Education, 1996.

© Copyright 1996 by the National Society for Experiential Education, 3509 Haworth Drive, Suite 207, Raleigh, North Carolina 27609-7229, 919-787-3263.

All rights reserved. No part of this book may be reproduced in any form or by any electronic or mechanical means, including information storage and retrieval systems, without permission in writing from the publisher, except by a reviewer who may quote brief passages in a review.

International Standard Book Number (ISBN) 0-937883-16-6
Library of Congress Catalog Number 96-69730

Design and Production by Zubigraphics,
Raleigh, North Carolina

Printed in the United States of America

Foreword

AS THE NATIONAL SOCIETY FOR EXPERIENTIAL EDUCATION CELEBRATES ITS 25TH ANNIVERSARY, WE REFLECT UPON THE VARIED CONTEXTS FOR OUR GROWTH AS AN ORGANIZATION. These environments have included a range of diverse experiences with educators and practitioners. Their work, in turn, encompasses the range of experiential education approaches to teaching and learning. Interwoven throughout has been a very fundamental belief in the necessity of engaging these experiential educators in dialogue with each other for their continued professional development, and in turn, their efficacy as facilitators of active learning with students.

And so it is that this publication symbolizes the very roots upon which NSEE was founded by individuals who 25 years ago recognized the need for and power of shared dialogue and exchange in the name of authentic, lifelong learning. For NSEE this publication represents the culmination of observing, listening, discussing, and exploring some less familiar territories for us as learners—a process not that dissimilar to what students experience as they take risks to become more fully involved in their own learning through community service experiences.

It is our hope that this book serves as a resource for you to draw upon as you embark or continue on your journey, enriching your work with students, as well as colleagues in your school setting and in the community as you renew yourselves as professionals.

NSEE comes out of this process more committed than ever to be learning partners with you as we refine our understandings of service-learning and its contribution to empowering learners for the common good.

Sally Migliore
Executive Director
National Society for Experiential Education

Acknowledgments

THIS PUBLICATION IS THE CULMINATION OF A YEAR-LONG PROJECT, WHICH REPRESENTS A TRUE PARTNERSHIP BETWEEN MANY INDIVIDUALS, INSTITUTIONS, AND ORGANIZATIONS. We extend a sincere thanks to all who contributed their time, talent, and support to bring this project to fruition.

The project was conceived by Allen Wutzdorff, NSEE's former Executive Director, and Sally Migliore, former Associate Executive Director, in 1994. Through their work with high school educators who participated in NSEE's two national projects, Allen and Sally recognized the need for a different kind of publication—a volume of case studies and personal essays on critical issues in K–12 service-learning. When Sally assumed the role of Executive Director, she articulated her vision for NSEE and the field of experiential education which would be more inclusive and representative of K–12 educators and issues. Sally's leadership and vision, not to mention her late-night and weekend reading, have been invaluable to this project.

Lisa Rhoades also assisted with every phase of the project. As Project Associate with NSEE's National Initiative, Lisa had developed a special perspective on the needs and motivations of K–12 educators. Her wisdom and sensitivity helped uncover the critical issues as well as the writing talent of many novice authors.

NSEE always practices what it preaches, and in that tradition we involved two interns in this project. Donald Miller was very helpful during the earlier stages of contracting authors, organizing various processes, and making sure everyone met deadlines. Andrew E. Fisher came on board during the later stages of copy editing, fact checking, and follow-up all the way through production. He also did a wonderful job of interviewing practitioners with some unique perspectives, and writing them up in the sidebars that appear throughout the book.

Longtime NSEE member, Consultant, and friend, Robert Sigmon provided his usual guidance, insight, and passion as we evolved the vision for this book, particularly the "Community" section and the Epilogue. Robert Serow, also an NSEE member and Consultant, was very helpful with some of the more technical aspects of the book, particularly the article on program evaluation. Zubigraphics literally visualized our vision through the beautiful cover design and the book's layout which is both readable and aesthetically pleasing.

We appreciate all of the K–12 service-learning practitioners who responded to our surveys that informed the content of the book. The National Helpers Network, the National Youth Leadership Council, and the Lincoln Filene Center at Tufts University were very helpful in identifying many survey participants. We are especially grateful to the contributing authors for taking precious time to reflect on and synthesize their experiences. We were constantly amazed by their selfless honesty and generosity in sharing their experiences—revealing both successes and struggles—with others.

This project would not have been possible without the tremendous support and trust of our funders: the Corporation for National Service, the DeWitt Wallace-Reader's Digest Fund, and The Hitachi Foundation. We especially enjoyed working and learning with our Program Officers, respectively, Nancy Murphy, Andrew Fisher, and Laurie Regelbrugge. Andy and Laurie worked with us on NSEE's two national projects focusing on high school educators. They shared in our vision to disseminate the lessons learned from those projects through this publication.

And finally, we offer our deepest appreciation and gratitude to our editor, William Finger. Bill provided technical expertise that surpassed our expectations. He masterfully preserved each author's individual voice, while also unifying each piece to the central theme and purpose of the book. Bill is a father, an educator, an artist, a community activist, and a learner, and he shared all of his selves with us and with this book. He has been a partner to everyone who participated in this project, and he has become a dear friend and mentor to me.

Gita Gulati-Partee
Project Director

fifth
four
seventh
eleventh
third
ninth
eleventh
twelfth
tenth
eighth
first
kindergarten
second
sixth

Table of Contents

III Foreword

IV Acknowledgments

1 Introduction

7 ISSUE 1   COMMUNITY

9   **Opening the Dialogue Between Schools and Community**
Jennie Niles with William Finger

14 **Defining Community**
Barbara Wysocki

19 **Identifying Community Needs and Resources**
Najwa Abdul-Tawwab

23 **Designing Meaningful Projects That Meet Community Needs**
Johnny Irizarry

29 **Forming Effective Community Advisory Boards**
Joyce McSpadden

35 **Training With Community Partners**
Partricia M. Barnicle

43 ISSUE 2   INSTITUTIONAL SUPPORT

45 **Sustaining Service-Learning through Political Change**
Fritz Crabb

52 **Integrating Service-Learning into the School Culture**
Joan Braun

56 **The Essential Concrete Elements of Success**
Beverly Hiott

61 **Getting Your Own Budget**
Nancy Russ

65 **Service-Learning as Educational Reform**
Andrew Furco

69 ISSUE 3   PROGRAM MANAGEMENT

71 **Matching Students with Service Sites**
Kathy Heffron

76 **Solving Scheduling and Transportation Challenges**
Jill Artus and Ivy Diton

82 **Risk Management**
    Cynthia Hubbard

87 **Marketing Your Service-Learning Program**
    Kathy Megyeri

90 **Fundraising and Collaboration**
    Janis Fries-Martinez

97 **Evaluation Helps Programs Function Better**
    L. Richard Bradley

---

103 **ISSUE 4**   CURRICULUM INTEGRATION

105 **Integrating Service-Learning Across the Curriculum**
     Dennis Brunton

110 **Under Construction: Knowledgeable, Committed, and Active Citizens**
     Helen A. Finken

116 **Creating Interdisciplinary Connections**
     Terry Deal Reynolds

120 **Assessment—An Integral Part of Experience and Learning**
     Marilynn Cunningham

127 **Reflection Leads to Real Learning**
     Wayne Harvey

132 **The Grand Reflection: How to Bring Closure to an Open-Ended Service-Learning Course**
     Audrey Wells

---

137 **ISSUE 5**   FACULTY INVOLVEMENT

139 **A Grassroots Approach for Enlisting Faculty Support for Service-Learning**
     Linda Knicely

145 **Rewards for Faculty**
     Rosalind Chivis

149 **Training Faculty in the Principles and Practice of Service-Learning**
     Elizabeth Gibbs

153 **Involving Faculty in Reflection**
     Deborah Genzer with William Finger

158 **The Faculty Committee—An Essential Ally**
     Paula Rowe with William Finger

---

163 **ISSUE 6**   STUDENT INVOLVEMENT

165 **Coaching Students to Be Leaders**
     Lana Borders Hollinger

171 **Recruitment and Diversity**
Lori Ebbighausen and Jennifer Batson

176 **Parents as Partners in Youth Programming**
Brenda Cowan

182 **Student Preparation—The First Step to Effective Learning**
Steve Zimmer

190 **How Do You Assess Service-Learning?**
Anne Purdy

196 **Recognition and Rewards—Stepping Stones for Good Citizenship**
Marianna McKeown

201 **ISSUE 7** RENEWAL

203 **Networking—A Path for Teacher Renewal**
Elizabeth Gibbs

207 **Consulting with Peers—An Exchange for Mutual Renewal**
Marilynn Cunningham

212 **Constructivist Professional Development**
Louise Giugliano and Jean di Sabatino

216 **Professional Renewal Through Reflection and Celebration**
Elizabeth Fugazzi

223 EPILOGUE

225 **Community Partnerships in Service-Based Experiential Learning**
Robert L. Sigmon

231 APPENDICES

233 Services and Publications of the National Society for Experiential Education

235 Other Resource Organizations for K–12 Experiential Education

Introduction

APPROXIMATELY FIVE YEARS AGO, THE NATIONAL SOCIETY FOR EXPERIENTIAL EDUCATION (NSEE) WAS AFFORDED TWO WONDERFUL OPPORTUNITIES to both contribute to and learn from the work of high school service-learning and internship program directors and faculty. The DeWitt Wallace-Reader's Digest Fund and The Hitachi Foundation funded two national projects whose goals were to strengthen and sustain service-learning and internships by integrating them more fully into the cultures, missions, and curricula of high schools.

BY **GITA GULATI-PARTEE, SALLY MIGLIORE,** AND **LISA RHOADES**

It is now five years later and we have practiced what we preach: we have stepped back from our daily work with these projects and reflected upon what we as an organization have learned through our rich and varied experiences with hundreds of high schools across the country. Five major lessons have emerged:

- teachers need to be active participants in a professional community for their own personal renewal and professional development;

- experiential educators are professionals who need continuous opportunities to reflect on their work, refine it, experiment with different approaches, assess the outcomes, and share their learning with others in the field—all part of a continuous process of growth for improved practice;

- educators need to be engaged with the broad spectrum of interests in service-learning as a tool for better teaching and learning, student leadership, and community collaboration;

- schools and communities need a wealth of creative approaches to develop or strengthen service-learning; while there are unifying principles of good practice, no one program model will fit the needs of every context or setting; and

- teachers need to be engaged with students in new roles as mentors, guides, and facilitators of student learning; this is what sustains educators, in schools and in our communities, who believe in the efficacy of service-learning as an approach to teaching and learning.

The case studies, first-hand accounts, and personal stories in this book capture the lessons we learned through our two national projects with high school educators and practitioners. The writers represent rural, urban, and suburban settings; public and private schools as well as community-based organizations; elementary, middle, and high schools; diverse student populations and communities; and various service-learning models.

Service-learning has grown significantly over the past several years. In fact, what was once an unknown term even in educational circles is now a field unto itself, and is cited in major newspaper and magazine articles about its connection to other movements in educational reform, responsible citizenship, and social change. With this explosion of interest and activity came an array of printed documents: definitions, principles of best practice, and program start-up guides and manuals.

As the service-learning movement was maturing, we asked ourselves and service-learning educators what type of resource was needed—what would honor your developing expertise and, at the same time, provide a guiding light for possible next steps to take on the path toward sustaining service-learning in the myriad settings in which you work?

Sketches of the book began to emerge as we engaged in conversations with you, our colleagues. We needed to create a book that you can use to take service-learning to its next stage of development in your setting. What we experienced and heard was that certain issues emerge at various points along the continuum of growth of your program or class. These issues often present themselves as challenges or critical junctures. From our experiences working with experiential educators over the past two decades, we knew that the most salient ideas and practical strategies for addressing these challenges would come from you and your peers.

It is time for all of us who believe in the efficacy of service-learning to step back and think a bit more about our collective experiences in this field. How do these case studies and vignettes speak to you? How can the stories embedded in these chapters connect with your stories about your work and how you would like to see it grow?

THE PROCESS The goals of this project were twofold: 1) to publish a useful resource for the field, and 2) to provide an opportunity for K–12 educators to reflect on their experiences and advance their own leadership through the publishing process. Participating in this project was an acknowledgment of their professionalism and the value of their experiences. By addressing practitioners' needs and critical issues, we wanted this book to be useful and applicable to the range of expertise in the field—for programs at the start-up, expansion, and sustaining stages.

From our 25 years of experience, we recognized that the best way to identify the critical issues that would be covered in this book was to survey the field. As practitioners in the field know, service-learning is not defined by only one model, and thus the context, circumstances, language, and dynamics are unique to each program and setting. With this in mind, we designed a survey with open-ended questions—we anticipated that this format would be a challenge for us during data analysis, but it ensured that we would receive the most authentic information. We sent the survey to our K–12 members and extended network, as well as to members of collaborating organizations working in K–12 service-learning.

Through the surveys, we identified seven broad issues that are critical to sustaining service-learning. The first six issues, correlating to the first six sections, represent the range of stakeholders and arenas that service-learning practitioners engage in their work: Community, Institutional Support, Program Management, Curriculum Integration, Faculty Involvement, and Student Involvement. The seventh issue, "Renewal," evolved from the "time constraints" and "burn-out" issues reflected on the surveys. While the first six issues focus on enhancing the service-learning experience for students, "Renewal" focuses on the professional's needs. Although we cannot create more time in the day, educators must be able to form networks, find support from their peers, and take advantage of opportunities for reflection in order to sustain themselves. These personal processes, in turn, have an impact on educators' schools, programs, and students.

The surveys also uncovered more specific aspects within each broad issue. These specific topics are covered in the individual case studies and essays. The process, at every stage, was organic, with topics continuing to evolve as the articles were being written. For example, we had originally thought we would include an article on identifying service-learning sites. But this issue was covered indirectly in several other articles, from a variety of perspectives that could not be captured in only one article. On the other hand, we found the issues of reflection and assessment to be so large and complex that they required two articles on each topic to thoroughly explore their nuances. Interspersed throughout the book are short "sidebars" that feature additional perspectives. In addition, many of the authors included sample forms, rubrics, charts, or graphics to enhance the concepts in their articles.

In general, each article reflects the experiences of one or two professionals addressing one specific issue or challenge. These are not program profiles. Rather, the idea was to take one issue, provide a clear definition or explanation for it in the context of a particular program, and uncover successful strategies to address the issue. In some cases, the articles took the form of traditional case studies, focusing on one example from start to finish. In other cases, the authors offered more general reflections on a variety of experiences around a specific issue they had faced in their careers. Regardless of the structure of the articles, the authors' individual experiences represent universal principles that can be adapted for any program model or setting.

In presenting their "lessons learned" to other practitioners, we encouraged the authors to reflect on challenges they were *not* able to overcome, as well as those they had conquered. As painful as they may be, some of our most powerful lessons emerge from those "unsuccessful" experiences. Many authors bravely acknowledged their own mistakes as well as the strengths of others in conveying these experiences.

Our project team consisted of three NSEE staff members who had experience with K–12 service-learning programs through the two national projects. We also worked with a professional editor, experienced consultants and advisors, and two college interns. Some of the contributing authors have been long-time members of NSEE or were involved in the two national projects. About half were identified through the survey process.

In addition to reflecting a diversity of institutional settings and program models, the writers also had varying levels of experience in writing for a publication. And so this process became a professional development opportunity for them as well. We recognize that the demands on K–12 educators are tremendous, and they are not often provided structured opportunities to sit down and reflect on their work, synthesize their experiences, and share them in writing with others.

Moreover, there are precious few venues or rewards for K–12 publishing. Many of the contributing authors commented on the growth, personal as well as professional, that they experienced by participating in this project.

While the articles have been edited, they do reflect the authors' unique voices. As a result, there are a variety of ways that the authors have chosen to deal with and share their stories.

THE SECTIONS Each section focuses on one critical issue, and includes four to six articles on more specific topics.

ISSUE 1— COMMUNITY Service-learning provides opportunities for educational institutions and community-based organizations to form meaningful, mutual partnerships. Doing so effectively requires all parties to be good listeners and learners, understand each other's goals, and work together through planning, implementation, evaluation, and celebration.

ISSUE 2—INSTITUTIONAL SUPPORT Even with the hard work and commitment of individual teachers or community members, service-learning will have limited growth without institutional support. Service-learning practitioners need the support and commitment of leaders at the school, district, and state levels. Institutional support provides the guarantee that service-learning programs are valued and will not be cut arbitrarily due to staff changes, budget limitations, or political ebbs and flows.

ISSUE 3— PROGRAM MANAGEMENT New and experienced practitioners alike need assistance in the "nuts and bolts" of administering service-learning programs. Effective program management is the key to meaningful and productive service-learning experiences for students, teachers, and the community.

ISSUE 4— CURRICULUM INTEGRATION For service-learning to transcend volunteerism or community service, it must be integrated into the curriculum. Only then will teachers, administrators, policy makers, parents, and students recognize service-learning as a legitimate and effective teaching method.

ISSUE 5—FACULTY INVOLVEMENT Often, it takes one dedicated and innovative individual to initiate service-learning. But educators cannot sustain themselves and their programs without the support and assistance of their colleagues. Faculty who are involved in service-learning can enhance their own professional and leadership development while helping to ensure long-term success for the program.

ISSUE 6— STUDENT INVOLVEMENT Student learning is at the heart of the educational process and teachers' work. Service-learning allows students a unique opportunity to take a more active role in their own learning, while making meaningful contributions to their communities.

ISSUE 7— RENEWAL In addition to their myriad responsibilities and concerns, service-learning practitioners must focus on their own personal and professional needs in order to sustain their interest, energy, and creativity. Service-learning provides opportunities for educators to renew their commitment to effective and innovative teaching and learning.

These seven sections are followed by an Epilogue, written by Robert Sigmon. In it, he challenges readers to deepen their thinking about the power and impact of service-learning and the necessity of forming meaningful, authentic school and community partnerships.

The book closes with further information about NSEE's services and a list of other organizations helpful to K–12 experiential educators and learners.

Community

issue 1

Service-learning provides opportunities for educational institutions and community-based organizations to form meaningful, mutual partnerships. Doing so effectively requires all parties to be good listeners and learners, understand each other's goals, and work together through planning, implementation, evaluation, and celebration.

JENNIE NILES opens the dialogue with a look at why and how authentic partnerships are formed.

BARBARA WYSOCKI shares her experiences in defining and redefining "community."

NAJWA ABDUL-TAWWAB explores strategies for identifying a community's needs and resources.

JOHNNY IRIZARRY demonstrates ways to design meaningful projects that meet community as well as student needs.

JOYCE MCSPADDEN shares her success strategies for organizing effective and supportive community advisory boards.

PATRICIA BARNICLE ponders how service-learning partners mutually train each other.

Opening the Dialogue Between Schools and Community

CREATING TRUE PARTNERSHIPS BETWEEN SCHOOLS AND COMMUNITY IS A CHALLENGE. At this point in our society, most community agencies do not see themselves as educators. They seek volunteers for their projects, not students. Likewise, most schools do not see their mission as providing services to the community, even though some of the most powerful learning can take place through such service.

BY JENNIE NILES WITH WILLIAM FINGER

Decision-making structures set up in an equitable way, with basic respect for each of the partners involved, can fundamentally change the way communities work.

Developing a true dialogue between a school and a community group requires the people working at the community agency to see themselves as educators, and the school staff and students to think of what they do as providing some meaningful services. Community agencies can take on some of the responsibilities of educators, and schools can take on part of the work of agencies. Schools can help with logistics, interpersonal skills, and other services, not just the intellectual, cognitive aspects; agencies can address some of the cognitive needs of students.

Combining the resources of community agencies and schools has been a powerful experience for us in Lawrence, Massachusetts, a city of 63,000, over 40 percent of whom are Spanish speaking. It has taken a great deal of planning, good strokes of luck, and dedication from many people, even to have small projects be successful. But we have found that a true dialogue between schools and community groups can be established. These partnerships have developed much like a solid, interpersonal relationship. There is a formality in the beginning, and you have to work on basic aspects of the relationship—identifying biases and assumptions, questioning them. This is the perspective at the core of service-learning. This type of education asks a lot of students, so people can understand many different perspectives.

ADULT LEARNING PROJECT We were able to develop a service-learning partnership in Lawrence with three committed partners: Lawrence High School, the Adult Learning Center, and Phillips Academy, where I was a biology teacher and the service-learning coordinator. Lawrence High has about 2,000 students, 85 percent of them low income and 85 percent Hispanic. It has developed partnerships with several area private schools and colleges in recent years, offering students advanced courses and other opportunities. The Adult Learning Center is a nonprofit agency, and a branch of the Lawrence Public Schools, that focuses on adult literacy, English as a foreign language, and high school equivalency preparation and testing (GED). Phillips Academy is an independent boarding and day school with 1,200 students in grades 9–12 and a teaching faculty of more than 200. More than 200 years old, it has vast resources compared to either Lawrence High or the Adult Learning Center.

This project, like many true partnerships, evolved through several paths. Phillips

Academy and Lawrence High have a 20-year history of various partnerships, including a residential program where Lawrence High students live on our campus for a term. The Community Service Program at Phillips, now in its 10th year, sponsors more than 40 ongoing projects and special events in conjunction with some 20 service agencies in the area, involving about 800 students a year.

Planning for the Adult Learning Project began in the spring of 1994, more than a year before it was implemented. Our community service office sponsored a series of brown bag lunches on service-learning with the language departments, which was the spawning ground for this and two other community-based learning projects. Dr. Margarita Curtis, a native of Colombia and chair of our Spanish department, had dreamed of engaging her advanced students with the Latino community in Lawrence. She and I began brainstorming about various types of projects. We knew that the equity relationship had to be obvious and real from the beginning of the project, and we knew that we wanted to involve Lawrence High students. We started working to find interested faculty at Lawrence High and to discuss possible projects with all of our community contacts. We imagined 10 different possible projects, depending on the agency, and didn't make any promises about working with any particular agency. Dr. Curtis put a course request in the catalogue for the next year, and I organized about five meetings with various agencies.

A negotiation about what is appropriate from each partner is needed, so that each shoulders an equitable portion of the commitment to the project.

During the summer, the community piece fell into place. Through a separate project, two Phillips Academy students had gotten more involved in the Latino community. They were working on a voter education and registration project, which led them to the Adult Learning Center. The students learned that illiteracy affected voting issues. These students and Dr. Curtis were having parallel conversations with the Adult Learning Center about citizenship issues. This agency expressed an interest in our project, and so our three-way conversation began—between Phillips Academy, Lawrence High, and the Adult Learning Center.

Over the fall, the details of the course evolved. The Adult Learning Center needed help teaching essay writing skills for the Spanish GED. The advanced Spanish students needed opportunities to use the language, learn more idiomatic speaking, and understand the structure of the language. Speaking only in Spanish, the students would work in pairs, one from each school, helping the adults to write essays on assigned topics, in preparation for the writing section of the GED test. In addition, Dr. Curtis met with the adult learners to provide more formal instruction.

During the first course, in the spring of 1995, the class met one day a week at a room in the public library, which is near Lawrence High. In the spring of 1996, the second year of the course, the class began meeting twice a week. The Phillips students met a third time with Dr. Curtis, although the Lawrence students were not able to attend that class. Dr. Curtis was the project coordinator and supervised each class at the library. The Lawrence High advanced Spanish teacher did not have the flexibility to leave the building for this project, but she did help with other co-curricular projects and field trips. She also was committed to the project and supported it among the Lawrence students and administration.

DIALOGUE EXPANDS LEARNING "On the way back from the class, a student told me she had spoken more Spanish in the last hour with her adult than she had spoken all of the winter trimester," says Dr. Curtis. While speaking that much Spanish was not a challenge for the students, the students also had to explain the structure of the language and had to work effectively with their high school counterpart. "But the most difficult aspect of the project for each high school tutor is how to motivate the adult with whom they work to return for the next class," says Dr. Curtis. "The students take it personally when 'their' adult doesn't arrive."

Elizabeth, one of the Phillips Academy students involved in the project, is a native Spanish speaker from New York City, so the fluency wasn't difficult. But the class pushed her in many new directions. "It really used all of my Spanish skills because I didn't just have to explain what the right grammatical answer was, but *why* it was that way. I had to become her teacher, and as such, be able to explain the same thing in multiple ways, logically. How could she remember all the grammar and sentence structure if I just said whatever was on the top of my head?"

Elizabeth knew when she was doing a good job, regardless of what grade she got in the course. "If we did a good job, our adult understood more about writing and grammar. We didn't have to take a test or get a grade to know how we were doing," she explains. "We all worked together, contributing different teaching ideas, sharing personal experiences, cooperating in every way. It was a whole different experience that I hadn't gotten in a regular classroom."

During the class, Dr. Curtis moved from table to table, helping the groups that got stuck. She encouraged the groups of three to help each other as well. The writing assignments were on current topics, often controversial, such as the death penalty, feminism, and the importance of sports in society. The GED students wrote weekly papers to practice their writing skills. The nature of the work prompted friendships, not just teacher-student relationships.

"The adults share their spoken language with us, while we share our knowledge of writing and grammar," explains Colleen, another Phillips Academy student. "Not only do we share information, but we also share stories about ourselves and our families. Most of us have been able to get to know at least one of the adults rather well."

Colleen got to know an adult, Marina. "I have talked to Marina about her four children, and she's asked me about my year in Spain," says Colleen, who recalls their interactions being formal at first. "But by the end of the term, we had long conversations that were great."

The students learned things that went far beyond skills related to the Spanish language. "I learned that I can't assume anything," says Colleen. "Since my life is centered around school, it never occurred to me that Marina wouldn't know where a sentence ends or that she would have trouble finding time to complete a short assignment." Marina is raising four sons by herself. "Her family is both the reason she is taking the class—to show her children how important education is—and the reason she occasionally doesn't finish her homework. I don't know how she does it."

The learning process went beyond the students. The staff at the Adult Learning Center also found the course a valuable approach to meeting their goals of adult literacy and more GED graduates. Terry Martin, who works at the Adult Learning Center, helps recruit the adults for the class, which includes an orientation, a discussion of the adults' goals, whether this course is right for them, and an explanation of the course. This spring 45 adults completed applications; more than 20 stayed for a week or more. By the sixth class, however, only eight adults remained. Several of those who dropped out mentioned the rigor and demands of the course, which were more than they wanted or could fit into their schedules. Others needed child care.

"It's wonderful to bring the two ages together, the adults and the high school students," says Terry. "They share personal experiences. It's a unique opportunity for such an exchange to take place." Terry and her colleague, Juan Cruz, want the project to continue and look forward to continued improvements each year. They hope that child care can be provided, which they think would help with attendance. They also hope that the time can be changed. Currently, the class meets at mid-day to accommodate the schedules of the high school students, but this is a difficult time for many of the adults. They also hope to have a graduation ceremony for the adults with certificates of completion, since the course is so demanding.

NEW MODEL FOR SOCIETY The project with the Adult Learning Center, as well as other community partnerships, involve many challenges for us at Phillips Academy. There are obvious differences in the three partners involved in this specific project—students in a prestigious prep school, students from an urban public high school, and adults trying to earn their high school equivalency in Spanish. If Phillips Academy shouldered all of the responsibilities or made all of the decisions, then it would not have been a true partnership. On the other hand, an equal amount of money does not have to come from each place. A negotiation about what is appropriate from each partner is needed, so that each shoulders an equitable portion of the commitment to the project.

In our case, Phillips had resources to offer, including my time as a paid staff person. Lawrence High couldn't put aside an equal amount of resources but did come with an equal commitment including their students. The Adult Learning Center offered the opportunity for our students to work with Spanish-speaking adults, and it recruited and prepared the adults for the class.

When these participants come into this Spanish GED tutoring project, they do not come only as individuals—as Dr. Curtis, Colleen, Elizabeth, and Marina. People come with a history, an ethnic and class identity, a life experience, a practical situation, and an institutional connection. As these individuals gather, there are biases and images that exist. But these cannot be the operating forces if a true partnership is to develop. The question in a true partnership is not who has the clout but rather, "Who has what skills and commitment?" People need to understand what skills each person and institution brings to the table. Decision-making structures set up in an equitable way, with basic respect for each of the partners involved, can fundamentally change the way communities work. That kind of model is not found in many places in our society. Putting emphasis on this model of an equitable decision-making structure can change communities one small step at a time.

We are attempting to involve students as much as possible in the development of and participation in such models. In contrast to being in a four-walled classroom, where the teacher has all the answers, this type of teaching approach changes the classroom dynamics. The students saw Dr. Curtis learning on her feet, reacting to the many situations that arose during the teaching sessions at the library. They also came to learn about aspects of the community, through people like Marina, that they had never experienced first-hand. They came to know each other as people with skills and experiences that they could share, which helped break down stereotypes and biases.

By creating such partnerships, we're creating structures through which individuals and the institutions they represent interact in new ways. Creating true partnerships between schools and the community offers a model for solving problems that students, hopefully, will take with them as they grow through adulthood.

Jennie Niles was the Director of Community Service at Phillips Academy in Andover, Massachusetts. She was also a Fellow in NSEE's Leadership Development Program, funded by the DeWitt Wallace-Reader's Digest Fund. Jennie is now attending graduate school, focusing on the development of school and community partnerships.

Defining Community

BROADENING THE CONCEPT OF COMMUNITY BEYOND THE OBVIOUS CONSTITUENCIES OF THE SCHOOL CAN HAVE A LASTING IMPRESSION ON STUDENTS, TEACHERS, AND THE LOCAL COMMUNITY. In the Urbana, Illinois, high school were I teach, for example, many of the students in our service-learning project had never been in the predominately African American neighborhood that was only half a mile from our school. Through an oral history project with a quilting group in that neighborhood, our high school students got to know the residents and their neighborhood. Moreover, the mostly white students and the African American quilters jointly produced a cassette guide to accompany a quilt exhibit that was part of a larger community event. The interaction between the students and the service site was a dynamic process with an impact that spread beyond the direct interaction between the two groups.

BY **BARBARA WYSOCKI**

...I attempt to make the definition of community as broad as possible.

Community is "a capacity for relatedness within individuals—relatedness not only to people but to events in history, to nature, to the world of ideas, and yes, to things of the spirit," explains Parker Palmer, a teacher and writer about public life. This definition can apply to any service-learning project that attempts to link learning with the broader community. Incorporating the historical roots of the subject, whether it involves an environmental issue or a local history project, can bring the community connection to life.

In the past 10 years, a colleague and I have developed and taught a service-learning course for seniors at University High School. This course, titled Social Advocacy: History, Theory, and Practice, involved students in studying serious social issues through volunteering at local social agencies and by hearing the perspectives of agency personnel, government officials, and those people struggling with unemployment, abuse, aging, and homelessness. Three years ago, changes in program goals challenged me to develop a service-learning component within an existing course and at a lower grade level. The biggest challenge has been defining community.

BEYOND OUR BUILDING University High School offers a five-year curriculum for its 280 students. The first grade level, which we call subfreshman, is comprised of 7th- and 8th-grade students. As they come together to form this class, they are also beginning a rigorous academic program in math, history, English, and a foreign language. The subfreshman history offering is called Ancient Cultures and History. The opening chapter of the text offers a discussion of what history is and how history is put together. While students can and do give intellectual assent to the discourse, nothing less than a real experience of history making drives home the importance of how history comes to be. If service-learning was logical anywhere in the subfreshman course, it would be in conjunction with this unit.

An oral history project seemed to address two vital issues. It would provide the students with a hands-on experience of history, and would offer an opportunity to interact with the community in a way that offered service and rich, meaningful learning. Since there would be a different topic each year, each project would allow us to redefine the community with which we would work. Three projects have been useful in taking our learning community beyond our own classroom.

To determine what special events or projects would lend themselves to student involvement, I began to assess the networks with which I was already involved: my church, the University of Illinois, United Way, League of Women Voters, and, most recently, a Black History Committee. At a regular meeting of the Black History Committee, an announcement was made about a traveling African American quilt exhibit that was scheduled to open in our community in about six months. The Committee brainstormed some possibilities to expand the exhibit and to highlight the talents and treasures of local quilters in our African American community. After some discussion, all agreed that the museum should feature local quilts with the traveling show and tell stories of these quilters through a cassette guide available to visitors and patrons of the exhibits. Our students would largely be responsible for the cassette guide.

University High School does not have a significant African American student population. The low visibility of this group on our campus, I felt, should not preclude our learning about their rich cultural heritage nor appreciating the contributions of African Americans in Champaign-Urbana. In fact, developing a service-learning unit precisely because we are unable to draw on our own resources was a terrific way to expand our horizons and extend the definition of community beyond the limits of the school building.

The preparations in the classroom began in earnest. The students learned about quilting styles and techniques and read stories where quilts figured prominently. I encouraged students to bring their own family quilts to class to show and relate the stories behind them. The manager of a local community radio station came to class and instructed the students on how to interview, handle equipment, and edit tape. While the classroom work proceeded, I arranged for each quilter to be interviewed by a team of six students, set up the schedule, and organized parents to transport the students to the senior center where the interviews would take place. For most of the students, it was the first time they had been in this neighborhood, and that experience, too, gave me an opportunity to raise issues of social and cultural isolation within the borders of a city.

The final step was editing nearly twelve hours of tape into a nine-minute cassette. Now our classroom was at the radio studio where we played and replayed the interviews, selected the best and best told stories, and mixed the segments with music and narration. For me, this was a real learning experience as I had never experienced this process and could not envision the final product. The piles of tape all over the floor were not very reassuring!

The opening of the show finally arrived and featured a reception that brought together the students, their parents, the quilters, community leaders, and the press. The combination of the bright colored quilts on the wall and the soft voices telling very personal and intimate family stories was a very moving and artful moment. It was also an opportunity to celebrate a very successful collaboration between the students and women who felt that their love and talent "was nothin' special."

The second project we did—interviews with family members and survivors of the Holocaust—offered a real contrast. The school does have a number of Jewish students, but I had no direct connection with any Jewish organizations. I approached the Jewish community of East Central Illinois to arrange for my students to hear the stories of survivors, including how and why they resumed their lives in East Central Illinois. The fact that a survivors' group continues to exist in the Midwest, and the extent of their work, was indeed a learning experience for me as I got to know more of the members and their reasons for remaining active. The English classes helped prepare for these interviews, since *The Diary of Anne Frank* was required reading in their curriculum. I supplemented with documentaries, two of which were produced by our local public television station. The students edited the interviews with the help of our local public radio station. The tapes aired on Holocaust Remembrance Day in late April.

Since 1996 is University High School's 75th anniversary, the focus of our current oral histories is the school's alumni, with at least one representative from each of the school's decades. One could argue that this topic is more in-house and lacks the community dimension of previous years. These interviews, in fact, helped students to see their school as much more than a haven for a good education, but rather as an integral part of their community. The students have seen how those alums in the local area have contributed to the community as developers, teachers, doctors, and elected public officials.

In each of these cases, defining community occurred on at least two levels. First, the group of people interviewed extended our learning community in various ways. In the case of the quilters, the walls of the school stretched to encompass a group of people who were in the community but not really part of our consciousness. The Holocaust survivors and the alums expanded the consciousness of our students in ways that books could not do. Second, community is the audience which benefits from the end product of the interviews. Museum visitors and a radio audience are certainly legitimate communities to serve through this type of project. In addition, if tapes can be donated to a local historical society or archives, the service goes beyond a particular time and purpose. In any event, I attempt to make the definition of community as broad as possible.

STIMULATING LIFE-LONG LEARNING To engage the students in this kind of service-learning really requires a knowledge and awareness of local resources and opportunities. Membership in or contact with organizations such as League of Women Voters or United Way is a terrific way to establish personal connections and to tune in to discourse beyond the school that could lead to an oral history topic.

This type of project also requires tremendous preparation and timing. Students need to be comfortable and knowledgeable both with the topic and the methodology of successful interviewing. To involve elements of the community, such as the radio medium for editing purposes, authorities on the subject for background information, or even parents who can serve as practice interviewees, are ways of broadening the scope of the project in terms of its community dimensions. Certainly a concluding celebration, which brings together all the stakeholders to recognize each other's contributions to the project, is not only recommended but highly appropriate.

I would encourage following five cardinal rules to guide you as you approach a broader community to enhance learning:

1. Broaden your definition of community beyond the obvious constituencies of the school. Moving outside the classroom enables you to design projects that are valuable, rewarding, and real.

2. Be a service-learner yourself. By modeling this methodology for your students, you are demonstrating how much there is to learn from the world at large and sending the message that learning is a life-long pursuit.

3. Accept and embrace the role of facilitator. Facilitating, as much as imparting information, is a part of teaching. Becoming comfortable in this role is part of your professional development and can make the difference between a project that's bogged down in confusion and one that runs smoothly, allowing the learning outcomes to emerge.

4. Have a tangible product as an outcome. Students need to know there's something real at the end; the segment of the community you're working with will also appreciate some result that benefits their group or interest.

5. Bring significant closure to the project. It's a great way to reward effort, allow all the parties involved to see and congratulate each other, and just have some fun.

My three experiences with oral history as a vehicle for service-learning confirm the importance of relatedness that Parker Palmer speaks about. Defining community through service-learning, it seems to me, helps an institution such as a school to know and recognize its place in the broader cultural, geographic setting. This process helps a school connect with people and groups who have much to teach, and to develop a partnership that is mutual and beneficial to all concerned.

RESOURCES AND SUGGESTIONS FOR FURTHER READING
Palmer, Parker J. "Community, Conflict and Ways of Knowing: Ways to Deepen Our Educational Agenda." *Combining Service and Learning: A Resource Book for Community and Public Service.* Ed. Jane Kendall and Associates. Raleigh, NC: National Society for Experiential Education, 1990.

...developing a service-learning unit precisely because we are unable to draw on our own resources was a terrific way to expand our horizons.

Barbara Wysocki is a history teacher and department chair at University High School in Urbana, Illinois. She and Audrey Wells developed and teach a service-learning class called Social Advocacy: History, Theory, and Practice, which has been in the curriculum for 10 years. Barbara was a Mentor in NSEE's Leadership Development Program, funded by the DeWitt Wallace-Reader's Digest Fund. Prior to her teaching career, Barbara was a VISTA Volunteer on the Navajo Reservation.

Identifying Community Needs and Resources

THE OLIVER WENDELL HOLMES SCHOOL, WHERE I TEACH 1ST AND 2ND GRADERS, IS NESTLED IN A TINY RESIDENTIAL PART OF THE DORCHESTER SECTION OF BOSTON. However, what was once a thriving area of single family homes is now a dangerous neighborhood, where ambulances often stop, sometimes hauling away dead bodies. Many of the children I teach live with grandparents or foster parents, their parents often incarcerated or in drug rehabilitation centers. A lot of my children don't feel safe. I often feel as if a tornado has hit their lives, throwing their spirit, emotions, and intellect all over the place.

BY **NAJWA ABDUL-TAWWAB**

When I received a grant for $350 from the Boston school office for a community service-learning project, I knew that finding community needs and resources appropriate for my students would be challenging. How could I create a true partnership between the school and our community? How would we even define our community? How could we match the community's needs and resources with those at our school?

These are difficult questions for any school environment, whether an urban elementary school in a high-crime inner city or a relatively calm suburban high school. Demographics, logistics, safety issues, parental involvement, and other practical matters may vary extensively, but some fundamental issues are common for all service-learning programs in terms of identifying community needs and resources.

Often, our first impulse in a service-learning project is to try to help a community, for example, by providing assistance to an understaffed social services program. Working with young children in an urban area short on obvious "resources," I had to think of "community" in a broader sense than the immediate geographic area. In our school, we have learned to explore the fact that we are all members of one family, the human race, and we really do have more in common with one another than the world wants us to believe. Once we acknowledge our commonalities, we need to find ways to honor our differences with dignity and respect.

Below are several approaches that are useful for any service-learning program to identify both the needs and resources of communities. This can help make service-learning projects enrich students' learning and their spirit, as well as meet actual community needs and foster a sense of caring for others.

IDENTIFY RESOURCES AROUND YOU Look at your classroom and local community as a treasure chest. The students, families, schools, neighbors, and local agencies are all jewels in this treasure chest. Find ways to discover hidden talents as well as obvious ones. You could use an informal survey,

Look at your classroom and local community as a treasure chest.

assign students to discuss some topic with their parents or guardians, or interview people in the neighborhood. Such efforts will build positive relationships, recruit potential volunteers, and identify local resources all at the same time.

This was true even in our neighborhood, which lacks many of the resources that other areas of the city have. With so many of our 1st and 2nd graders living with grandparents, we decided to do an intergenerational unit. "Grandparents Week" gave us an obvious time. Our young children asked their grandparents for their stories and memories. Eventually, we put together songs and poems into a small production, working with a local theater. Some of the grandparents taught us the dances they used to do. We began to use grandparents as one of our best resources.

The local theater became a regular resource for our school. It lends itself to cultural involvement with schools and families. Our Asian students and any other children who were interested were able to attend a Chinese New Year celebration, for example. We got community outreach tickets for the students and the parents that wanted to participate. At school, we talked about theater dress and etiquette, and the children made simple books about the theater. Even these young children were able to serve their community by connecting their families with cultural opportunities and reflecting about these events.

IDENTIFYING A THEME AND FORMAT Focusing on a theme often helps match ideas generated in the classroom or curriculum with genuine needs and resources in the community. What do you and your students want to study? Discuss and plan participatory activities for you and your partners. Or use your needs assessment to seek out logical partners, who may be beyond your immediate neighborhood or area of the city. Involve your students. Let them make suggestions and help make decisions. Your theme should provide your students with opportunities to use academic skills and knowledge in real-life situations in their communities. Think about relationships between school and community activities and build upon them.

With our young children, we had decided to focus a unit on illnesses. The children wanted to look at AIDS. I asked them if they thought children could get AIDS. Many said yes. Some didn't know. "Let's learn about it, Mrs. Abdul-Tawwab," they said. We were well on our way to becoming a community of learners, which hopefully one day would lead to a connection outside the classroom.

One of the connections we made was with the Boston Pediatric AIDS Foundation. We had to struggle to make a connection with this community. On the one hand, it seemed like a wonderful opportunity for our children to learn about AIDS. But on the other hand, we had to respect the privacy of those who were sick. It is important to respect the needs and goals of the agency involved, to consider their needs as well as those of the students.

In my classroom, I started by asking the children how they feel when they are sick. We talked about ringworm and some illnesses, real situations. Then, we decided to write and decorate small books for the children with AIDS in the hospital. Several other classes became involved, as well as parents.

Eventually, about 120 children made books, dictating their stories if they were too young to write them out. They decorated them so that about half the pages were illustrations. The project was building vocabulary while working on handwriting and storytelling skills. They wrote stories about a flower, about green beans, about Jack and the Beanstalk. They got excited and the project took off.

FOLLOW-UP ACTIVITIES The children had one success with writing books for children, so I jumped at another chance for a similar connection. A history professor, who was a friend of my husband, was spearheading a statewide drive to collect and send a million books to the new South Africa under President Nelson Mandela. He knew I was a school teacher and asked if I wanted to help. I created a parent flyer and developed a mini-unit on South Africa, using materials I had saved when Nelson Mandela had visited Boston in 1990.

The connection between the AIDS project and the South Africa project, while not obvious at first, was perfectly natural in the classroom. The young elementary school children were sharing stories of their lives with other children. Each primary project can lead to more partnerships, service, and learning with creative follow-up activities. Watch for opportunities and for the appropriateness of linking specific academic disciplines to community settings, even if your community expands internationally.

Following up the initial project led to a new and exciting community partnership, this time with children in South Africa. We wrote more stories. The children wrote stories about their lives in America. It was a real learning experience for the children to write and publish. We would have class reflection time on a regular basis to check in on our thoughts and feelings about what we were doing. The project organizer came and spoke at our school, showing pictures of the schools where the books were going. Many of the children in my classroom looked like the ones in the pictures, but their lives were so different.

What began as a unit on illnesses in my classroom eventually evolved to a school-wide project connected with South Africa. The small grant that I began with took me to the copying machine where other teachers learned what I was doing. It was a start. We also enlisted a lot of other help.

Seeking financial support and commitments from other people is crucial in identifying and building genuine community partnerships. Encourage as many groups as possible to become involved and responsible for some phase of implementing the project. Write grant proposals, look for free materials, and ask for in-kind services, donations, and time. Ask your local businesses, colleges, banks, and community residents to contribute their support.

Publicity and promotion are also important. Put up notices on bulletin boards, send notes to families, friends, and colleagues. Put up posters, pass out flyers, and leave announcements in the local "Y," library, restaurants, movie theaters, laundromats, cleaners, banks, and religious institutions. Contact your local television station, radio station, and newspaper for public service announcement opportunities. Eventually, the word gets out. The Boston City Council learned about our book project and honored us at City Hall. The city provided free bus service

Think about relationships between school and community activities and build upon them.

for us after school one day, and we attended a special session of the City Council to receive a certificate of commendation.

At such moments of success and celebration, remember to invite everyone to share the success. The local media should be there to capture what you all have worked on. Your partners should be there too, if possible. Put on performances and let people take note of what you have accomplished. Display projects and pictures or show video tapes of work.

LOCAL ACCOUNTABILITY Even in the busy life of a school teacher, it is important to evaluate what you are doing, especially in terms of community partnerships. It is helpful to interview residents and agencies about their concerns and to offer your own reflection as well as those of your students and partners about joint projects.

Because of the type of neighborhood where I teach, I feel it is important to connect with human service agencies. I work through a group called the Dudley Street Neighborhood Initiative, where I have learned about various human service resources for children. Often, informally, I'm able to direct parents to the services they may need. This may overlap with a specific community service unit that I'm doing with the students or it may not. But the starting point for my involvement is the idea of community service-learning.

I see my mission as a teacher as a collaborative effort. I need to know the needs of different agencies, students, faculty, the principal. Then we can develop the best partnerships possible. Community service-learning is also a collaborative effort. For my students, the process is about changing attitudes. Even in this neighborhood where a lot of children don't feel safe, we are trying to help build positive habits of mind.

Najwa Abdul-Tawwab is a teacher at Oliver Wendell Holmes Elementary School in Dorchester, Massachusetts.

Designing Meaningful Projects That Meet Community Needs

FOR THE LAST SEVEN YEARS, TALLER PUERTORRIQUEÑO (THE PUERTO RICAN WORKSHOP) HAS BEEN ORGANIZING AIDS EDUCATIONAL PROJECTS THROUGH THE ARTS. In contrast to a direct-service approach, we use artistic methods to provide people a way to learn about, talk to each other about, respond to, and contribute to the community's education on HIV/AIDS. In the process, we have worked with two local middle schools in particular in developing a number of AIDS education projects. In these partnerships, our agency has pursued its mission as an educational institution, complementing the educational mission of the schools. Together, we have worked to design projects that meet an urgent need of these students and our community. Sex and HIV/AIDS had not been addressed openly in our area, even though the virus is spreading rapidly in the Latino population.

BY JOHNNY IRIZARRY

Taller is a community-based cultural center, located in a North Philadelphia neighborhood rich in history. Poverty has taken hold of the area as the collapse and flight of industry and work opportunities has occurred. With so many needs in our area, Taller has to make careful program choices. This is not easy when the needs are so great. In our 22-year history, our mission has been for the arts and culture to be at the core of what we do. Our guiding question in assessing community needs is "How can Taller best influence the overall well-being of the community it serves through the arts?" We seek to develop multi-disciplinary arts and cultural programs in which the community can participate in a significant way.

Within this overall mission, we have pursued many types of projects to meet community needs. In recent years, AIDS has deeply touched the life and work of Taller. A number of artists and others who have worked with Taller are either infected or have passed because of AIDS. This has created in the organization a special interest in establishing programs that address HIV/AIDS and the dramatic impact it has in our local community, as well as the national Latino community.

A commitment to social justice and to an interest in serving as a partner in the continued development of the Latino community has led the organization towards becoming more involved in collaborative projects with schools and other non-arts-specific organizations. As demand for our participation and involvement in collaborations has continued to grow, we found it important to identify a "philosophical definition" to guide us in making choices and decisions on our organizational role in partnerships. We pursue collaborations that operate on principles of cultural pluralism and provide additional resources to our community's cultural educational development. We also seek equal planning and creative power in the projects and equitable financial contributions,

The active involvement and personal commitment of the teachers greatly affect the project.

if possible. We want the projects to build bridges that can be strengthened in the future, fulfill specific needs, and move beyond stereotypes with sincere intentions of assisting the community on a long-term basis. We seek projects that recognize the expertise of community members, including their knowledge of and access to our community's resources, audiences, art, artists, history, and culture, as well as their capacity to identify problems and implement solutions. We want to break social barriers, exchange ideas, and build on community and organizational stabilization and empowerment.

Our experience has been that once initial trust is established between our agency and specific dedicated teachers and the principals, schools are extremely interested in working with community agencies in special projects, especially if the community agency brings financial resources and creative projects that can enhance the students' learning. We have had less success when schools approached us with major project ideas but without major funding. Smaller projects developed by schools have been more successful, such as murals, cultural workshops, and presentations.

AIDS PROJECTS Our AIDS projects over the last seven years have included a number of quilting projects and workshops involving people of all backgrounds and ages, from children to seniors. Several of these have involved two middle schools that are located near our center. The National Names Project inspired the idea of a community-wide AIDS quilt-making project, which we did with the schools. The staff at Taller developed a sketch of our idea and approached specific teachers and the principals at the two middle schools that are near our center. We had direct contacts at those schools, had done other arts and cultural projects there, and had "adopted" one of the schools through a school district "Adopt-a-School Program."

At one school the collaborating teacher in the AIDS Quilting Project involved her special education students and her academically gifted students in a mentor-partner relationship between the students and seniors at a community senior citizen center. Her students traveled to the senior center on one Monday and the seniors would travel to the school the following Monday until the Quilt Project was completed. The loving relationships established between the seniors and the students was one of the most rewarding results of the project. In addition the project provided a rare opportunity for special education students to work together with the academically gifted students on a specific project at the school.

Other AIDS projects with the schools have included a "Youth Speaking to Youth About AIDS" project, where students made educational posters, and a bilingual AIDS Educational Comic Book Project called *Think Twice, An AIDS Story/Piensalo Bien, una historia sobre SIDA*. In the poster project, two final posters were printed, bilingual and in full color, with 4,000 copies distributed throughout the city. The comic book, which received a 1994 Arts and Culture Award from the Philadelphia Commission on Human Relations, was also distributed citywide, after 3,000 copies were printed.

These and other community-based projects were youth and student centered for the most part, and involved a curriculum developed by a team of visual artists, writers, teachers, AIDS educators, social service workers, community members, students, and members of Taller's staff. Most of the projects involved activities directly in the schools, at the Norris Square Senior Citizen Center, and at Taller's Education Building. Our after-school and Saturday programs in arts education also served as a host for the implementation of many of the components of these projects.

MAKING THE PARTNERSHIP WORK In designing projects that meet community needs, community agencies and schools should emphasize several important elements to ensure success. These will apply to all projects, with the emphasis changing depending upon the circumstances of your situation.

1. Build "working teams" to implement the project. One of the most challenging and important components of our AIDS educational programs was developing a team where all of the members were equally committed to the concept of the project, to its educational and social mission, and to the community. The team members must have the same information and plan of action and know and respect each other's role in the project. This component has presented the most work for us in the planning and beginning stages of the project. Once this groundwork was accomplished, implementing the rest of the project was much easier.

2. Be sure the school principal is committed to, and well informed about, your project. For the Taller staff, the coordinating artists, AIDS educators, community partners, and the school staff to work on our AIDS projects, we had to have the cooperation of the principal.

3. Establish trust among the groups involved. Having a working team and keeping a principal well informed are the first steps toward establishing trust. It is needed between our organization, the principal, the teachers at the school, and the other team members throughout the project implementation and beyond. In such a diverse partnership, conflicts and differences of opinions will surely arise. These need to be addressed immediately. The solution lies in the commitment of all the participating partners to confront each other honestly when problem issues do arise, and continue to work together.

4. Constant communication and trust must be maintained with any outside consultants. Our staff and project coordinating artists have to work very closely together. The responsibilities of the artist need to be clear, especially when he or she is the creative guide to the project. This is a role of guidance and artistic support allowing for the ideas and concepts of the students, teachers, and other project participants to determine the creative and collective outcomes. The logistics need to be clear as well. At times, the artist would establish a working schedule with the teacher and arrive and realize that special situations had arisen that altered the schedule— a shorter period was in effect, citywide testing was taking place, or some other schedule adjustment. The artist was at first frustrated, but learned to call the main office before coming to be sure that no special situations had arisen.

5. The active involvement and personal commitment of the teachers greatly affect the project. In our projects, the teachers need to negotiate and share control and power with the project artist and AIDS educator in order to guarantee effective involvement and a successful project. We have

We want to break social barriers, exchange ideas, and build on community and organizational stabilization and empowerment.

discovered that teachers who enjoy team teaching and have a personal investment in the lives of the students beyond the classroom make excellent partners for our AIDS educational projects within schools. We have found many teachers willing and receptive to participating in collaborations of this kind, and they find the time and appropriate way to integrate the project into their curriculum and teaching requirements, sometimes even beyond the project concept.

Art teachers at both schools were especially interested in participating in the project but other teachers were also involved. The home education teacher took on a main role, for example, involving her students in sewing the quilt panels together. Our teacher contact at one school was a Taller board member, and she got other teachers interested in AIDS education, even if their project wasn't related to our arts projects. At the time we began working on this project, the schools did not have a formal way of teaching the students about AIDS, so our projects prompted a number of AIDS-education projects.

A science teacher had his students study and artistically interpret the scientific composition and breakdown of the human immune system caused by HIV/AIDS. The students created individual art panels demonstrating this scientific process. A social studies teacher had her students study the local and national demographics of the spread of the AIDS virus. The students studied how maps are created, the racial and economic composition of the neighborhoods, and the health resources available to the neighborhoods. They also created maps showing how the disease has spread locally and nationally.

...the implementation of these projects would not have been possible without the support of so many people willing to make the project a reality.

6. Mutual investment is important, but funding often comes from only one partner. Funds for our school-based projects have usually been raised by Taller Puertorriqueño from sources specifically interested in supporting AIDS educational alternative and experimental programs, especially within under-served communities. These funds pay for artists fees, supplies, and production costs, such as printing the comic book. Community-based social service agencies have provided the services of bilingual AIDS educators, informational materials, and other technical assistance to the project. These services were essential with the comic book and poster project.

The schools have adjusted their class schedules to include the effective implementation of the project, integrated the project into their regular curriculum, hosted project receptions, provided supplies and sewing equipment, and offered other vital support to the project. Artists, community-based printers, and others have brought to the project artistic guidance, knowledge, and technical assistance beyond what they have been paid for.

The cultural educational work that Taller and many community agencies provide is urgently needed and in growing demand. It has become clear to many educators that traditional educational methods have failed to prepare communities of color to progress educationally, economically, and socially. Many of Taller's projects are designed to help address and counteract racism, build self-esteem and awareness, create respect for differences, identify commonalities, and build and promote community pride and unity.

With the comic book project, for example, it was important to create a bilingual publication because of the bilingual population we were targeting. We had a bilingual Latina writer and educator work with the youth in developing the story line. The opportunity to teach reading, writing, and creative skills in developing the story line was a key component of the project. We also had a visual artist work with the youth doing the drawings. She and the students brought in lots of comic books to study options, emphasizing anatomy, graphic arts techniques, and how to use many different art materials.

The youth had a direct and determining role in the entire story line development and in the final images used. We were committed and willing to end the story whichever way the majority of the youth in the schools felt it should end. The AIDS educator worked with both the writing group and the drawing group as well and did an excellent job in keeping the information accurate and clear for what people needed to know.

Reprinted with permission from *Think Twice: An AIDS Story*, published by Taller Puertorriqueño, 2721 N. 5th Street, Philadelphia, PA 19133, 215-423-6320.

Reprinted with permission from *Think Twice: An AIDS Story,* published by Taller Puertorriqueño, 2721 N. 5th Street, Philadelphia, PA 19133, 215-423-6320.

LASTING VALUE The administrative responsibility of managing these special grants and the full burden of fundraising for the projects, on an organization the size of Taller Puertorriqueño, has been difficult for us to sustain. The lack of appropriate funding for programs such as these is a limiting factor. At the same time, the implementation of these projects would not have been possible without the support of so many people willing to make the project a reality. We have discovered that participants have made deeply personal connections to their involvement in the projects and to the opportunity to address a difficult issue such as AIDS, and its effects in their lives and that of the community, through the arts.

The seniors at the Norris Square Senior Citizen Center used the AIDS Quilt Project to search for understanding and provide emotional and community support to a fellow senior who had recently lost a son to AIDS and had stopped attending the Senior Center due to fear of rejection. The quilting workshops, discussion sessions, ecumenical service, video documentation, and exhibition of the final quilts associated with the project served as a friendly and "easier" method to address their fellow senior's loss and fear of rejection and to facilitate a better understanding of the AIDS epidemic and its direct impact in the community's life. In the video that documents the projects, the seniors and others involved in the project speak to many issues that extend beyond the issue of AIDS, such as intergenerational relationships, politics, race, class, gender, sexuality, and other factors in our ability to confront and find collective solutions to the problems that deeply affect our community.

Johnny Irizarry is the Executive Director of Taller Puertorriqueño (The Puerto Rican Workshop) in Philadelphia, Pennsylvania.

Forming Effective Community Advisory Boards

ADVISORY BOARD. WHEN I FIRST HEARD THOSE TWO WORDS 20 YEARS AGO, OUR EXPERIENTIAL LEARNING PROGRAM, IN CHARLOTTE, NORTH CAROLINA, HAD BARELY BEGUN. How could I organize a board when I was up to my neck in trying to recruit community sponsors and place interns? Nevertheless, it was a grant requirement. Little did I know that this group would become one of the most enjoyable parts of my work and the lifeline to preserving our program through multiple superintendents.

BY **JOYCE MCSPADDEN**

We were two months into our school year when we had our first advisory board meeting. I invited all the community sponsors that had become involved with our students to date. An anthropology professor at the university was our first chair. He had one of our interns and seemed to understand what our overall program was trying to do. Some key parts of our advisory board meeting format began that night. We gave the group an update on how many students were involved, where they were placed, and what kind of community sponsors were needed. Several students reported on their internship experiences—their interests, hands-on observation activities they experienced, the types of projects they did, and how the internships benefited them.

Our board members tell us that the student reports are the best part of each meeting. Over the years, an intern reported on his research on why pneumonia contacted by hospital patients is much more resistant to treatment than pneumonia strains contacted outside the hospital. One intern organized an entire junior docent program at a local art museum. This was a tremendous help to the museum, especially in the summers when many youth groups wanted museum tours. In another example, a local plantation has been restored as a living museum, and their intern developed a booklet identifying herbs and their uses in early American life. The museum printed the booklet and distributes it to visitors.

By the end of the first year, we had targeted some key persons to serve on the advisory board and had established a regular meeting time agreeable with the majority. After three years our night meetings became lunch meetings hosted by various board members every other month during the school year. Day meetings with lunch boosted attendance.

Inviting all the participating community sponsors to serve as advisory board members did not last long because of the program's growth. All eleven senior high schools in the Charlotte-Mecklenburg County school system participate in the program. Each student intern is supported by a faculty advisor, the internship coordinator, and a community sponsor who help the student plan worthwhile objectives and learning activities. Most students participating in the program

...our advisory board members know their suggestions can lead to meaningful change.

are not paid, but they do receive elective academic credit. Internships range from 45-180 hours and take place after the regular school day. Students must furnish their own transportation. Approximately 500 high school students participate in the program each year.

Our program, called the Academic Internship Program (AIP), seeks to: 1) provide opportunities for high school students to explore areas of academic, career, or service interest through internships with local governmental and civic agencies, businesses, industries, and individuals; 2) establish positive relationships between the school and the community; and 3) enable students to earn credit for extracurricular experiences of an academic nature. Each student keeps a journal and most of them complete a project.

WHO SERVES ON THE ADVISORY BOARD An advisory board is a group of volunteers representing various segments of the community such as businesses, nonprofit organizations, parents, and educators whose expertise and valuable insights can be helpful to the staff who are charged with implementing a particular program. An advisory board's purpose is to give advice, not to function as a governing board. An advisory board can be invaluable in pointing out the community's resources, identifying prospective community sponsors, and serving as an advocate for your program.

Our program has 25 advisory board members, mostly representative of business and nonprofit agencies, plus two parents and several educators. We have students at each meeting, but not the same students each time, since they must miss school to participate. Your board will be more successful if it reflects as much diversity as possible in terms of gender, race, ethnicity, etc. We include our immediate supervisor, who always attends our meetings, and two other central office staff, who attend when possible. Rely on protocol and intuition in deciding who and how many central office staff to include.

Board members have sometimes made the impossible happen.

If your experiential learning program emphasizes service-learning, you still can benefit by including business representatives on your advisory board. Corporate resources may be the backbone of your community sponsors' budgets and will give your board added power to accomplish those things that you and social service agencies cannot do alone. For example, our board member who was vice president of a large bank hosted a lovely luncheon for the advisory board to welcome an incoming superintendent. It was arranged for the publisher of the local newspaper to attend the meeting. The following Sunday, the publisher's weekly column highlighted the students who spoke and the community sponsors who participated. More importantly, the column quoted the new superintendent saying that the program was a "top priority" and invited others in the community to participate as sponsors.

One reason board members are eager to serve is because they believe firmly in the mission and goals of our program. There is a tremendous nationwide emphasis on the total community working together in the education of our youth. The School-to-Work Opportunities Act and the National and Community Service Trust Act stress the need for students to be involved in learning experiences that are hands-on, meaningful, and connected to the real world.

In North Carolina, school reform has been the focus of many groups, including the Governor's Commission on Workforce Preparedness and the Charlotte Chamber of Commerce's Education Council. Various businesses, the Charlotte Chamber, and Charlotte-Mecklenburg Schools held a system-wide School-to-Work Summit last fall and Career Expo 1996 this spring.

Publicity about national and statewide efforts has saturated our community with the need for school reform. Because experiential education is on the cutting edge of school reform by involving students in real world experiences, our advisory board members know their suggestions can lead to meaningful change. They enjoy the opportunity to influence and support a program that exposes students to real world-settings. They are eager to involve students in their own organizations as well as promote the program so that others in the community will participate.

Advisory board members consider it an honor to be asked to serve. Some members may be alumni from the very schools you serve and want "to give something back." Members enjoy both a social and intellectual environment by participating on our board. Often they feel it is their duty to find a replacement for themselves on the board if they can no longer serve. Many members commit to serving more than one three-year term. Over time, a rich camaraderie has developed among members, and they have a strong loyalty to the program and each other.

WHAT IS THE ROLE OF THE ADVISORY BOARD Responsibilities range from attending meetings to helping the community support the mission and goals of our program. Each board member must be an advocate for the program and help enhance its public image. In the early years the advisory board sponsored a year-end gathering honoring all our students and community and teacher sponsors. This event was a reception or supper program with all three groups taking part. As our program has grown to the size it is today, it is difficult to hold such an event. When our program has a shortage of sponsors in a certain area, board members often furnish staff with leads and help to develop community resources. There have been times when our board members have visited internship sites. This visitation has been done to thank new community sponsors for their participation or to provide extra support for the students.

Our board has provided orientation for new members, sponsored an in-service luncheon and teacher appreciation reception for teacher sponsors, and hosted a panel to recruit additional community sponsors. A special board committee raised funds for these projects. Members have written letters or phoned businesses or organizations to explain the internship program and recommend that their group become involved. Board member roles remain flexible in order to take on new challenges as they may develop. At a recent board meeting, our host was BellSouth who hooked together interns and board members with interns and NSEE staff in two other cities by way of North Carolina's information highway.

Board members have sometimes made the impossible happen. For example, a student's application to the state university had been rejected. After the school received a letter from an advisory member who had worked with the student, she was admitted with full financial aid. Our program began with a three-year federal grant, and had little hope that it would be continued when those funds expired. Our third-year advisory board organized a letter writing campaign to persuade the school board and administration to continue the program with state and local funding. Community sponsors, parents, and students wrote more than 250 letters requesting that the AIP continue. Several of our board members made a presentation to the school board explaining how the program benefited the students, schools, and community. Using graphs and charts, they showed the growth in the number of students and community sponsors involved over the first three years. This was much more effective than a staff person's presentation would have been. This involvement was very helpful in getting our program adopted into the local budget, where it has been for 17 years.

Finally, board members can provide important linkages with other agencies, programs, or individuals. For example, the chairman of the Chamber of Commerce's education committee is a member of our program's advisory board. He keeps our board informed about community leaders' views on school reform. His participation and advice are helpful in keeping our program on target, and he lets other community groups know what we are doing.

Advisory board "rescue" of our internship program became a reality again this spring as I was writing this article. Because our administration was directed to trim the system's budget by a sizable amount, one of our two internship coordinator positions was being considered for a redirection of funds. We learned about this possible cut one week before our school board was to vote on the budget, a time that fell during spring break. Immediately, our advisory board met and launched a campaign to inform many of our parents and key community supporters of this threat to our program. A bombardment of letters, faxes, and phone calls to the interim superintendent and school board members followed.

A group of supporters attended the school board meeting and an excellent presentation was made by two of our board members, an intern's parent, and a former intern. Since many of our school board members were new, we looked at this meeting as an opportunity to inform them about the Academic Internship Program in general, its accountability, and what this program has meant to students, parents, and community sponsors. Packets of information included materials used, names of community sponsors, and the number of interns involved in various areas. One of our board members who spoke ran a cost-benefit analysis and found that the Charlotte community had contributed more than $500,000 to this school year's internships. This amount was based on employers' time, materials, and equipment involved in the average internship. The school board voted unanimously to keep both coordinator positions in the budget proposal.

Your advisory board will be an effective way to integrate your schools with the world outside. It may also be one of your most successful academic ventures. You will find your board to be a wonderful support group, and members can be a sounding board for new ideas or frustrations. After a time your members will begin to share ownership of the program. Broadening the program's support base can be very helpful as you meet new challenges in the future.

Through our experiences, we have found some tips for success that might be useful in your program as well.

LOGISTICS
- Schedule meetings well in advance and try to keep the same time. For example, our board meets at 11:45 a.m. on the second Wednesday every other month during the school year beginning in October.

- Day meetings will be better than night, even if you schedule them late in the afternoon.

- It is best to have board members serve terms of a fixed length, such as three years, and staggered so that one-third will expire each year. You can always ask your best supporters to sign-on again.

- You can probably count on two-thirds of the members at each meeting. If you want 20 people to attend, have membership of 30.

ORGANIZATION/FUNCTIONING
- You may need school board and/or administration approval to organize an advisory board for your program.

- Have advisory board members representing various walks of life, guaranteeing fresh ideas and faces coming to the board each year.

- Use advisory board members as officers; you plan the meeting agenda and provide all the help and information for the chairperson to conduct an organized meeting.

- Encourage board members to offer assistance in their areas of expertise. For example, someone in graphics or advertising might be of help in designing a brochure for your program.

- If your program involves teacher sponsors, the advisory board can undertake special projects to show appreciation to teachers for assuming this extra responsibility. This could include luncheons, teas, or simple gifts such as sticky note pads printed with your program's logo.

- Thank board chairs with appreciation plaques for their service. Other gestures, such as cards or flowers if a board member becomes ill, are also a good idea.

- Your board can take on the responsibility of fundraising for special projects, but this should be kept to a minimum.

- When important staff changes occur, your advisory board should have input into the selection process.

MEETING CONTENT
- Always provide program accomplishments and statistics at each meeting.

- Your board members have a natural interest in the schools you serve. In addition to hearing from students, provide opportunities for them to hear from school administrators regarding the

...board members can provide important linkages with other agencies, programs, or individuals.

mission and objective of your school system and how your program integrates the system's overall goals.

- Provide opportunities for board members to hear from each other about how they involve students with their organizations.

- Invite several guests to your meetings. You might include a high school principal or other school staff member or a new community sponsor who has become involved with your program.

REFERENCES AND SUGGESTIONS FOR FURTHER READING

Dyer, Delwyn A., and Oscar M. Williams. *Developing Effective Boards, Councils and Commissions.* Blacksburg, VA: Virginia Cooperative Extension Service at the Virginia Polytechnic Institute, 1991.

Silver, Gerald. *Advisory Boards: Academic Partnerships That Work.* 1992, unpublished.

Teitel, Lee. "The Advisory Committee Advantage: Creating an Effective Strategy for Programmatic Improvement." *ERIC Digest.* Washington, DC: ERIC Clearinghouse on Higher Education, George Washington University, 1994.

Joyce McSpadden is Coordinator of the Academic Internship Program for the Charlotte-Mecklenburg Schools in Charlotte, North Carolina. She has also been a Mentor in NSEE's Leadership Development Program and a Consultant with NSEE's National Initiative, funded by the DeWitt Wallace-Reader's Digest Fund.

Training With Community Partners

"WHAT IS THE MEANING OF 'COMMUNITY' IN THE TERM 'COMMUNITY SERVICE-LEARNING'? Are we talking about working with nonprofit agencies, parents, elder citizens, interested community members, our schools, or all of the above? Should we focus our community service-learning initiative on our communities—the five towns that make up the regional school district—or go beyond that to the larger towns that surround us, where 'problems' are more evident? What is the role of the community in the education of its children?"

BY **PATRICIA M. BARNICLE**

These were some of the questions being explored at the second meeting of the Tantasqua Community Service-Learning Advisory Board, being held in a school library in a suburban area of Boston. Present at this meeting were teacher representatives from all five towns in the regional school district, the Superintendent of Schools, three principals, several high school students, and six community members.

Tension was high that night as educators, community members, and students exchanged their beliefs about where the focus should be in this year's community service-learning small-grant program. The tree warden, head of the local veterans group, hospital volunteer coordinator, and planning board member all argued for funding programs in the local communities where they saw the greatest need. Educators and students wanted to go beyond the local town boundaries to homeless shelters and veterans homes in nearby towns. They asked the community representatives to give them ideas about possible local projects. The planning board member from one local town rattled off three such ideas that came immediately to her mind. Then she added, "I have absolutely no idea where these fit in the school's curriculum or at what student developmental level we should aim them. I need your help in that." Silence filled the room as a realization surfaced. We needed each other to really make this work!

Most educators, community members, and students have had little training in leading groups or other interactive process techniques. Community projects can bring these diverse groups together in new and thought-provoking ways. However, it is important to structure this process well and build on it incrementally to avoid frustration at all levels. In a well facilitated model, agency staff are able to describe their organization's mission, goals, and daily services. Educators are able to put forth desired curriculum outcomes. Students can describe how they learn best and where their skills and interests lie. Discussing and developing programs as a team with all participants present avoids a common pitfall of community service-learning—isolated and, therefore, limited thinking. Exploring issues that arise in a supportive, well facilitated environment

We are asking them to stop working as though school and community are two separate and isolated entities....

builds a bond of trust between participants that hopefully will transfer to the initiative as a whole.

Many community service-learning trainers make the mistake of viewing their training through only one lens. They work diligently with educators alone to teach them how to integrate community service with academic learning. They develop orientation sessions for volunteer coordinators to help them create appropriate service opportunities for students. Or they work with youth, teaching them the skills necessary to lead community service projects. What is missed with this approach is the complex and exhilarating result of an ongoing dialogue that is cross-generational and diverse. The same degree of attention is needed with community agencies and with all of these groups meeting together. The learning then happens both in the process and in the program. Programs created in this way have greater depth, perform real service to the community, and are ultimately more sustainable.

TRAINING MODELS Integrating community service-learning partnerships into a school and community culture in a sustained way can be daunting. We are asking educators, students, and community members to shift roles and structures—to give up individual power in one area in order to gain a greater success for the team. We are asking them to stop working as though school and community are two separate and isolated entities, and begin to look at themselves as a vibrant "system" of education in which they and students are full participants. The challenge and the risk of community service-learning is what takes it beyond "a good thing to do" into an exemplary model of teaching and learning—a way to build strong schools and communities that can meet the complex challenges of the 21st century.

An effective group can be the spark that lights the fire under the whole district.

Over the past several years, the Lincoln Filene Center at Tufts University in Medford, Massachusetts, has piloted some training strategies to build strong community partnerships. Funded by grants from the DeWitt Wallace-Reader's Digest Fund, the W. K. Kellogg Foundation, the Filene Foundation, and the Corporation for National and Community Service, these strategies have included:

- the development and training of community service-learning advisory boards made up of students, educators, and community members to work together to build community service-learning initiatives,

- an intensive training of trainers model to build a state leadership cadre for community service-learning, and

- local training model that brings together educators, community members, and students to develop and implement community service-learning projects.

In the **advisory board model** we train participants to build an effective team. Through short on-site trainings and intensive summer institutes, we help members become more skillful facilitators, introduce them to group process and team-building techniques, and lay a strong base for the discussion of issues critical to community service-learning. Why is all this so important to the development of their initiative? An effective group can be the spark that lights the fire under the whole district.

The **training of trainers model** builds the capacity of educators and community members to lead initiatives. This intensive two-year process training is spread over seven day-long sessions. Participants learn to view their initiative through a "wide lens." Using strategic planning and organizational development techniques, they design a plan of action for their site. Some of the training activities include:

- Learning about institutional change and how to lead peers through reform and restructuring of systems. Starting with the impact of any kind of change on their personal lives, they learn techniques for preparing school staffs to deal with the kind of changes necessary to implement educational reform.

- Assessing their community needs and resources. Too many community service-learning projects look only at needs and not at what vital and rich resources the community can contribute to education.

- Learning to strategize politically within their districts. Using a SWOT (Strengths, Weaknesses, Opportunities, Threats) analysis, they design a plan that shows good entry, connecting, and focus points for their work. They explore where the "power" is at their site and how to connect with it.

- Participating in the making of public policy that affects community service-learning at the local, state, and national levels. They learn to map strategies and write legislation.

- Building community and school partnerships that will last beyond the life of a grant. Participants explore techniques for "hearing all voices" and working together in an ongoing way to evaluate and assess work.

The Lincoln Filene Center has collaborated with the Louis Feinstein Public Service Program at Sharon Public Schools, Mmapeu Consultants, and the Massachusetts Department of Education over the past two years to develop this exciting program for all Learn and Serve sites in the state of Massachusetts. This partnership has developed a team of trainers from diverse backgrounds who design and implement the trainings together. This approach models for participants the collaborative teaching techniques so essential to the development of community service-learning initiatives.

In the **local training model**, on-site presentations ensure the largest number of participants. These are highly interactive day-long trainings that encourage exchange of ideas and opinions, building of group process skills, and exploration of case study models and prototypes. With this approach, a project that is integrated into the curriculum can be developed on site. It is absolutely necessary to have educators, community members, and students participate in activities in mixed groups. When these groups discuss, develop, implement, assess, and evaluate their ideas in an ongoing way, what happens might be called "Civic Arts Learning." In their book, *The Quickening of America*, Lappé and DuBois show the difference between traditional community service and civic arts learning (227):

	COMMUNITY SERVICE	**CIVIC ARTS LEARNING**
Primary value for students	Making students "better people" —more altruistic and empathetic	Learning the arts of public life and building knowledge
Program direction	School faculty and staff	A partnership between school and community
Function	Service to others	Collaborative community problem solving

In order to prepare young people for effective living in the modern world, today's successful schools are involving everyone who has a stake in education—students, parents, teachers, community residents, taxpayers, all of us. They are discovering the value of using democratic approaches in preparing students who will have to think for a living. From the ground up, they are building on a long tradition of democratic schooling to reinvent education appropriate to our 21st century needs.

The Community Service Learning Project Work Sheet is an exercise we developed and have used time and again with groups of 30–100 people broken into mixed teams of 8–10 participants. This interactive team experience walks participants through the steps of creating a community service-learning project tied to curriculum. Team members discuss and come to consensus on expected outcomes (academic and community based), assessment of community needs and resources, classroom activities and connected community service work, the building of community collaborations, and planning ongoing evaluation and assessment of the initiative.

An overlay on all of this is a discussion of the skills and interests of the students involved. The results are great initial community service-learning curriculum ideas that build on community, educator, and student goals and interests. Often, these trainings are the beginning of a large community service-learning initiative in that school or region.

MODELS WORK All of these training techniques are necessary to ensure a comprehensive approach to building community service-learning initiatives. The most sustainable programs will implement all three simultaneously and develop an inclusive process that promotes rigorous academic learning and meaningful community problem solving.

The Boston Public Schools, for example, has used all three training approaches. It has developed community service-learning training that ensures the broadest participation, the highest level of

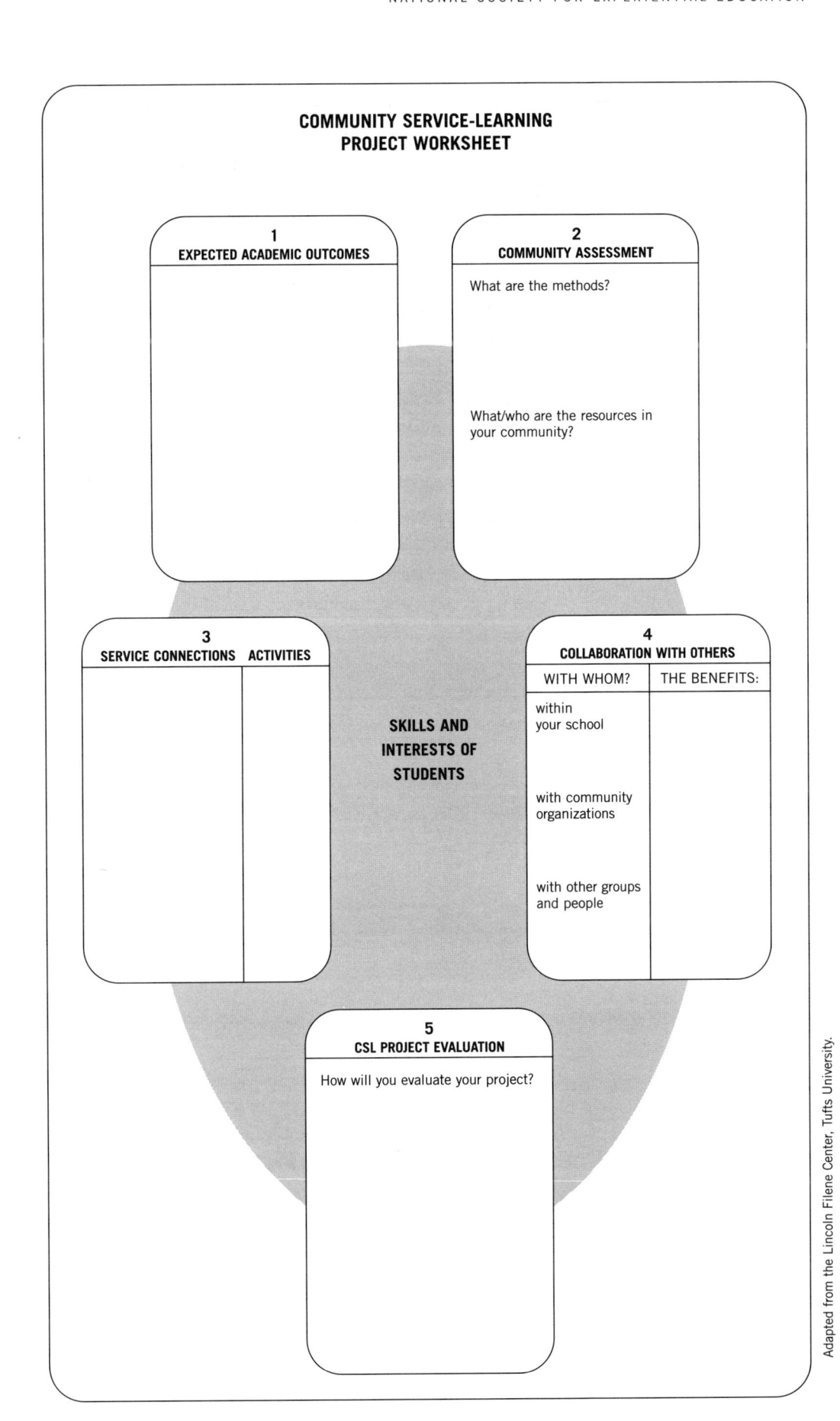

COMMUNITY SERVICE-LEARNING PROJECT WORKSHEET

1. EXPECTED ACADEMIC OUTCOMES

2. COMMUNITY ASSESSMENT

What are the methods?

What/who are the resources in your community?

3. SERVICE CONNECTIONS | ACTIVITIES

SKILLS AND INTERESTS OF STUDENTS

4. COLLABORATION WITH OTHERS

WITH WHOM?	THE BENEFITS:
within your school	
with community organizations	
with other groups and people	

5. CSL PROJECT EVALUATION

How will you evaluate your project?

Adapted from the Lincoln Filene Center, Tufts University.

rigorous learning, the most thoughtful use of community resources, and optimum provision of service to school and community needs. Using these three training models, the service-learning program in the Boston Public Schools went from 60 teachers to more than 300 teachers, in 33 schools, involving more than 9,000 students in the 1994–1995 school year. Some of the resources used in this effort include:

- A diverse Advisory Board that strategizes consistently to "grow" the initiative. Last year this group wrote a public policy for community service-learning and presented it to the School Committee in June, where it was passed unanimously.

- Strong liaisons with the Mayor's office and city agencies that have participated in the development and implementation of curriculum initiatives.

- An alliance with the Private Industry Council (PIC) and Boston's School-to-Career program, which is building a continuum of community service-learning, K–12, for Boston Public Schools.

- A large group of teachers who, through the training of trainers model, have become peer leaders for community service-learning. They organize and present expositions of their work for schools and agencies in Boston.

- A collaboration with the Impact II Teacher Training Network for Boston Public Schools, which provides on-site training, technical assistance, and general guidance through the system.

- Strong community partners such as the Food Project, City Year, Citywide Parents Council, United Way agencies, and the YMCA. These groups have become advocates for community service-learning in the nonprofit world.

Whether in a large urban system like Boston or a smaller system, well integrated, academically challenging, and truly useful curriculum initiatives can be developed. To help ensure success, several training points should be kept in mind.

- Think systemically when designing training models. Point out how community service-learning fits into the larger educational scheme.

- Be sure all players are present at training sessions even though they may resist this method.

- Through your training, model the behaviors you would like to see exhibited in the development of community service-learning. Train in teams using interactive models and be open, knowledgeable, and respectful of all participants' points of view.

- Be willing to concede that there isn't a prescription for "perfect" community service-learning. Explore many entry points with trainees and help them develop a strategy or strategies best suited for their site.

...learning to work effectively with diverse teams of people is absolutely essential....

- Don't sacrifice the process work. Although it may seem tedious at times, learning to work effectively with diverse teams of people is absolutely essential to the success of community service-learning in the classroom and out.

REFERENCES AND SUGGESTIONS FOR FURTHER READING

Lappé, Frances Moore, and Paul Martin DuBois. *The Quickening of America: Rebuilding Our Nation, Remaking Our Lives.* San Francisco: Jossey-Bass, 1994.

Stiles, L., and M. Dorsey. *Democratic Teaching in Secondary Schools.* New York: Lipincott, 1950.

Patricia Barnicle is Director of Programs and Training at the Lincoln Filene Center, Tufts University, in Medford, Massachusetts.

Institutional Support

Even with the hard work and commitment of individual teachers or community members, service-learning will have limited growth without institutional support. Service-learning practitioners need the support and commitment of leaders at the school, district, and state levels. Institutional support provides the guarantee that service-learning programs are valued and will not be cut arbitrarily due to staff changes, budget limitations, or political ebbs and flows.

issue 2

FRITZ CRABB begins the section with an overview of how practitioners in Michigan have sustained service-learning through various political changes.

JOAN BRAUN writes about the importance of service-learning becoming integrated into a school's culture and mission.

BEVERLY HIOTT shares her experiences in securing some of the practical necessities for service-learning programs.

NANCY RUSS follows with her success story of getting a separate budget for her program.

ANDREW FURCO closes the section with a look at how service-learning can be connected to broader educational reform.

Sustaining Service-Learning through Political Change

SUSTAINING NEW PROGRAMS IN THE MIDST OF DECLINING REVENUES AND CHANGING POLITICAL CLIMATES IS A RECURRING PROBLEM FOR URBAN PUBLIC SCHOOLS. Two issues stand out. For the past 10 years, urban districts have experienced declining revenues and greater pressures to increase student performance. In Michigan, funding and school accreditation is tied to statewide tests. The governor and legislature have also created a network of charter schools which decrease funds available to traditional public schools.

BY **FRITZ CRABB**

Besides issues of student performance and declining revenues, there have been political attacks on service-learning in Michigan and across the nation. The most frequent of these attacks likens service-learning to involuntary servitude, expressly prohibited in the Constitution. Where lawsuits have been filed, all cases have been decided in the school's favor. Another attack has questioned "payment" for volunteering. The "payment" by the school level is generally course credit, although some programs purporting to be service-learning actually give students a stipend. The "back to basics" movement in education has also attacked service-learning as a vehicle for teaching values and as unnecessary to the core educational processes.

These issues—concentration on student performance in traditional academics, lack of adequate funding, and attacks on service-learning—could have combined to derail service-learning in Grand Rapids, Michigan.

STRATEGIES Service-learning is still alive in Grand Rapids because of the strategies the district has used to implement it as an integral part of the curriculum.

The Grand Rapids Public Schools is the second largest school district in Michigan. It has 48 elementary schools and six specialty elementary programs; four comprehensive and two specialty middle schools; and four comprehensive and four specialty high schools. It serves 28,000 K–12 students in Grand Rapids, the state's second largest city. The percentage of minority students has grown to 55 percent, with 62 percent of students now living in poverty.

Service to the community is a cultural norm in Grand Rapids. The community's strong religious base encourages volunteerism. Major community events such as the Arts Festival and the River Bank Run never suffer a lack of helpers. Therefore, community service is also ingrained into the Grand Rapids Public Schools. Because of this community history, the district was well positioned to accept the challenge of implementing service-learning.

An example of the predisposition towards service was the creation, by the school district in 1984, of an Office of Student Activities, staffed by a full-time director. This office encouraged participation in community

In times of decreasing funding, only programs that show a clear link to student learning will be able to survive.

service activities. It helped form partnerships with local agencies, foundations, and the Heart of West Michigan United Way. Many clubs and organizations such as Young Educators, National Honor Societies, and student councils required or strongly encouraged community service.

Another factor that bolstered the move towards service-learning was a district-wide strategic planning initiative begun in December, 1992. A steering committee of citizens, parents, and educators drafted three objectives which continue to guide the district. Two of these objectives relate directly to service-learning:

- Students will serve the community in a manner of their choice as defined by their individual educational plan.
- Students will have learning experiences outside of the regular classroom.

This community endorsement of service-learning moved service-learning to the district's list of priorities. When it began its service-learning programs, the school district faced five questions:

1. How can it create a common understanding of service-learning?
2. How can it account for service-learning in the organizational hierarchy?
3. How can it show the impact of service-learning on student learning?
4. How can it provide adequate funding for service-learning programs?
5. How can it leverage community support and resources?

The answers to these five questions can guide any service-learning program through difficult political changes. The strategies our district used can be adapted to any community as it begins or expands its service-learning programs.

STRATEGY 1—CREATE A COMMON UNDERSTANDING There are several definitions of service-learning in use. Most programs prior to 1990 required students to complete a number of hours of service in an approved setting to get credit and/or to graduate. Few programs linked service-learning directly to the classroom.

Through state and national contacts and through meetings with school and community leaders, a definition of service-learning was crafted in the district to match the definition found in the National and Community Service Act of 1990 (NCSA). This definition required that service-learning meet a real school or community need, connect to the students' academic programs, and provide for reflection.

Grand Rapids used this definition, placing special emphasis on the connection to the academic program. As a learning organization, the Grand Rapids Public Schools is responsible for seeing that its students learn intended objectives. In times of revenue shortages, any program that does not positively affect student learning is subject to reduction or elimination.

All training and communications to teachers, parents, and the school board used the NCSA definition. Programs that applied for service-learning funding had to meet this definition. The

Facilitator of Service-Learning used this definition as the focus for presentations to all school and community groups.

Other terms were used to describe activities, even though districts sometimes called them "service-learning." "Required service" was used to describe programs that require a certain number of hours in the community. "Community service" was used to describe volunteer activities that did not meet the NCSA definitions.

The district never wavered from its insistence that service-learning be directly tied to classroom learning. This meant that many service activities could be accomplished in the classroom and in the school. There was no direct measurement of hours; what was measured was what students learned through the project. For example, at Stocking School, students create books which are donated to new mothers at a local hospital to encourage them to read to their children. What is measured is not the time the students spend on the book, but how their books meet stated objectives in the language arts and fine arts curriculum. Over the intervening years, programs that could not demonstrate a clear connection to student learning have been cut or severely scaled back.

STRATEGY 2—PLACE SERVICE-LEARNING CORRECTLY IN THE ORGANIZATIONAL HIERARCHY Service-learning was first assigned to the Coordinator of Student Activities, a position which was in charge of all extra-curricular student leadership programming. The position reported to the Director of Athletics and Student Activities. This office and position had no connection to the curriculum division of the district.

Research was beginning to show that service-learning could be a powerful teaching tool if it became a part of the curriculum. It could not be seen as an extracurricular activity nor could it be seen as an "extra" activity to add to an already full curriculum. It had to be seen as a tool to help teachers teach the existing curriculum.

The lack of a firm connection to the curriculum division became very apparent as teachers were recruited to participate in service-learning programs. They had to agree to use service-learning methodology in their classes. As the Coordinator of Student Activities had no previous contact with the curriculum division, it was hard to make teachers and administrators understand the scope and importance of the service-learning programs and hard to get them to agree to "add" this component to their classes.

Service-learning and student activities continued to be linked during the 1992–1993 school year which slowed implementation of district-wide service-learning. Realizing this, the Coordinator of Student Activities met with the Director of Curriculum Services and developed a plan to move service-learning to the curriculum division.

The superintendent announced the new position of Facilitator of Service-Learning in the spring of 1993, which was full time and reported to the Director of Curriculum Services. This gave the program the curriculum status it needed with teachers. The Facilitator was able to bring the resources of this division to bear on the implementation process.

STRATEGY 3—SHOW THE IMPACT OF SERVICE-LEARNING ON STUDENT LEARNING This is a critical aspect of program development. It was the one that was done least well in Grand Rapids.

What is measured is directly related to the definition used. If the district had defined service-learning as hours spent on service outside the classroom, simple measurement tools could have been constructed. Because service was defined as directly linked to student learning, different indicators had to be devised to measure the impact of service-learning on student learning.

Most outside funders will not fund a program unless they can see that the district is firmly behind the program...

There were a number of reasons this was not done well in Grand Rapids. In the start-up phase of the program, major effort did not go into measurement tools that could prove the validity of service-learning. They went instead to creating and instituting the definition, developing the training materials, recruiting teachers and administrators, making the necessary connections with community organizations, and securing funding. Even if measurements were developed, there were not sufficient numbers of teachers employing similar service-learning strategies to make them meaningful.

When the review of the 1992 Strategic Plan was completed in 1995, all objectives related to service-learning remained unchanged. There was, however, a change in direction regarding measurement. The committee felt that classroom-based service-learning was the means for teaching students the skills and providing them the motivation for continued community service, and it recognized the need to develop effective measures of student learning.

STRATEGY 4—PROVIDE ADEQUATE FUNDING FOR SERVICE-LEARNING Despite new state funding programs in Michigan that promised to equalize and stabilize public education funding, the reality is that per pupil funding across districts remains unequal and the amount school districts are able to spend on instruction is declining. Even though actual education dollars in the state budget are increasing, per pupil outlays are decreasing. The state has passed many costs down to the local districts and the number of students in the state is increasing at a greater rate than the increase in funds. Service-learning in Grand Rapids was not as affected by these cuts as other district programs because of the availability of outside funding, which the district has aggressively pursued.

The district was invited to apply for an Active Citizenship Today grant from Constitutional Rights and Close-Up Foundations. It was one of five in the nation to receive the grant in January of 1992. The strength of this grant was the very firm and necessary connection between the service and the classroom. In addition, three staff members from the district were selected to participate in NSEE's Leadership Development Program, funded by the DeWitt Wallace-Reader's Digest Fund. Through this program, we received professional development, technical assistance, and mini-grants to strengthen service-learning programs.

The district has received Learn and Serve Michigan grants for four years. These grants were both politically and economically important. Economically, they helped institute programs that could not have been undertaken otherwise. Politically, they were a message to the superintendent and school board that Grand Rapids was on the cutting edge of a national trend.

The district currently has a proposal before a major funder. If funded, this project will provide the training and curriculum development for full implementation of service-learning.

Most outside funders will not fund a program unless they can see that the district is firmly behind the program, which Grand Rapids has demonstrated. Besides the grants mentioned above, the district had committed over $100,000 per year to the program. This funding includes the director's salary, clerical help, training costs, office expenses, and materials development.

STRATEGY 5—LEVERAGE COMMUNITY SUPPORT AND RESOURCES For service-learning, a vital resource is community links. Students need a place to undertake their service. The community needs to understand the purpose of the program and its role in planning and implementation.

These links were established in the first year of the program. The Facilitator became a member of the United Way Community Connections Committee, the Grand Rapids Service Corps (AmeriCorps) Board, the United Way Youth Initiative Board, and the area-wide Service-Learning Advisory Board.

These community connections fostered program development in various ways. First, the Facilitator could point community agencies to school resources for help with projects. Second, the Facilitator was given many opportunities to speak before agencies to explain the Grand Rapids Public Schools program of service-learning.

The most important partnership is with the Heart of West Michigan United Way. This provides direct connections to all major social service agencies in the city. Its Volunteer Connections Office secures outside speakers and visitation sites for each of our teacher trainings. In addition, it oversees the Youth Initiative Program, a service and philanthropy program for high school youth from the metropolitan area. This program takes the message of service-learning to high school student leaders. They, in turn, carry it back to teachers, principals, other students, and parents. In 1995, the district collaborated with the Heart of West Michigan United Way and a local neighborhood association to write a grant that supported a summer school service-learning program for at-risk middle school students.

These collaborations have expanded the circle of community leaders who understand and support service-learning.

The appointment of Michelle Engler, wife of Governor John Engler, as chairperson of the Michigan Community Service Commission (MCSC) also helped leverage political support. The MCSC oversees all community service activities in Michigan and is the conduit for federal funds through the National Community Trust. Her direct involvement in the movement probably helped Michigan avoid some of the political problems that have plagued service-learning programs in other states.

LESSONS LEARNED Service-learning can be the hub around which many current educational reforms revolve. At its core, it asks that students find information, make decisions based on that information, take action, and evaluate the results of the action. Employability skills, cooperative learning, and higher level thinking skills are central to this process. The experience of sustaining service-learning in a changing political and economic climate taught us many valuable lessons. What Grand Rapids learned can serve as a guide for other schools or districts seeking to establish a curricular-based service-learning program. Our experience suggests that any district that seeks to implement a service-learning program should consider these issues:

Decide on a definition. This is critical. Make sure that the definition fits current definitions being used across the country. If you plan to seek outside funding, make sure that it is a definition that is generally accepted by funders.

Decide on indicators of success. Program sustainability depends on letting others know how service-learning affects student learning. In times of decreasing funding, only programs that show a clear link to student learning will be able to survive. Grand Rapids' failure to do this up front slowed development of the program.

Link service-learning to your strategic plan or district mission. Service can be linked to almost every district mission statement. Don't depend on others to do this. Find the links and point them out whenever you can.

Integrate service-learning into the curriculum and appropriate administrative structures. Ideally, service-learning should be in the curriculum division of your school's administrative structure, rather than student activities. This will give service-learning credibility with teachers as an effective teaching tool.

Find state and national support. Many of the state and national curriculum goals relate directly to service-learning. They may not call it service-learning, but they are saying the same thing. Point this out to district administrators and school board members.

Show the value-added nature of your program. Even if you cannot demonstrate the direct link to learning early in program development, you can show value added. Value-added aspects of service-learning include the value of service to the school and community and the increased positive connections with community organizations. Networks established by the Facilitator in Grand Rapids have brought many other resources to the district. Even though it is not central to the program, the number of hours students contribute can be quantified. This information can be valuable in community relations.

Be a broken record. Someone needs to "carry the torch" for service-learning. Talk about it at every opportunity. Look for links to all areas of the curriculum. Look for existing programs that either follow the service-learning model you are using or can follow it with minor modifications.

Program sustainability depends on letting others know how service-learning affects student learning.

Publicize, publicize, publicize. Create newsletters, fliers, PSAs, and videos to publicize your program. Send press releases for every good news story that has any possible link to service.

Network. This is one program that cannot be done in isolation. You need to make the community links and pave the way for teachers and students to initiate projects.

Frederick (Fritz) Crabb is currently the Facilitator of Grants for the Grand Rapids Public Schools in Michigan. Formerly, he was the Director of Student Activities, and then Facilitator for Service-Learning for the district. Fritz was a Fellow in NSEE's Leadership Development Program, funded by the DeWitt Wallace-Reader's Digest Fund.

Integrating Service-Learning into the School Culture

FIVE YEARS AGO, THE LOCAL SCHOOL BOARD OVERSEEING CHAMPLAIN VALLEY UNION HIGH SCHOOL, at the urging of the superintendent, passed a policy that required all students to "be involved in a program of community service" and the service "be integrated into the curriculum."

BY JOAN BRAUN

The most important result of our efforts is that service-learning is now a part of the school's and community's language and conversation.

That action prompted a pivotal change in the school's Direction Center, which had administered a service-learning and a school-to-work program for about 20 years. We began a shift in efforts from providing direct services to students to developing new initiatives, forging new connections with the community, and providing direct services to faculty and staff as well as students. Our goal centered on facilitating connections between the school and the community.

To accomplish our goal, we sought to facilitate the integration of service-learning and the school-to-work initiative into the culture and curriculum of the school. In the process, we hoped that serving and caring for others would become a part of the values that operated here at Champlain Valley Union.

Moving service-learning from alongside of the curriculum to the core of the school has been a challenge. We began this shift with a highly respected program with a 20-year track record, knowledgeable staff, an administrative charge, and a clear board policy that complemented the stated school mission. The mission of Champlain Valley Union states that "every student is capable of learning" and can "master the behaviors, skills, and knowledge essential for a contributing member of a democratic society."

The school board policy on integrating service-learning into the curriculum provided an explicit link between a school system's stated mission and using service-learning to achieve that mission. While this link looked good on paper, the faculty and administrators had not incorporated service-learning as part of their operating philosophy. We had to develop a plan that could shift both the fact and the perception from what "they do there" at the Direction Center to "what we do here" as an integral part of Champlain Valley Union High School.

"What you all do over there is wonderful, but I don't have time to even begin to think about having community people involved with my class," one of our English teachers told me in 1993, two years after the new board policy was adopted. "I can barely manage to work with the students I have in class. How could I possibly cope with 20 additional adults?"

MOVING SERVICE-LEARNING INTO THE SCHOOL CULTURE Located in suburban/rural Vermont, Champlain Valley Union has 900 students grades 9–12, about 90 percent white (the same proportion as the state), from diverse socio-economic backgrounds. The staff of the Direction Center, long part of the school structure and budget, is composed of a director, community coordinator, Graduation Challenge coordinator, and secretary. Before the new school policy, we had been working with students on an individual basis to explore their interests, to find sites in the community, and to develop learning goals with the agency. A staff member oversaw each project, provided required reflections throughout the year, and concluded with evaluations and a year-end celebration. Students received elective credit.

Shortly after the new school board policy, we were fortunate to be selected as a pilot site for NSEE's project, supported by The Hitachi Foundation, to strengthen and sustain high school service-learning programs. The grant provided us with outside support and resources in beginning to find ways to integrate service-learning into the daily life of the school. It also increased our visibility and provided outside consultations.

Initially, however, we had considerable difficulty in even finding adults in the building willing to meet with our consultants. The frustration of having to go around the building and sell people on the value of spending time with national figures was very discouraging. We had verbal support from the superintendent and the principal, but no push for second tier administrators or faculty to become involved.

We started by developing three committees called "Learning Circles"—one of students, one of faculty and staff, and one of members from our Community Advisory Board. During the three years of the grant, members attended regional conferences, read materials, and engaged in stimulating discussions about service-learning and ways to nurture and develop it at our school. We also held two full-day retreats.

During the third year we brought two members from each group together with the Direction Center staff in a retreat setting to develop a new vision and mission for the Direction Center. The group worked on this at three meetings over a period of several months. The final recommendations included three steps to reach that vision: 1) the establishment of a committee to develop a formal implementation plan for the board policy; 2) the development of a database of community resources to be available to faculty, staff, and students throughout the school; and 3) the development of a comprehensive Career Resource Center that will utilize service-learning and career materials, community resources, and experiences for the entire community. We are still following through on these recommendations.

While this process was extremely helpful to us, it had some weaknesses. We would have preferred to have the groups meet jointly for the entire time, and to continue to do so. While community members are extremely supportive and willing to meet with us in a very flexible manner, this is very difficult in a rural setting. Transportation and convening during non-school hours is difficult for students. Also, the faculty, staff, and students are heavily involved in various school restructuring efforts, spending much energy on other committees. The best way to produce quality planning work for integrating service-learning into a school, I now believe, is to have professional development time during the summer and during the school year with in-service days and full-day retreats.

WHERE ARE WE NOW? After five years, we are slowly integrating service-learning into our school mission, in terms of how it functions in the daily life of the school. But we still have a long way to go. A year after the English teacher told me he would be overwhelmed adding 20 adults to his class, I approached him again.

"Would you be interested in working with residents in a retirement community, partnering them with your students to improve their language skills, and having your students teach computer skills to their elderly partners?" I asked.

This time, I got a different response. "It sounds like an interesting idea. Let's try it." Why such a change in just a year?

The groundwork laid by the grant enabled the conversation and ideas to spread beyond our immediate committees to larger portions of the school. The administration's emphasis on collaboration among faculty and staff and the structuring of faculty meetings and in-services to facilitate this process has helped immeasurably. The growing national prominence of service-learning has certainly boosted our credibility.

The inclusion of community involvement in the designing of curriculum is now strongly encouraged. Barriers to our work have significantly disappeared. This year the school had 438 students, from 10 different areas, contributing to the community, and 1,434 adults sharing their skills with the school and our students. We have also established a professional development section of the Direction Center's library, and an increasing number of articles about students' service-learning opportunities and experiences have appeared in both the school and community newspapers.

In conversations in the building, whenever it is appropriate we suggest ways to integrate service-learning into particular topics of study or activities. Whenever possible, we follow up these conversations with articles from our library. Many exciting initiatives have been generated as a result of casual hallway meetings, which feed into and off of intentional planning by the Direction Center.

The most important result of our efforts is that service-learning is now a part of the school's and community's language and conversation. There is an understanding that it is an additional way for students to learn, a way of developing caring, contributing citizens, a way of making students' learning relevant to them and their community, and a way to engage the community as teachers and resources. We keep an informal tally of every time we hear a student or faculty member use "reflection" in a conversation. It has become both an accepted word and a common teaching technique.

This year two-thirds of our freshmen have had group interview experiences with a neighboring retirement community. Each student in the remaining third gave five hours of service in self-selected projects to their community as part of their curricular studies. All 10th graders now have an individual, five-hour service-learning experience in conjunction with their English research papers and presentations. We are recommending that all 11th graders have individual community experiences leading to their required Senior Graduation Challenge, which is community/experience based.

Many school activities also have added service-learning components, such as the Key Club, class councils, athletic teams, House Teams, the hiking club, and Friday Night Coffee House, to name a few.

It is no longer unusual to see community adults in the building at all times of the day. By participating in a variety of short- and long-term activities here, they serve as constant role models of service to our students. We have spearheaded a county-wide service-learning network in conjunction with United Way's Volunteer connection and The Governor's Commission on Volunteerism. In the spring of 1996, all freshmen participated in a summer opportunities fair which featured service-learning openings for their vacation time.

I see the changes continuing and service-learning flourishing. Service-learning and the school-to-work initiative will begin to blend together, providing our students with a firm foundation for life-long commitments to community service and learning.

The one clear understanding I have gained through this venture is that change is a process not a destination. It takes a strong belief in what you are doing, patience, resources, and support from a variety of constituencies. But perseverance has many rewards.

"I could not have gotten through the semester without the help of our partners," the English teacher told me in June of 1995, after completing the project with the senior citizens. "What they taught our students and what our students taught them was truly life changing."

The growing national prominence of service-learning has certainly boosted our credibility.

> Joan Braun is Director of the Direction Center at Champlain Valley Union High School in Hinesburg, Vermont. She has been a Mentor in NSEE's Leadership Development Program and a Consultant with NSEE's National Initiative, funded by the DeWitt Wallace-Reader's Digest Fund. She was also a key liaison for NSEE's Pilot Project, supported by The Hitachi Foundation, to strengthen and sustain high school service-learning programs.

The Essential Concrete Elements of Success

IN THE SPRING OF 1993, FOUR STAFF MEMBERS BEGAN CONSIDERING IF IT WERE POSSIBLE TO INSTITUTIONALIZE SERVICE-LEARNING AT SPRING VALLEY HIGH SCHOOL IN COLUMBIA, SOUTH CAROLINA. Each of us had some previous success with integrating service into the curriculum. All of us were constantly searching for strategies that would motivate students to take more responsibility for their actions, attitudes, and learning. We believed in the benefits of linking community service to curriculum and promoting lifelong learning among students to ensure success, self-reliance, and personal growth.

BY **BEVERLY HIOTT**

...you will need allies in administrative positions to move an idea to a functioning program on any substantial level.

We had a beginning—our individual commitment to the concepts involved and the energy of our group, which we came to call the "Core Four." We also had an application to NSEE's Leadership Development Program, funded by the DeWitt Wallace-Readers' Digest Fund, given to us by the then Assistant Principal for Curriculum. But we did not have adequate concrete supports—an office, phone, equipment, secretary, time away from courses for planning. We had conceptual support from our Assistant Principal. But could we take that to a functioning, service-learning program that added flesh and bones to our ideas?

The task we faced is not unlike that of teachers and administrators throughout the country. A few teachers might be interested in service-learning and have some personal experience. They want to make that sporadic effort more of a part of the operations of the school. Perhaps a grant helps get things started. But what key factors get the concrete elements in place to help ensure that the program doesn't die when the grant ends? While every situation is different, there are some common pitfalls and guideposts that can help a program obtain the concrete support it needs. Our situation in Columbia over the last three years illustrates many of these factors.

FINDING SUPPORT TO START Perhaps the most important factor for anyone trying to advance service-learning is to draw on group support. An isolated voice is less likely to develop concrete administrative support than a core group is, especially in a large school or district. Our school had 2,400 students at the time with a new school under planning to relieve overcrowding.

Our core group completed the NSEE proposal in the spring of 1993 and two of us—Marianna McKeown, who taught leadership courses and a seminar in the Gifted and Talented program, and myself—were selected for the Program. I was then coordinating Spring Valley's dropout prevention program and teaching social studies courses within the program. This grant allowed us to get leave time to attend various training workshops, including a national meeting in the fall of 1993, where we drafted a two-year action plan for a service-learning program at our school.

An important first step in the plan was to expand the core group into a more formal Task Force. We added students and community representatives to the group. We recruited students through an application and interview process, emphasizing diversity and leadership potential. The Task Force met regularly to carry out the action plan, each member taking on certain responsibilities. We met during lunch and after school, and we had release time from classes at various critical points. This was manageable because of the grant and other factors. I worked with a teacher team, for example, and Sherrill "Marty" Martin, another member of the "Core Four," had an administrative position, Student Activities Director, so our schedules were more flexible and could adapt to the needs of others. Students also had excused absences for meetings. Having initial administrative support helped us get professional leave and excused absences for students when necessary, which helped a lot.

The Task Force established a number of programmatic goals, but we still had no space or point person to implement them. For example, we wanted to provide personal assistance and practical hands-on workshops to help faculty integrate service-learning into the curriculum. We wanted to develop service courses to be offered for credit. We wanted to develop evaluation tools and procedures. We had the energy of the Task Force members and several extracurricular school-wide initiatives to build on. For example, our school sponsored a Winter Days drive, which was an extracurricular effort to provide service to foster children, the council on aging, and others. We wanted to bridge the gap between extracurricular and academic-based service-learning.

We felt that if we experienced success, if the power of the program motivated and benefited students, that the administration would do everything possible to ensure continued growth. The more success, the more growth. Then we would approach the key question of getting a service-learning coordinator with a functioning office. After a year, I knew I wanted to be a service-learning coordinator, but didn't know if such a position could be carved out at Spring Valley. We needed a coordinator's position for the program to grow more quickly and strategically. Initially, we felt we could move forward gradually without a designated coordinator. But our experience and that of our colleagues nationwide indicate that curricular integration is more likely to happen with a full-time coordinator.

FINDING ADMINISTRATIVE ALLIES Regardless of your situation, you will need allies in administrative positions to move an idea to a functioning program on any substantial level. This is particularly important during times of staffing changes, administrative turnover, budget cuts, and other unexpected situations within the typical educational environment.

In our first year, we managed to increase staff and student interest in service-learning and develop linkages of this concept with existing reform efforts, such as school-to-work. This helped to establish the need for a coordinator's position. By 1994, our school was going through a major transition. The opening of a sister school, Ridge View High, would greatly relieve overcrowding at Spring Valley, but it would result in significant downsizing of our faculty. In the fall of 1995, we would have some 40 fewer faculty members and 700 fewer students.

At this point, we had an unexpected surprise that helped us tremendously. The Assistant Principal for Curriculum, who had passed the original NSEE application to us, became the principal of the new high school. One of the core group, Marty, was chosen as the new Assistant Principal for Curriculum at Spring Valley. He was determined to find a way for us to create a service-learning coordinator's position, even with fewer overall faculty. A less visionary administrator might have missed the opportunity to pursue the coordinator's position during the 1995–96 school year, when the downsizing occurred.

We had to develop a structure for the coordinator's position that would be possible within the changing staffing arrangements. Marty, Marianna, and I designed the coordinator's position to include instructional, administrative, and technical assistance responsibilities. (See the chart at the end of this article.) The coordinator would teach three courses, about 120 students, in peer assistance leadership, community service leadership, and community service internship. Because of the way the block schedule system works at Spring Valley, students could spend two weeks of each semester in course information and training sessions and subsequently be placed in volunteer positions throughout the school and community under adult supervisors. Students would meet periodically during the semester and again for end-of-course presentations. This would leave the coordinator the flexibility to work with other faculty and community groups in various ways.

Marty took this plan to other key administrative decision makers and was able to show them the benefit of having a coordinator who could serve in multiple capacities as both a program coordinator and teacher/facilitator for service-learning. The administration agreed to create the coordinator's position. A major reason was that the design allowed the position to be created without new funding. The position actually became an asset in a time of downsizing and restructuring.

The value of having a key administrator on your side cannot be overemphasized. Marty is highly regarded among our staff, runs Curriculum Action Team meetings every class period twice monthly allowing all faculty to participate, and is leading the redesign of Spring Valley's curriculum into career clusters. If you're not as fortunate as we were to have "one of our own" in a position of authority, build and nurture relationships with key people who understand the benefits of service-learning to the students, the school, and the community.

DOING MORE WITH LESS After the beginning of the semester, when students in my three courses are in their placements, my role becomes largely facilitative and administrative. I provide other staff with information, resources, and direct assistance in linking service to their respective curricular areas. I also establish and maintain school and community connections. This keeps our program, called "VikingServe," in the forefront both on campus and in the community. The Task Force and I have become wonderfully adept at "plate spinning."

The overall impact of the coordinator's position as it exists at Spring Valley far surpasses what one teacher could do in one classroom with 120 students. My major job focus is to coordinate service-learning—not teach four history classes, act as department chair, and take on service-learning as an extra, as is often the case in many schools. I have so many resources from which to draw, far beyond the Task Force itself. I have 60 students from the Peer Assistance Leadership class in any given semester to help run the program. These students may choose in-school placements in guidance, administrative offices, science and math labs, and special needs classes, to give just a few examples.

The VikingServe program itself is one of the placement choices for students. So the program has a staff whose payment is not money but course credit. The students visit on-campus placement sites and take attendance, communicate between other peer assistants and me, conduct observations of peer leadership students in their placements, provide clerical assistance, serve as spokespersons for VikingServe, and assist other teachers with on-going service projects. A substitute is not required when I'm absent.

Having a coordinator's position is important, but other supports are also needed. Funding for materials and supplies, student transportation, staff and student training, and other services has come largely from grants and fellowships, including NSEE's Leadership Development Program and Learn and Serve America grants. We have generated small amounts of money for our program by conducting staff development, training, and consultation for other schools and districts both in and out of the state. We share computers, printers, cameras, and other equipment with the dropout prevention program. As with most rooms in the Technology Center, where we are located, we have a phone. I have quick access to the building's fax and copy machines as well as a long-distance telephone line. I manage a local school fund and a Learn and Serve grant, with the assistance of school bookkeepers.

As an administrator, Marty has been able to show top decision makers the benefits of using one person's time differently and more effectively. For 1996-97, he will ensure that VikingServe is included in the school budget process so that we can engage more students and teachers in service-learning. This should make us less dependent on dwindling grant funds and help service-learning become more deeply entrenched in the curriculum.

Part of my personal and professional strength is relationship building, for myself, my students, and our program. This adds to the high visibility of the program, both in school and in the community. More importantly, the program has developed through the collaborative efforts of teachers and administrators. Service-learning became part of the school's strategic planning in 1995. More administrators and teachers see it as a way to carry out school and district missions, especially in regard to personal responsibility, citizenship development, and lifelong learning for students. Many of our faculty embrace our mission. They "get it." Many see VikingServe and the students as important resources. Many staff members supervise Peer Leadership students on placement. As more and more teachers incorporate service into sociology, biology, Spanish, art, building construction, journalism, and other classes, they generate excitement and camaraderie. Service becomes a tie that binds traditionally isolated curricular areas.

As mundane as it seems, what can make this connection grow are the practical elements of a functioning program—a coordinator, an office, a phone, basic materials, operating funds, and other support services. We get so much administrative and teacher support because we give so

Service becomes a tie that binds traditionally isolated curricular areas.

much. We were fortunate to have Marty move from the "Core Four" to a key administrative position. He remains an active member of the VikingServe Task Force. We were fortunate to have a core group to begin with. We have had to *seize* other opportunities as they presented themselves. But we have had to be intentional, deliberate, and strategic.

Regardless of our situation as teachers and administrators, we need to set goals and start with the end in mind. Have a vision of what we want. Collaborate. Plan strategically. Gain support of key players, critical among them, administrators. Clear principles help set priorities, guide decision making, solve problems, communicate rationale, and gain commitment from others. This kind of foundation building helps to ensure that, in crisis moments, our programs don't get the axe. When something becomes the lifeblood of our school, no one would consider taking it away. Practical support services, along with solid collaborative planning and implementation, are fundamental to making service-learning programs an essential part of public schools.

ADMINISTRATIVE DESIGN FOR SPRING VALLEY HIGH SCHOOL SERVICE-LEARNING PROGRAM

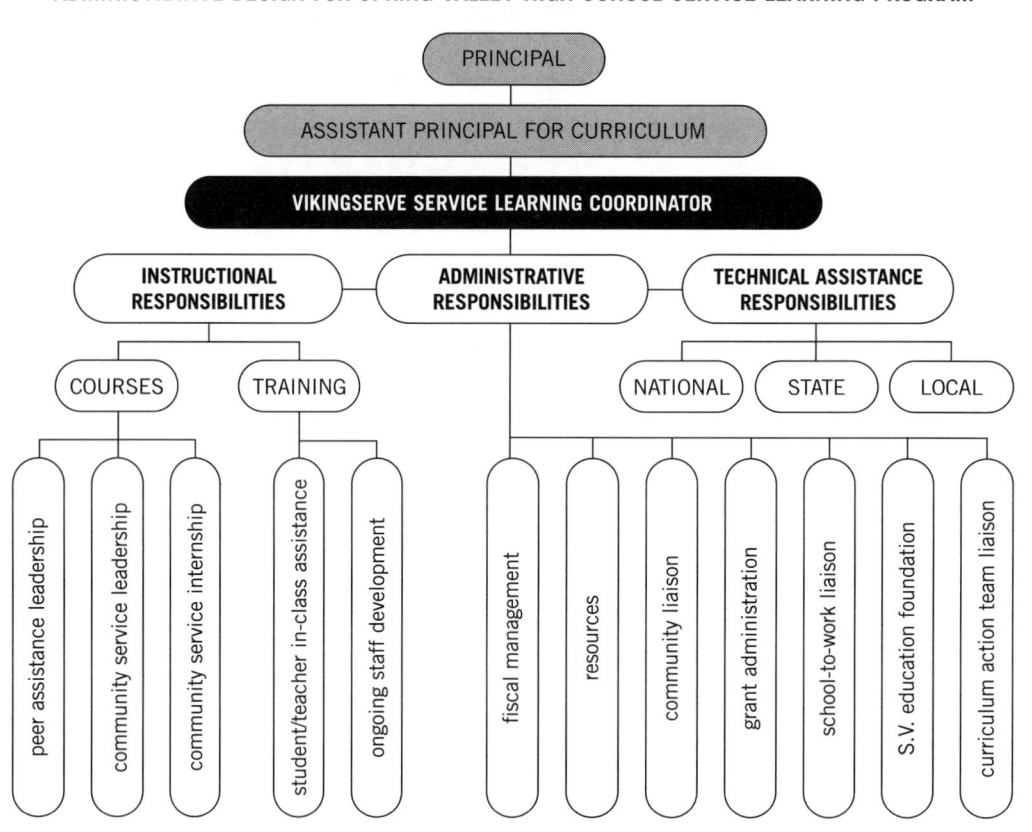

- PRINCIPAL
  - ASSISTANT PRINCIPAL FOR CURRICULUM
    - VIKINGSERVE SERVICE LEARNING COORDINATOR
      - INSTRUCTIONAL RESPONSIBILITIES
        - COURSES
          - peer assistance leadership
          - community service leadership
          - community service internship
        - TRAINING
          - student/teacher in-class assistance
          - ongoing staff development
      - ADMINISTRATIVE RESPONSIBILITIES
        - fiscal management
        - resources
        - community liaison
        - grant administration
        - school-to-work liaison
        - S.V. education foundation
        - curriculum action team liaison
      - TECHNICAL ASSISTANCE RESPONSIBILITIES
        - NATIONAL
        - STATE
        - LOCAL

Beverly Hiott is Service Learning Coordinator at Spring Valley High School in Columbia, South Carolina. She was a Fellow and a Mentor in NSEE's Leadership Development Program, funded by the DeWitt Wallace-Reader's Digest Fund.

Getting Your Own Budget

AT IRONDEQUOIT HIGH SCHOOL IN ROCHESTER, NEW YORK, I TAUGHT BUSINESS AND LAW COURSES FOR MANY YEARS. In the late 1980s, I started seeing a new trend in education. School counselors were beginning to request field placements not just for business students but for math, science, foreign language, and technology students. The guidance counselors handled whatever requests they could but did not have the time to follow-up with a student who spent a day with a professional person. The district administrators were aware of the frustration over this lack of continuity in field experiences as well as the growing national initiatives in experiential education. In response, they created a new position at the school, a "Career Connections Coordinator."

BY **NANCY RUSS**

Spring 1991. I interview and am chosen for the job. I remain under the school's Business Department and budget, teaching two law courses per day but with the rest of my time to develop this new program.

After five years in this job, I know I've found my niche in public secondary education. I love what I do. I'm probably like hundreds of secondary education teachers across the country trying to infuse experiential education into the school's curriculum. Like most of these teachers, I've had to fight for funds from the school system. It has never been easy. Operating on a shoestring budget, I realized early into my new job that I needed my own budget within the school budget. But how can one person, starting with only an idea and a niche in an existing department, secure an independent budget?

During the summer of 1991, Dr. Stewart Agor, the school principal, and I had a training session on starting and managing an effective program. Kathy Heffron of nearby Pittsford Central School District, who had developed an experiential education program there, led the training. Dr. Agor and I then met with the school counselors to establish program objectives and outcomes. We agreed on a basic philosophy that all students should be able to try the work today that they might pursue as a career tomorrow. Students needed help in making intelligent choices about the future. I designed the initial program to be attractive for all students, freshmen through seniors. At this point in the program, it was primarily career oriented; the concept of service-learning would become a larger focus in the district later.

There were four options in the original program. In "Shadowing Days," a student would be matched with a mentor for a day. In an internship, a student could learn more about a profession by becoming involved with an organization for a semester. A work/study program allowed a student to be employed in an area related to future career goals. A "Career Explorers" program allowed students to meet at night with professionals on tours, workshops, and presentations.

A desk and a phone, file cabinets, and folders. It was a simple request.

Having gotten the administration's support and designed the initial program, what would I need to run this new program? A desk and a phone, file cabinets, and folders. It was a simple request. The program funding would come from the Business Department budget.

September 1991. We blitz the school with bulletin and public address announcements about the new program. Seniors express the most interest. By the end of the month, 42 students are enrolled in the semester internship.

The program picked up interest as the year progressed. By October, there were 29 students enrolled in the work/study program, 12 in shadowing days, and nine in Career Explorers. As the year went on, the interest in the shadowing days grew, with 113 students participating by the end of the year. Also, we discovered that many students were already participating in Career Explorers, a Boy Scout program, and now wanted it on their transcript, along with those participating through our program. I was accomplishing the district's goals all with a desk, a phone, file cabinet, and folders—and no budget.

What we didn't expect, however, was the deluge of requests that came into the Career Center, a separate program in the high school. The participation in the internships and other exposure to possible careers prompted requests for information on careers, majors at particular colleges and universities, career days, and seminars. Parents wanted to come in and investigate opportunities for their child.

I began to have a vision of taking over the guidance Career Center, turning this classroom size room with windows into a Career and Community Connections Center. I would need computers, eventually with CD-Rom capability, career guidance books and materials, and college search programs. I wanted the ambiance of the room to be inviting yet professional. Posters of schools and professionals in their fields would be on the walls, along with pictures of our students engaged in their placements and bulletin boards and a glass showcase to highlight the experiential learning opportunities for students. The Center would be a place to help students find opportunities for community work. This would help build the service-learning aspects of the program. I would become knowledgeable about a variety of academic disciplines and career possibilities by researching, speaking with professionals, and developing a core of academic advisors.

Yes, I had a vision, but it would cost money. I was under the budget of someone else who had an entire Business Department's needs to think about. My goal was to create a functioning career and community service center and to be able to sustain it. I needed my own budget!

June 1992. I approach the principal and the coordinator of the Business Department and ask to be relocated to the Career Center. Dr. Agor sees the importance of my work being in a central location to serve all students. The head of the Business Department agrees and is willing to continue funding the phone, desk, and basic office supplies. But he cannot fund the computers and laser printer we need. Who will fund them?

When school opened in the fall for my second year in this new program, everything I requested was in the Career Center, including the computer equipment. There had been a dramatic increase in student requests for placement for the new school year. With this evidence, Dr. Agor helped get the funding we needed for the computer from the district general computer budget. This included two computers and printers for students to access a program called the Guidance Information System, which helps do college searches, interest inventories, and related functions. Despite these successes, the room still needed a lot of improvement—paint job, carpeting, curtains. To justify these expenditures, I made sure Dr. Agor, the district curriculum coordinator, counselors, the Business Department head, and the district superintendent saw the room at its busiest—when college recruiters and career speakers were visiting, students were working on the computers, and group guidance sessions were taking place. During the fall parents night, I made sure the Career Center was open, letting parents have a chance to use the computers and get a printout of a profession or college. If I could convince the administrators that this was a high-visibility room, I could get the cosmetic uplift.

I met with Dr. Agor and Mr. Cardamone, our vice principal, over coffee. They had seen the students actively engaged in their own learning, and they saw community partnerships developing. They wanted the Career Center to be a resource room for anyone seeking outside placements and took steps that eventually led to the renovation with funds from the capital improvement budget.

That fall, I had a wonderful surprise to be selected to participate in NSEE's Leadership Development Program, sponsored by the DeWitt Wallace-Reader's Digest Fund. NSEE paired me with an experienced mentor and supported my participation in training institutes. This gave the program more credibility and gave me a chance to learn more skills. My administrators supported me completely in this. Also, I was able to get a small grant for our program for conferences, books, supplies, and other expenses.

My coordinator's role continued to expand during the second year, along with the number of students involved in the program. I had to screen potential placement sites, take students on contract signing appointments, do formal evaluations, and attend meetings. The students needed more help in my absence. I needed a staff assistant to create the weekly guidance chronicle, schedule student appointments, help students on the computer, and answer the phones in my absence. The weekly log report of activities, student participation, and community use of the Career Center justified the need for a staff assistant. But where would the money come from?

Because of the inflexible school schedule, some students cannot do an internship or service project during the academic year and wanted a summer program. I requested five days of work in the summer to find placements, accompany students on placement appointments, and do follow up site evaluations. For this, I requested my regular contract salary rate, not the lower, summer curriculum writing rate. Dr. Agor looked surprised when I asked for my regular rate, but I got it.

Kathy Heffron from Pittsford, who had assisted me and Dr. Agor at the beginning of the program, called me regularly to lend her support. She encouraged me to think about an appreciation breakfast. Even in the fall, I chose a date in late May and began the planning. The cafeteria manager would transform the cafeteria and provide an elegant buffet breakfast for students,

My goal was to create a functioning career and community service center and to be able to sustain it.

mentors, administrators, school board members, and faculty advisors. Our total guest list would exceed 280, and it would cost about $450. But we had enough from the small grant to pay for it. Dr. Agor knew about the plans. Our credibility was growing.

December 1992. Dr. Agor leans over the counter in the main office and hands me a packet. It's the 1993–94 budget request packet. SUCCESS! I am to develop a separate budget for the Career Connections. It is being moved out of the Business Department.

Many factors contributed to this success—bringing the program from a handful of students to more than 150 in two years, the support of the administration, the community mentor involvement, the appreciation breakfast plans, receiving a small grant, and participating in leadership training seminars. Dr. Agor decided that the Career Connections program needed its own budget. Funding for the program was coming from too many sources and directions. My goal had been to have our administrators see that one person should assess the funding needs of the program and put in a budgetary request every January, just like other curriculum areas. Then, if the taxpayers in the community supported the annual budget, I would know in advance how much money I had to work with the following year.

Getting funds to run any program or department is difficult. School budgets are tight. Every department needs money. How we go after it is the challenge. As I look back on the start-up pains of my program, I realize that to justify my future expenditures, the administration would have to see student success, a positive impact on our educational programs, and support from the community. I'm thrilled at the outcome. I now prepare my own budget. My needs are still quite simple in comparison to larger curriculum areas. Professional growth and development, through conferences, will by be my biggest challenge since my NSEE grant expired.

My program is largely career oriented but service-learning projects are becoming a larger focus of our district. I find myself helping more students and faculty look for opportunities to connect classroom learning to a service setting. I've asked my principal to consider changing the name of the program formally to the Career/Community Connections Program. I've casually adopted that title since it best reflects the services we provide.

May 1996. The Service-Learning Coordinator at the junior high school and our Latin Teacher want to work with me to develop a stronger service-learning program at the high school. We have a service-learning course called Citizens in Action and general volunteer workers in place, but want to expand the service-learning concept. Tentative plans are to meet over the summer to plan strategies and activities. No compensation from the district. No budget...yet. Just motivated people interested in working together.

Nancy Russ is Coordinator of Career Connections at West Irondequoit High School in Rochester, New York. She was a Fellow and a Mentor in NSEE's Leadership Development Program, funded by the DeWitt Wallace-Reader's Digest Fund.

Service-Learning as Educational Reform

SERVICE-LEARNING IS CHANGING THE EDUCATIONAL REFORM PARADIGM IN CALIFORNIA. Throughout the state, service-learning programs are providing enriching opportunities for students, teachers, schools, and school districts to connect, unite, and collaborate. Unlike traditional categorical programs that separate out certain groups of students to receive "special" assistance and services, service-learning operates under the assumption that all students have many strengths that can be combined to make important contributions to the betterment of society.

BY **ANDREW FURCO**

In California, a growing diverse student population has spurred on the implementation of a variety of educational reforms—migrant education, special education, bilingual education, vocational education, Gifted and Talented Education, Limited English Proficiency, student leadership, and programs for at-risk youth, among others. Most of these reforms are designed to separate out certain groups of students to receive much needed "special" services. Unfortunately, however, because these well-intentioned programs focus on students' differences, they contribute to the perpetuation of student factions and program stereotypes. In contrast, the inherently unifying and inclusive nature of service-learning allows for a more effective means to achieve fundamental educational reform.

According to education analyst Michael Fullan, "There are currently many reform initiatives from school to district to state aimed at changing the structures of school work and the norms and practices within them. If we are not careful, we can easily witness a series of non-events and other superficial changes that leave the core of the problem untouched (47)." Reforms that only focus on certain subjects, engage particular communities, target specific groups of students, or are applicable to certain types of schools are likely to reform one part of the educational system without really changing the core.

Thus, to be effective, an educational reform effort must embrace all parts of the educational system. This reform must involve all aspects of the educational process, and be able to piece together parts of a whole without having the parts lose their individual shapes and character. It must be inclusive, unifying, and universal. It must be applicable to every student in the system. It must involve every academic discipline. It must engage all teachers.

Genuine educational reform must promote the self esteem of students and instill critical thinking in their learning process. It must draw on the multiple types of abilities inherent within students and provide authentic learning experiences. And, it must find ways within the K–12 educational system to connect learning with life experiences rather than separating the learning

...service-learning can be applied to any school program, operate within any academic curriculum, and involve any student.

process away from basic human issues of maturation, growth, and awareness of the needs of other human beings.

As a universal educational reform, service-learning can be applied to any school program, operate within any academic curriculum, and involve any student. Today in California, 575 schools engage more than 50,000 students in a wide variety of service-learning programs through the state's Department of Education CalServe project. These programs are found in almost all academic disciplines, grades, and types of communities located in the state. While each of the programs is unique in its approach and the types of service activities its students provide, all the programs are predicated on partnerships and collaborations that help unify the educational system.

Service-learning is inherently a unifying agent—it brings people together to work toward important common causes. The CalServe projects are creating places of learning that are unifying and collaborative. Although these schools may have unique approaches to and goals for teaching and learning, all of them have embraced service-learning as a means to bring together students, teachers, schools, and districts. They are functioning as an antidote to the exclusionary model of today's categorical reform programs.

As an inclusive approach, service-learning encourages the involvement of all students regardless of age, ability, or ambition. It supports students from diverse backgrounds and experiences in addressing important social issues that are common to all. Because service-learning is based on cooperative learning and partnership building, it fosters collaboration among teachers across discipline areas and grade levels within a school, among K–12 schools, and across school districts and counties. In California, these reforms are occurring in four primary ways: by fostering student partnerships, by developing teacher collegiality, by fostering school partnerships, and by building inter-district consortia.

FOSTERING STUDENT PARTNERSHIPS Service-learning programs in California have provided opportunities for students to work with peers from other classes and schools. Some programs combine students in different courses (e.g., English and science) to work together on a service project, while others pair older and younger students through tutoring and mentoring activities.

In Oakland's Commencement 2000 Program, for example, elementary, junior, and high school students work in cross-aged teams on science projects revolving around creek restoration, community gardening, and tree planting and nurturing. Students are assigned age-appropriate tasks that are integrated with their particular science curriculum. The program is based on a cascading leadership model in which high school students teach science to junior high school students who, in turn, teach science to elementary school students. This model allows the older students to serve as role models for the younger students. As the students work together on their service projects, they form important kinships that often remain long after the service projects end.

In the Los Molinos CalServe Partners in Education program, elementary and high school students work together on a local creek preservation project. Using a multi-disciplinary approach, this project is connected to all K–12 core academic curricula, including drama and art. The creek restoration project serves as an ongoing theme in students' classes as they progress through their schooling.

Similarly, in a Fresno program, high school students can complete their service project in either education, the environment, or public safety by developing a project that engages them in service-learning with older and/or younger learners. Students who select these types of projects discuss and work through issues of role modeling, respect for elders, conflict resolution, and team building.

All three of these programs help foster unity among students by providing them an opportunity to work collaboratively. Students are encouraged to work with other students from diverse backgrounds. Because students can rally around a common social or educational cause, students' differences are not an issue. Rather, the focus of the program is on what each student can contribute to the project. Each student is seen as a resource who has something to offer.

DEVELOPING TEACHER COLLEGIALITY Many of California's service-learning programs have brought together teachers from various disciplines to collaborate on projects that cut across curriculum lines. Typically, the service project becomes a theme that is incorporated into the students' various academic courses.

At Delta Sierra Middle School in Stockton, for example, eighth-grade students identify a series of community needs and develop community-based service projects to address these needs. These projects utilize a cross-disciplinary thematic curriculum approach that provides opportunities for the eighth graders to work on their projects in their various classes (English, science, social studies, and math). The theme is incorporated into each course, providing all eighth graders with a sense of how their various courses are interrelated. Because the teachers meet regularly to discuss how their disciplines can be taught through the service projects, they learn from each other and are able to share their experiences with one another. Teachers can discuss the same group of students and talk about the students' work habits and team dynamics. Teachers also feel part of a team and feel more valued and involved. For teachers who spend much time isolated in their classrooms, the opportunity to work with other teachers in developing a mutually beneficial program can be invigorating and enjoyable. If the collaboration is ongoing, it can help foster strong teacher collegiality, help streamline the school's curricula, and build a more open, united, and cohesive school.

FOSTERING SCHOOL PARTNERSHIPS A number of California's service-learning programs have brought together two or more schools to work toward common educational and social goals. In Los Angeles, three neighborhood high schools—John Marshall, Franklin, and Eagle Rock—work together in developing a comprehensive service-learning program that is focused on violence prevention. The program is coordinated by a counselor at one of the schools who works with teachers at each school in developing the program at their respective sites. Although each site's program is based on the same violence prevention curriculum, it is unique in the way it integrates the service-learning component into curricula. Throughout the year, students and teachers at the three sites are brought together to share resources and work collaboratively on a large violence prevention project.

In programs that operate across schools, teachers from throughout the district can share curriculum ideas and work collectively through similar service-learning programmatic issues (such as transportation and liability). For a district, such a partnership can assist in the adoption of universal service-learning standards and regulations such as wording on student service contracts and criteria for grading. Developing universal standards and regulations are especially helpful to a community organization that works with students from many schools.

BUILDING INTER-DISTRICT CONSORTIA Service-learning projects also have been used as a tool for uniting educators across school districts and communities. In Northern California's Alameda County, 10 school districts have banded together to form a county-wide service-learning partnership. School representatives from 10 of the county's 18 school districts come together each month to share resources and support one another in their service-learning endeavors. While each district has a different focus and approach to service-learning, all the districts work toward the common goal of strengthening communities and enhancing all students' learning experiences.

The partnership is coordinated by the county's Office of Education, which also serves as the partnership's fiscal agent. This partnership has allowed the district representatives to become better aware of what is happening throughout the county. They have been able to share the knowledge with many schools in their neighborhoods. The strength of this approach is that it is generative; information on service-learning can be used at all school sites to establish programs. It also helps build unity across schools and across districts.

REFERENCES AND SUGGESTIONS FOR FURTHER READING
Bolman, J.V., and Deal, T. *The Dynamics of Organizational Change in Education.* Berkeley: McCutchan Publishing Corporation, 1983.

Fullan, M.G. *The New Meaning of Educational Change.* New York: Teachers College Press, 1991.

Little, J.W. "The Persistence of Privacy: Autonomy and Initiative in Teachers' Professional Relations." *Teachers College Record* 91.4 (1990): 509-36.

Andrew Furco is Director of the Service-Learning Research and Development Center at the University of California at Berkeley. He has worked as a research associate at the National Center for Research in Vocational Education, directed a high school service program in Northern California, and worked as a middle school vice principal and teacher.

Program Management

issue 3

New and experienced practitioners alike need assistance in the "nuts and bolts" of administering service-learning programs. Effective program management is the key to meaningful and productive service-learning experiences for students, teachers, and the community.

KATHY HEFFRON begins with the basics of identifying service sites and monitoring students on site.

JILL ARTUS AND **IVY DITON** team up to deconstruct the mysteries of scheduling and transportation for service-learning activities.

CYNTHIA HUBBARD explores the nuances of risk management.

KATHY MEGYERI suggests strategies for marketing your service-learning program to various stakeholders.

JANIS FRIES-MARTINEZ shares her success stories in fundraising.

RICHARD BRADLEY outlines methods and rationales for program evaluation.

Matching Students with Service Sites

MATCHING THE RIGHT STUDENT WITH THE RIGHT SITE CAN MAKE OR BREAK A SERVICE-LEARNING PROGRAM. By establishing a process for accomplishing this goal, a program coordinator can enable a student to have a successful and relevant experience. The time and effort used in selecting an appropriate placement at the beginning of the program allows the coordinator to spend more time with the student on reflection and learning and less time on troubleshooting and putting out fires.

BY **KATHY HEFFRON**

Several years ago, we added service-learning to a 16-year-old career internship program. High school juniors and seniors have an opportunity to work with professionals in business, government, or a civic organization gaining hands-on experience. Students are not paid but receive school credit and a written evaluation for employment, college, or scholarship applications. By integrating a service-learning philosophy into our internship program, students now experience a broader learning process. The process we have developed for site placements grew out of the internship program, which is the way we have involved service-learning into our curriculum. This model involves an in-depth review of the student's needs and strengths before beginning the placement, which is usually a semester-long program.

Regardless of the type of service-learning program you have, the steps I describe below can be useful. You will need to modify them to your own circumstances. For shorter placements with more students involved, you will not have the time to do as much interviewing with the students, for example. Some classes may be placed in group situations without individual interviews. But when an in-depth placement is involved, where a student functions with specific responsibilities in an agency, the steps below will be a good checklist to follow. These steps allow the coordinator to track the student from the time the student applies for admission into the program until credit is granted at the conclusion.

STUDENT APPLICATION The application form should include information about the student that can help determine what type of placement might be appropriate. This includes interests, whether the student has transportation, what courses the student has taken that might be relevant to the interest, the quarter or semester preferred, and extracurricular activities that might create a conflict. The student might also express interest in specific placements.

Preliminary screening of students through conversations with other adults can help avoid problems as the program progresses. Send a list of potential students to guidance counselors and administrators asking about any possible concerns—such as attendance, reliability, behavior problems, and motivation—before the placement is made.

Sometimes you may request a brief résumé

By building the monitoring process and techniques into the initial planning, you can prepare the student for a positive experience.

along with the application form. If the student has never prepared a résumé, provide a generic form which the student can use as an outline. This is helpful to the community advisor who may want more information on the student's background. Stress neatness, clarity, and accuracy. Remember, this is the community advisor's first introduction to the student.

STUDENT INTERVIEW This is the time to focus on what the student expects from the experience and what you expect from the student as a program participant. Review the application form with the student and add or delete any information the student requests. Make sure the two of you are talking about the same thing. Ask the student to explain what he/she thinks the placement is about. Show evaluations and descriptions from students who have completed the program in that particular area.

Communication is extremely important in supervising the student.

Probe into the interest the student has listed. If a student writes "social work" as the career interest, for example, find out what age group and type of social issue he/she wants to work with. Find out other helpful information such as whether the student is comfortable going into certain areas of the city or community. Are the student's parents uncomfortable with any aspect of the program? Would the student like to go on off-site visits or remain in the agency office? Would the student be uncomfortable working in a hospital emergency room, jail, or other stressful situation?

All of these questions will give you a better understanding of the student to make a compatible placement. Be honest and realistic! If you feel the student does not have the appropriate academic or social background for a particular placement, suggest and encourage another or related field. This can save a phone call from an unhappy community advisor who feels the student isn't interested or doesn't have the basic course work.

Go over the descriptions of possible placements and discuss how the student intends to get to the internship, the schedule, and specific logistics. Ask the student again if he/she understands the program requirements and responsibilities. Then, let the student decide if he/she wants to make the commitment.

CONTACT THE COMMUNITY ADVISOR Marketing the internship or service-learning program takes a lot of work. Developing a network of community placements is essential in matching students with good placements. Where programs have been functioning for several years, you will build up relationships with certain agencies and community advisors. In other cases, you will need to contact some new agencies. I find an initial telephone call a useful way to begin, followed up with a letter, program materials such as a brochure, and the student's application.

Developing a vital network of placement sites allows a program to continue serving students over the years. While an advisor may need to seek placements for most students in high school, some students can take the initiative to find their own placements. "A student's experience of exploring and negotiating the position can be one of the most valuable aspects of the internship," explain Robert Inkster and Roseanna Ross, in their handbook *The Internship as Partnership* (18). Again, while there are differences between a semester-long internship program and many service-learning projects, this model can be useful.

STUDENT PLACED Once the community advisor has agreed to accept the student, talk to the student and prepare the paperwork. This should include an acceptance letter stating the placement site, the name of the community advisor, and requirements such as weekly reports, time sheets, daily journal/log, who to call if they cannot attend on their scheduled day, and final project. The contract/commitment form should include program requirements, community advisor's requirements, student expectations, and signatures of the student, school program coordinator, the community advisor, parent, and an administrator.

"By completing a process of self-assessment, goal-setting, résumé-writing, interviewing, and negotiating a learning agreement with the site supervisor and faculty advisor, the intern will develop confidence, positive attitudes, and more realistic expectations," explain Inkster and Ross. "This process helps the intern become an active learner. Your goal in advising is to empower the student to take an active role in this process (63–4)."

STUDENT PROGRESS MONITORED Communication is extremely important in supervising the student. The program coordinator cannot respond appropriately to a problem if he/she has not been informed by the student or community advisor. Make sure all those involved in the experience know how to reach you. Designate a place where students can leave messages, weekly reports, journals, or final projects. Encourage students to ask questions or express concerns they may have about their placement. Reassure the students that you are available for them if needed.

In the same manner, keep the lines of communication open between you and the community advisor. You want to know if there is concern about the student's grades or incidents that have taken place in school. You want to know from the community advisor if the intern is having a problem at the site. Is the student consistently late? Does the student fail to notify the community advisor of a schedule change?

In supervising the student's experience, refer to the program requirements that you established earlier in the process. These guidelines will now assist you in keeping track of the student's progress. Keep a list of the program requirements to see if the student is working on schedule.

The checklist could include weekly reports/time sheets, a journal, group seminars, and site visits. The program coordinator is responsible for monitoring these various types of information on the student's progress. If the student is behind in hours, find out why. Reviewing the journal enables the coordinator to be aware of the student's personal observations. Informal group seminars can be held at lunch period or after school. Students have the opportunity to discuss their service-learning experiences with other students involved in the program, share problems, and find solutions. Site visits can be valuable for many types of reasons, so be clear about your goals. They could be to see the student at work or to meet with the site supervisor. By building the monitoring process and techniques into the initial planning, you can prepare the student for a positive experience.

REFERENCES AND SUGGESTIONS FOR FURTHER READING

Inkster, Robert P., and Roseanna G. Ross. *The Internship as Partnership: A Handbook for Campus-Based Coordinators & Advisors.* Raleigh, NC: National Society for Experiential Education, 1995.

Kathy Heffron has been the Career Internship/Community Service Coordinator for the Pittsford, New York, Central School District for 16 years, building it from infancy to a state and national model. She has written A Guide to Developing and Managing a High School Career Internship Program. *Kathy was a Mentor in NSEE's Leadership Development Program, funded by the DeWitt Wallace-Reader's Digest Fund.*

SERVICE-LEARNING IN RURAL AMERICA

by Andrew E. Fisher

Chuck Ericksen, Community Education Director with the School District of Flambeau in northwest Wisconsin, knows the challenges that rural service-learning programs face. Flambeau finds itself at the bottom of the economic spectrum with high unemployment. Many of the students involved in his service-learning program are at risk. But, "we have a tenacious bunch of folks," Ericksen says. "Their creative, entrepreneurial spirit is what allows service-learning to thrive in this rural area."

Due to the void of local businesses and companies, service-learning opportunities are more disguised than in other places. But opportunities exist; it just takes creativity to uncover them. For instance, a science class took an interest in a local paper company that produced a lot of waste. Although the company was not violating any laws, the students' testing discovered that clay could be filtered out of the waste and perhaps used for another purpose. The students contacted a neighboring town, and it turned out that a turkey farm was able to use the clay as a binder for turkey feed.

In the Outdoor Education program, Flambeau students run their own outfitting business and serve as guides on the Flambeau Hiking Rivers as well as in the Blue Hills. Some students apprentice themselves to local naturalists and orienteers. Other students provide nonprofit groups with marketing services for free.

The logistical challenge of transportation is overcome through the sharing of vans with other programs in the county. This pooling of resources and overall collaborative attitude within the community is vital for service-learning in remote areas.

Such innovative thinking is crucial for the survival of service-learning, and, Ericksen contends, for the rural community in general. In each of these cases, students are learning and practicing skills that enable them to grow more as individuals. At the same time, the community is reaping the benefits of quality services.

Solving Scheduling and Transportation Challenges

"WATCH ME GROW! I'M CHANGING! WHO AM I? WHERE DO I FIT IN?" These are the voices of some typical 6th-grade students entering W.T. Clarke Middle School, a school of approximately 625 students, located 20 miles from New York City in a suburban middle-class community on Long Island, New York. These students eventually find themselves in a 6th-grade health class, a one-semester course, covering a variety of topics including mental health, growth and development, diseases including AIDS, alcohol, consumer health, first aid, and other New York State mandated subjects. The students enter with few expectations. They leave with incredible insight, an eye on the future, and some answers to their existential questions.

BY JILL ARTUS AND IVY DITON

We are constantly reassessing and renewing our own experience and the experience of the students.

How did this 6th-grade health curriculum take on such vitality? Teacher Jill Artus felt that the health curriculum should be connected to the world outside of the classroom. When the new assistant principal, Ivy Diton, came to Clarke Middle School in the fall of 1993, they discussed the possibility of coupling the middle school health curriculum with meaningful experiences within the community. With encouraging support from the principal and district health administrator, they began integrating community service-learning projects into the 6th-grade curriculum.

In order for this program to work, however, it was important to overcome the challenge of scheduling and transporting more than 100 students to various agencies in and around the middle school community. Some possible placements included the Community Reform Temple Preschool with a focus on child development; the A. Holly Patterson Geriatric Center with a focus on the final stages of the life cycle; the Henry Viscardi School for the Physically Challenged with a focus on overcoming stereotypes of the physically challenged; the Helen Keller National Center with a focus on developing an understanding of the handicapped; local elementary schools with a focus on drug and alcohol prevention for younger students; and our school's own special education class with a focus on growth and development.

Most of the projects involve transportation away from school, and the activities, therefore, require flexibility in scheduling. Activities have included the assignment of pen-pals, sporting events, planting flowers, holiday entertainment, producing videotapes about drug prevention, students teaching students, greenhouse planting partners, "Contract for Life" circulation, arts and crafts, bus rides around the local community to plan for the creation of community booklets, and a "Celebration of Service," a gala culminating festivity organized to recognize the students for their outstanding work in the community.

We have found that the driving force behind our successful program is good relationships with each other, our colleagues, and the community at large. As teacher and administrator, we see this program as a collaborative venture. Through mutual respect, common goals, and on-going support, we have been able to overcome many of the challenges that encumber other middle school community service-learning programs, particularly scheduling and transportation difficulties. With support from our colleagues, our program has grown and blossomed. Most important, we nurture our relationships with the field site program leaders because they enable our program to exist. Our needs dovetail with their needs, creating a very gratifying experience for all involved.

Our program operates on the assumption that middle school students need appropriate support and guidance when they visit the various field sites. We plan our visits during the school day, and students travel together as a class with their teacher to each field site. Hence, scheduling and transportation, which are the lifeline of our program, become important issues as students perform the service as part of the regular school day.

SCHEDULING Scheduling is a significant issue because, ideally, we want to have as many field visits as possible without disrupting the regular schedule of each student. The time slots for visits must coincide with the needs of the selected field sites, so it is essential to plan visits with the site personnel before the program begins. Generally, early morning classes are the most difficult to schedule. For example, an early morning class could not visit the local senior center because the residents are not out of bed, dressed, and fed until later in the morning. The local preschool students, as well as the physically challenged students, do not arrive until 10:30, which also poses a scheduling problem with an early morning service-learning class. In-house projects, pen-pal projects, local community-based projects, and in-house visits work best in these situations.

We have found that adjusting the student schedules is an effective strategy to overcome these problems. Students need to spend at least one hour away from school to have meaningful service experiences. Generally our field sites are no more than ten to fifteen minutes away from school. Field sites located at a greater distance would require more time away from school. Using a traditional school schedule, "double periods" are ideal for the service-learning experience, especially when they are connected to a lunch period resulting in three class periods for a site visit. Block scheduling will also enable the teacher to have this flexible use of time for site visits.

In addition, we actively encourage support from other staff members who teach the same group of students because cooperative relationships greatly affect the students' experience. If students need more time at the field site and it overlaps into another class, the teachers work cooperatively to develop a solution. Through these relationships, the teachers share a common interest and incorporate the service experience into their own curriculum. For example, the teachers may use the service experience as a unifying source for making interdisciplinary connections among the various subject areas. Using this model, students who are visiting with seniors as part of their service experience may read stories about senior citizens in language arts class, discuss cultural difference as they relate to aging in social studies class, or analyze statistics about aging in mathematics class, just to name a few of the possible curricular connections. Hence, the service experience becomes an enhancement of the content curriculum, and the students' time away from school an acceptable part of the middle school program.

Listed below is a sample 6th-grade student schedule. We can combine two and sometimes three (periods 4th to 6th), which are sufficient for scheduling challenges.

8:30–8:40	Advisory
8:40–9:25	1st period: Language Arts
9:25–10:10	2nd period: Reading
10:10–10:55	3rd period: Physical Education/Music (alternating days)
10:55–12:15	4th and 5th period: Science/Health or Computers (alternating days)
12:15–1:00	6th period: Lunch
1:00–1:40	7th period: Social Studies
1:40–2:25	8th period: Math
2:25–3:10	9th period: Library/Art/Foreign Language (alternating days)

TRANSPORTATION Transportation to and from the field sites is a major issue for our program. In our community, public transportation is not readily available for our students. As a suburban school, we are located several miles from the local railroad and at least three quarters of a mile from the nearest public bus. We therefore need to rely on the school district to provide transportation to and from the field sites. These buses are very costly, and the school district is financially unable to provide the number of buses needed to sustain our program. The scheduling of double periods enables us to walk to several sites, but the walking time significantly cuts down on the amount of time we are able to spend at each field site. At times, students have missed other classes. This has not become a problem in our school because we have respected the needs of other teachers. However, we recognize that if students miss many classes, other teachers may become intolerant of the program.

We realized, early on, that we needed additional money for the buses. The first year of our program we relied on the district to provide as many buses as possible. Our classes were limited to two visits a semester. By the second year, we began to apply for grant money to support our program. By the third year, we have successfully secured enough grant money to support our buses for field trips.

Writing successful grant proposals has been an important aspect of our program. We have been able to raise over $10,000 to sustain our program through the Learn and Serve America: K–12 School Grants program. In addition, our school is part of a research grant sponsored by the City University of New York and has received free service-learning training and technical assistance. Effective proposal writing and networking skills are critical for all educators but are particularly significant for programs that rely on outside funding. The focus of our grant proposals is to enhance student involvement in the community and encourage the development of an active and critical citizenry. We state that in order to realize this goal, buses are needed for field trips. Transportation, therefore, becomes the largest budget category in our grant proposals. We are not writing the grants for buses per se, but in order to achieve the objective set forth in our proposals, we need to transport the students from school to the various field sites.

It is important to note that publicity has played a valuable role is helping us secure these additional funds. As the community became aware of the success of our program, perceptions of our school were enhanced. We are frequently featured in the local newspapers and have even had a spot on a local TV news show. These perceptions become a self-fulfilling prophecy; the better the perceptions, the better you become. Our school was recently highlighted as a model middle school service-learning program in a Department of Education training video. This recognition will enable us to gain more stature in other grants competitions as we seek additional funding to support our buses to and from field sites.

REFLECTION Flexibility plays an important role in program implementation as you must be willing to try new ideas and strategies. Reflection and constant re-evaluation make scheduling as effective as possible for an exciting program. Personal reflection allows you to re-evaluate what you have done, and how you could do it better. For example, perhaps it is better to visit the seniors right after breakfast when they are more alert, or you may want to suggest (as we did) that sites visit your school a few times to relieve both the transportation and scheduling difficulties.

We invite the site staff to meet with our classes in school as an orientation session before the students visit their sites. These visits eliminate the need for an orientation field visit and also give the students a sense of knowing before they actually visit the site. We have also invited preschool students to our school for a carnival and party that were planned and implemented by our students at the conclusion of the project year. Students from the physically challenged school were guests at our school for an entire day with our health students as tour guides. These visits are particularly important for schools who are unable to transport their students. Using this model, they can bring the community into their schools and promote active learning without the students ever leaving the schools. In addition, several of our students volunteer to work with our special education students in our own school.

Parents and community members are potentially good sources of funding and transportation to community agencies.

We are constantly reassessing and renewing our own experience and the experience of the students. We do this through active personal reflection and through the recommendations of our students. Their input is very important to us and we encourage active dialogue. We have learned that the more interaction with the community, the more the students learn from the experience. In addition, we have learned that sustaining relationships with community members greatly enhances the experience for the students. However, we have also learned that too many different field sites become difficult to schedule and maintain.

Staying organized has enabled us to schedule and transport over 100 6th-grade students each semester to various field sites on Long Island. A checklist with necessary programmatic steps is essential in making your preliminary arrangements. This checklist may include scheduling notes, ideas for student preparation in class, transportation arrangements, and necessary forms (e.g., transportation, permission slips, consent forms for photo-documentation, administrative procedures to be followed, etc.). A sample checklist follows this article.

At first, all these ideas and "things to do" were maintained on scribbled notes of paper. Eventually a three-inch-wide heavy-duty binder with plenty of subject dividers became the personal journal of the integration of community service-learning into the 6th-grade health curriculum. The book is divided into nine sections: (1) Introductory Activities, (2) Reflection Activities, (3) Service Sites, (4) Service Projects, (5) Quotes from Students, (6) Media and Press Coverage, (7) Grant Applications, (8) Correspondence, and (9) Future Project Ideas. A second binder contains photo-documentation of projects. These binders are used to record scheduling or transportation problems, and other issues that may have occurred. They also provide an opportunity to reflect on personal and program development and improvement.

Above all, as a teacher and assistant principal, we have become appropriate role models for our students as we are involved in aspects of our own school community. We include, as part of our own schedules, time to attend community meetings to learn about potential field sites and share program ideas and insights with community members. We encourage community involvement and strive to get parents involved in all aspects of the program. Parents and community members are potentially good sources of funding and transportation to community agencies. We share the volunteer experience with our students and have learned, first hand, the importance of this contribution to the life of our community.

"Who am I? Where do I fit in?" We believe that after the semester in the health curriculum, our students can address these important question with a far greater sense of purpose.

Jill Artus is a health teacher at W.T. Clarke Middle School in Westbury, New York. Her community health education experiences working for the American Heart and Lung Association and the New York City Police Department's Health Services Division have helped her to bring the community into the classroom.

Ivy Diton is the Assistant Principal of W.T. Clarke Middle School. She is a doctoral candidate at New York University's School of Education, and her current research focuses on community service-learning at the middle school level and the development of an ethic of caring in early adolescent students.

SERVICE-LEARNING PROJECTS CHECKLIST

PROJECT NAME _____ YEAR _____

SITE ADDRESS _____

_____

TELEPHONE NUMBER _____

CONTACT PERSON _____

CLASS/TEACHER _____

PERIOD/DAYS _____

_____

THEME _____

DATES _____

MATERIALS _____

CHAPERONES _____

_____

○ FIELD TRIP REQUEST (BUS REQUEST) FORM

○ FIELD TRIP ROSTER (COPY TO OFFICE WITH PERMISSION SLIPS)

○ ROSTER OF STUDENTS NOT GOING ON FIELD TRIP

○ WRITTEN CONFIRMATION OF BUS RESERVATION BY _____ (ONE WEEK PRIOR)

○ FIELD TRIP VEHICULAR INSPECTION FORM (GOING)

○ FIELD TRIP VEHICULAR INSPECTION FORM (RETURNING)

Adapted from W.T. Clark Middle School.

Risk Management

PINGREE IS A COEDUCATIONAL COLLEGE-PREPARATORY DAY SCHOOL (GRADES 9–12) LOCATED IN A RURAL TOWN NORTH OF BOSTON, MASSACHUSETTS, KNOWN PRIMARILY FOR HORSE FARMS AND EXTENSIVE RIDING OPPORTUNITIES. While we aim for diversity in the student body, our location away from any major urban area makes that undertaking difficult. Our students, however, do come from a wide area and represent some 50 different communities, some as much as an hour away. Community service activities need to be squeezed in as time permits, which is a challenge in a day school where time is both limited and precious.

BY **CYNTHIA HUBBARD**

...risks clearly need to be considered, evaluated, and, whenever possible, avoided or at least controlled.

Community service at Pingree School had its beginnings thirteen years ago when a dedicated math teacher felt it appropriate to have a student activity club dedicated to social concerns, and to make volunteer activities in the surrounding communities available as an after-school option, along with athletics and drama. Any community service done was entirely voluntary, and the student club aimed primarily to educate and engender awareness of social issues and concerns. In 1989, the Trustees approved the implementation of a 50-hour community service graduation requirement. The school purchased a van for community service use and hired a staff person to administer and oversee the program. The program now coordinates the graduation requirement, the Social Concerns Club, after-school volunteer activities, Community Service Day, class projects, school-wide projects, a Homeless Outreach Program, a service component in some courses, and the promoting of various assemblies and other activities such as an annual Blood Drive and the sponsorship of an international child.

As with any school where outreach into the community involves student driving, working with diverse populations, and the natural ebullience of youth, there is always an element of risk. Perhaps nowhere in Pingree's program are the risks more obvious than in our once-a-year Community Service Day. On this particular day, classes are canceled and the entire school—students, faculty, many of the staff, and several parents—are out in the community in groups of four to 40 at various shelters, soup kitchens, day care centers, nursing homes, programs for the disabled, and outdoor park facilities. It is a wonderful day. The students look forward to it; the faculty cooperate enthusiastically; and some parents offer their assistance year after year. However, the day is not without its risks. A few years back, in fact, a near miss with hepatitis B exposure in a facility for the mentally challenged raised a serious question as to whether Community Service Day could or should be continued. As the various risks were considered, however, the school decided that the rewards outweighed the risks and the decision was made to continue the program.

Nonetheless, over the years, we have become much more sensitized to the risks involved and the various ways they can be managed. Similar to most schools, Pingree carries a comprehensive liability umbrella as part of the school's insurance coverage. This means that any student involved in any school activity, on or off campus, is covered beyond his or her own individual insurance in the event of an accident. Many community agencies also carry insurance which covers both paid and voluntary helpers, but such insurance is not guaranteed. For this reason, the risks clearly need to be considered, evaluated, and, whenever possible, avoided or at least controlled. Charles Tremper and Gwynne Kostin, in their helpful book, *No Surprises: Controlling Risks in Volunteer Programs*, outline a method for risk management. The process utilizes five steps:

1. Looking for risks;
2. Assessing the risks;
3. Deciding how to control risks;
4. Implementing a risk control strategy; and
5. Reviewing and revising the process.

We have utilized this model at Pingree. These five steps serve as a valuable process for evaluating any service-learning program.

LOOKING FOR RISKS In Pingree's Community Service Day with 280 people out in the community at various organizations, some as much as an hour away, there are several areas that offer potential risk. There are obvious risks involved with transportation. Students help with the driving, although we do try to keep student driving to a minimum.

Once at the sites, a variety of risks are present. There are infectious diseases within certain populations. Students could accidentally damage property or not handle a patient in a nursing home properly with the resulting possibility of personal injury. A student might spill or splash toxic cleaning materials while doing clean-up work in a soup kitchen or shelter, and we all know that no one is completely immune from allegations of sexual abuse from children in day care facilities. Then there are all the outdoor risks of slipping, falling, working with power equipment, and cutting oneself. This year approximately 80 students were working cleaning up river beds that were muddy and slippery. We had to ensure ahead of time that all students assigned to this site were able to swim and had the proper equipment so as to avoid the danger of slipping into the water.

Finally, the risks are there and they are real. Pretending they are not is neither realistic nor practical. Denial can also be very dangerous as it "substitutes deliberate ignorance for thoughtful planning" as Tremper and Kostin put it. Furthermore, in the event of an accident, the various constituencies involved are much more likely to come to some sort of harmonious resolution when there has been some open acknowledgment and discussion of the risks from the very beginning.

ASSESSING THE RISKS Given the presence of risks, they need to be assessed and evaluated on an on-going basis. The likelihood of a student being in an automobile accident is very real.

However, these same students drive themselves and other students to school on a daily basis. Parents know that their children are taking this risk whether they are driving or being driven by another student. They are also taking a risk every time students go anywhere from the school for athletics or for a field trip. As far as exposure to diseases, the relative risk is higher than it would be at school, although, as with many schools, mononucleosis and other viruses do periodically make their rounds. Generally speaking, those facilities where the risk of infectious disease is an issue are very careful about informing the students about proper hygiene and necessary precautions. Similarly, outdoor projects carry about the same amount of risk that students encounter doing comparable projects in their own yards and are probably less risky than the sports in which they engage on a regular basis.

Risking the school's good will is perhaps the hardest to evaluate and measure. For the most part, students are polite, thoughtful, and considerate. That is not to say that there are not from time to time misunderstandings and the occasional inappropriate behavior, all of which can usually be remedied by a follow-up conversation and/or letter of apology.

DECIDING HOW TO CONTROL RISKS Implementing the necessary strategies to control risks must be an on-going process as the possibilities for new dangers present themselves. The driving situation is controlled first by having as few student drivers as possible, and choosing those students known to be responsible and to have good driving records. Communication with the parents is key, and it needs to be consistent and continuous. About a month before Community Service Day, a letter goes to all parents explaining the situation and informing them to let the school know if they do not want their son or daughter driving with a student. We then ensure that the student in question rides with an adult. Each year, we hear from about three or four parents. Permission slips are of questionable value in the event of a major law suit and, for this event, would be prohibitively cumbersome. Each school should consult with its legal counsel for help in deciding whether or not to use these forms and the appropriate language for them.

The system we use may not be ideal, but at least it does communicate with the parents so that there are no surprises. We also ask parents to inform us if they specifically do not want their children to drive, and we are instituting a new policy that students bring in permission notes from home if they plan to drive. We also utilize willing parents as drivers and have chartered buses for projects that involve large numbers of students who will be traveling a long distance.

With regard to the issue of disease, in addition to relying on the individual agencies to instruct students in proper care and hygiene, we are very careful about where we send students. Having had an incident which could have been quite serious, there are programs to which we simply do not send students. The risk of a student contracting hepatitis B is not a risk we are willing to take knowingly. There are others projects that can be just as meaningful without putting students' health at risk. For students working outdoors, we always try to make sure that they have the gear and clothing necessary for the job: long pants, gloves, work boots, and the like. There have been occasional incidents of poison ivy, but nothing that we would consider sufficiently serious to forego opportunities.

IMPLEMENTING A RISK CONTROL STRATEGY One way that we try to avoid risks in general is to communicate very clearly and very specifically with the various agencies we visit. Initially, we ask them to write out what the students will be doing and what specific equipment/clothing is necessary. In a return letter of confirmation, we repeat to them our understanding of what the students will be doing. Invariably, in spite of everything, there is always one group that gets a surprise. This year, a group of students who were planning to work with children found themselves painting and thus without the appropriate clothing—not a serious risk, but an unpleasant surprise nonetheless. Each year, the faculty/parent in charge of each group calls the site the day before to reconfirm the planned activity. This policy was initiated after several years of having a group arrive at a site unexpected, in spite of a letter of confirmation. In future years, we intend to include a review of the specific tasks as part of that conversation.

REVIEWING AND REVISING THE PROCESS In order for Community Service Day and any service project to be successful, the element of risk has to be considered. However, there is always some inherent assumption of risk of which parents and students need to be aware. The school also must take its responsibility seriously, continuously reviewing sites, policies, and procedures. Each year we solicit feedback from the sites, the students, the faculty, and the parents who took part. We review and evaluate the feedback and take it into consideration in formulating the future program.

THE THREE "C"S Successful service-learning programs ultimately revolve around the three "C"s of risk management: commitment, communication, and consistency (Tremper and Kostin). We must be clear and consistent in communicating our commitment to service-learning to all constituencies involved—students, community agencies and organizations, parents, and faculty. Our *commitment* to service-learning reflects the mission of the school and the community service program in particular—to maintain a program that is safe, beneficial to the community, and a learning experience for the students

Communication with parents, students, the agencies, and the school at large must be clear, consistent, on-going, and two-way. Feedback must be welcomed, accepted, and responded to. We must be willing to deal with problems openly and honestly as soon as they arise, be able to admit a mistake, apologize, and take whatever steps necessary to ameliorate an unhappy or unfortunate situation. We must be *consistent* in what is expected of the students, the adult members of the community, and the agencies, as well as in our responsibility to review risks and in communication at all levels.

Risk is a given, and we must be open to its presence and willing to work with it through responsible risk management procedures. The five steps of risk management reviewed here specifically in light of Pingree School's Community Service Day apply to all service-learning projects no matter how large or small. They are a valuable process for any project to follow. Looking for and assessing risks, constantly evaluating them, and implementing risk control strategies should be a part of the on-going responsibility of the Community Service Director. By clearly and consistently communicating awareness of the risks involved, much can be done not only to avoid problems, but to deal openly and creatively with difficulties when and should they

Implementing the necessary strategies to control risks must be an on-going process....

arise. With this five-step process and the three "C"s of risk management one can conclude that it is indeed better to live with risk than not to live at all.

STEPS TO TAKE FOR GOOD RISK MANAGEMENT
- Check your school's umbrella insurance policy.

- Inform parents of student projects, especially where they are working and who will be driving. In the event of an accident, an uninformed parent is an unhappy parent!

- Get to know your placement sites and the contact people. Knowing the person at the agency makes problem solving much easier.

- Utilize student drivers only when absolutely necessary and then, only with the parents' knowledge and consent.

- Be realistic about students and student behavior. They are not yet adults.

- Communicate in advance with the project supervisor. Ask about risks at the site, the need for special equipment or clothing, or any other unusual precautions.

- Include, whenever reasonable, other members of the school community in service-learning projects and planning. The more people feel "left out," the more negative they will be should problems arise.

- Pay attention to near misses. They are accidents waiting to happen.

- Deal with rumblings or rumors of discontent as soon as possible.

REFERENCES AND SUGGESTIONS FOR FURTHER READING
Goldstein, Michael B. "Legal Issues in Combining Service and Learning," in *Combining Service and Learning: A Resource Book for Community and Public Service*. 3 vols. Ed. Jane Kendall and Associates. Raleigh, NC: National Society for Experiential Education, 1990.

Tremper, Charles, and Gwynne Kostin. *No Surprises: Controlling Risks in Volunteer Programs*. Washington, DC: Nonprofit Risk Management Center, 1993.

Cynthia Hubbard is Director of the Community Service Program at Pingree School in South Hamilton, Massachusetts. She is an ordained priest in the Episcopal Church and served as the Associate Rector of Trinity Church in Topsfield, Massachusetts, prior to joining the faculty at Pingree.

Marketing Your Service-Learning Program

MARYLAND IS THE FIRST STATE TO REQUIRE THE COMPLETION OF 75 HOURS OF SERVICE-LEARNING FOR HIGH SCHOOL GRADUATION. To be meaningful, students' experiences must include reading, discussion, writing, and action. Service-learning is based on the belief that given the opportunity, today's students will bring the energy and do what is necessary to make their local communities and their states better places. All students—honors students, vocational students, general education students, special education students, ESOL (English for Speakers of Other Languages) students, and even those severely disabled—have something to give to their communities. I've seen better grades, higher test scores, and improved attendance as desirable by-products of service-learning.

BY **KATHY MEGYERI**

Whether your program is required or voluntary, marketing the program is of utmost importance if community support and student enthusiasm are to continue year after year. Marketing also helps advertise the pluses of the program, especially to those few parents who still do not understand its value. It generates interest, enthusiasm, and curiosity, particularly from counties and school systems still debating whether or not to offer service-learning. Marketing also helps motivate faculty members to play a more active role, recruits community sponsors, and aids in student recruitment. Generally, people want to be part of a winning service program, and marketing is a means to bring people on board.

My suburban high school enrolls almost 1,600 students and is located 22 miles north of the nation's capital. My particular service-learning students are engaged in four types of service: working with elementary pupils, the disabled, ESOL students, and the elderly. Our population of recent immigrants have been among our most dedicated and enthusiastic volunteers. Their reflection pieces indicate that service-learning has helped them adapt to America. For the last six years, we have nurtured our service-learning program and have seen it grow to become internationally recognized. Last year, we were filmed by the Munhwa Broadcasting Corporation of Korea to be showcased on their "Today Show" to promote service-learning in that country.

Service-learning has brought about more student activism. Some decide to be advocates by lobbying, speaking, writing, or performing for their cause. For example, one student's letter to the editor on behalf of refugees was printed in a Washington, D.C. daily newspaper and is still quoted by refugee advocates. Another student is now serving an internship on Capitol Hill because of her testimony on world hunger. Whether their service is direct (tutoring or mentoring) or indirect (collecting, constructing, or fundraising), when the students become advocates, they personify "hope" for a better tomorrow. Thus, based on my

...marketing is a means to bring people on board.

experiences, I offer other service-learning programs suggestions on how to market their work successfully.

APPROACHES THAT WORK

Use "volunteer" stickers or buttons. Students wear these in the community as they go about their service. They are "badges of honor" for student volunteers and reinforce their sense of pride in their work. Functioning like billboards for the school, they let the community know which school is involved in the service activity. They remind the community agency or individuals of their partnership with the school. Security guards at various institutions are grateful for the displayed badges, which inform agencies that the students represent your school.

Recognize the value of public relations. Feature students who are models of service-learning. Plan early for an awards night for parents, volunteers, and agency sponsors to share each student's success and to publicize your program.

But don't become possessive. Involve as many people as possible in activities. Remember, this is not just your program; it also belongs to the school, the students, the parents, the principal, and the community. Ask them to join you as you address community groups, and book speaking engagements at community functions as often as possible. Students are your best salespeople, and if the Kiwanis, Optimists, and Lions Clubs are impressed, as they usually are, time and again they will offer you needed funding or exposure for future activities.

Feature an outstanding student service provider each month in the school's newspaper and in the school's front showcase. Then, call the local media to feature that student as well. The story will convince readers, parents, and other members of the community that your school's program is worth promoting. For example, one of our students babysits and volunteers her time after school free of charge to help care for quadruplets born to a local family. The local Moms Club of Olney, Maryland, saw to it that she was featured in the local paper for her efforts and awarded her a "babysitter of the year" award.

Publicly thank local businesses that support your program. There are many ways to do this. End-of-the year awards programs can be a good opportunity to honor local businesses. For example, our local Sandy Spring National Bank offers service-learning coordinators from county schools the use of its meeting rooms free of charge, a small gesture but so welcome to those of us limited to meeting in school classrooms. Consequently, this year, we nominated the bank for a School-Community Partnership Award. It was great publicity for the business and helped strengthen our partnership.

Highlight projects that fulfill a community need. For example, the local hospital called to request students to translate into other languages signs and informational booklets given to patients prior to surgery. Of our 1,600 students, 260 come from 43 countries representing 28 languages. Many of these committed themselves to translating such documents and signs into Korean, Bengali, Chinese, Spanish, and Russian. This project was so successful that it is currently being shared with other hospitals in the metropolitan area to meet the needs of our ever-increasing immigrant population. The student who translated the documents into Bengali even wrote home to Bangladesh for a typewriter so that her translation would look polished enough to be printed. Many hours were devoted to the project. All participants agreed that their time and efforts were well spent because they felt that others of similar backgrounds benefited and appreciated reading such work in their native languages. Accolades for participants have appeared in the local paper, and students' reflection pieces were shared with the local media and foreign publications. For example, *Senior Edition, USA*, a magazine based in Boulder, Colorado, sent each writer a small royalty check, quite a heady experience for a teen who has probably not written for publication before.

Enlist parental support and testimony. The mother of one of our student firefighters told a TV camera crew of the impact service-learning had on her son who was not a good student but who felt he had a sense of responsibility toward others. When she completed her testimony, there was not a dry eye in the studio. Another mother spoke of the benefits of service-learning at an awards ceremony. "The accolades were wonderful, and the exposure and attention were terrific," she told the audience. "But the most valuable prize by far was the lesson that good deeds do get noticed. My son learned that people appreciate the efforts of citizens who give of themselves and that it isn't only the bad guys who can get their names recognized." A county publication printed the statement.

Record program accomplishments. Remember, if it isn't in writing, it doesn't exist. Share students' reflection pieces, which are a validation of the inherent goodness in today's youth. Students, parents, and community agencies love to hear volunteers' and clients' responses. They are easy to get published if you target a particular readership by using *Writer's Market* in your local library, or if you mail them to associations to be used in their newsletters. The reflection pieces help solidify students' impressions of the experience.

Reflection writing can also help some students focus on possible careers. For example, the local Heart Association enlisted two of our students to travel to elementary schools with their heart-health-care kit to present seminars on good eating habits and the need for exercise. This experience of teaching good health care to 2nd graders convinced one of the girls that she wanted to become an elementary school teacher. Her reflection piece was published in the local Heart Association's new brochure.

CONCLUSION In sum, effective marketing can enhance your service-learning program in several ways. By promoting the activities and accomplishments of student volunteers, you can help sustain their enthusiasm, which can be contagious and helpful in recruiting other students as well. Faculty members, administrators, parents, and community members will also become more supportive of service-learning if it is positively marketed.

Kathy Megyeri is the Volunteer Coordinator at Sherwood High School in Sandy Spring, Maryland. She has taught freshman high school English for 30 years.

Fundraising and Collaboration

IT IS 6:45 IN THE MORNING. MORE THAN 4,000 STUDENTS ARE ARRIVING FOR ANOTHER DAY OF SCHOOL. They originate from 80 countries, speak 40 first languages, and make John Marshall High School one of the most diverse and challenging high schools in the country. I am the coordinator for the school's Technology Academy and Health Careers Academy, two experiential reform programs on our campus in downtown Los Angeles. I also coordinate four grant programs, two service-learning grants, and two school-to-career grants. My job is to help as many of these 4,000 students as possible to connect their learning with the real questions of life—all part of the mission of John Marshall.

BY JANIS FRIES-MARTINEZ

Fundraising should not become a goal for its own sake.

As I sit in my office, a teacher comes in and tells me about a great conference on service-learning taking place in San Francisco in two months. I know the next question will be, "Do we have the funds to pay for it?" Fifteen minutes later, my phone rings and a teacher asks, "Do we have enough money to pay for a substitute teacher to cover my class next Thursday?" He wants to attend a meeting being held by the construction workers' association. Five minutes later another teacher asks, "Can we possibly get a hospital bed for the certificated nursing program classes?" Ten minutes later, just before the first bell rings, a teacher hurries in to ask, "Will there be funds to pay for the printing of a Domestic Violence Handbook my students have targeted as their service-learning project?" As a result of various grants and business/community agency partnerships centered around experiential education programs, I am able to accommodate each teacher's request. The question is, "How were we able to get these additional resources?"

The short answer is, we have sought and received funds outside of our school budgets.

Like many schools working to implement various types of experiential education programs, regular budgets and funds are not sufficient for our service-learning goals. The two general ways to seek additional resources for experiential education programs are through grants and through in-kind contributions of goods and services, usually from your local community.

Seeking outside resources requires long-term commitment of people, energy, and time. Grant funding is provided by corporations, foundations, government agencies, public agencies, and sometimes by private individuals. Grants are varied. Consortium grants, block grants, and individual teacher grants are just a few examples. School districts are often eligible to apply for grants that individual schools cannot apply for. In-kind contributions can be equally varied.

GRANTS I never write for a grant just because it will give us funds. I try to assess the needs of the school, students, and teachers first. Will this grant fulfill an already identified need? For example, our school has a dropout rate of close to 40 percent. This means that two out of every five 9th graders who enter our school do not graduate. One year ago, a group of teachers made a presentation to our school-based-management council. They asked for money to pay for a teacher to coordinate a program that would identify and work with at-risk 9th-grade students to address the school's growing concern over the dropout rate. Although the presentation was excellent and the implementation plan simple, it was not doable due to the level of funding needed for the coordinator's position and support services ($72,000). A teacher position would be lost in order to fund this position. The plan was put on the back burner.

One month ago, I attended a service-learning conference. One of the sessions was about a new mentoring grant aimed specifically at helping at-risk students with their academic endeavors. Bingo, this was the grant that could possibly help us implement our 9th-grade dropout prevention program. The mentoring grant award listed at $65,000, enough to meet our program goals with minor modifications. Instead of funding one coordinator position to implement the program (something this grant committee would probably not fund), we could pay for one period of class time on each of our school's three tracks. Using these three periods of class time, we could offer a class where 11th- and 12th-grade students could be trained as academic mentors. Each class would carry approximately 30 students. We would assign one mentor to three at-risk students. In this way we could offer positive academic mentoring for 270 9th-grade students. The cost for all three classes would be approximately $21,000. We could then hire a teacher as a program coordinator for two additional periods of time, at another $14,000. The total cost in teacher and coordinator time would come to $35,000. We would have $30,000 left over to purchase student/teacher instructional materials, substitute time, conference time, mentoring consultant fees, and other identified programs needs.

The important thing is that this grant helped us to ferret out another way to implement our original plan. If we do not receive this grant, we can continue to search for other grants aimed at working with at-risk students' academic endeavors, dropout prevention, student mentoring, and/or service-learning mentoring projects. Each time we find one of these grants, we need to remember to adapt our grant to meet the necessary guidelines provided by the grant. We have learned that one grant generally does not fit the criteria of another grant, even though the target audience or cause is the same. We need to rewrite the grant each time we attempt to fund it or enhance it with additional grant funds.

Through many efforts such as the example above, we have found seven factors to be essential in grant writing:

1. Know the funder and do pre-application research. Find out what background information is needed to write a successful proposal. This can be accomplished by contacting program officials, application reviewers, or veteran grant writers to get tips. Don't ignore a funder's guidelines in the hopes of "fitting" your proposal into their niche. It's been estimated that your chances of success improve by as much as 300 percent when you make contact with the funder before and during the proposal-writing process.

2. Before starting the application process, be clear about what you want to accomplish. Draw up a long range plan that projects goals at least five years ahead. If you are able to preview related grants, only preview successful applications from grant seekers whose projects are similar to yours.

3. Write with honest, clear language. Don't ask for more than you need. Never lie. Avoid filling your proposal with jargon. Never use the same application twice. Be up front about asking for money. Get to the point. Try to look professional. Involve key community figures where possible. Tell the funder about the existence of the problem you intend to solve and prove it with statistics, case studies, testimony, and any other measurable data.

4. Always work to a timetable. Make sure you have enough time to complete your application so it meets the funder's deadlines. If you don't have time to do it properly, don't compete for the grant at all.

5. Give thought to the idea of cooperation. Many funders, particularly federal agencies, like applications where more than one organization is involved. If you submit a cooperative proposal, remember to make sure that there is both a formal and informal relationship between grantees.

6. Know your budget. It's probably the first thing a funder will look at in your proposal. It needs to be realistic and give credibility to your entire proposal. Present the budget separately from the rest of the application. Make sure the figures are correct, and that the budget accurately reflects your needs. Keep a record of how you arrived at your costs.

7. Read the instructions before applying. It sounds simple, but grant competitions live by two rules: The funder is always right, and when in doubt, refer to the rule. Check with the funder to see if there's a preferred format.

IN-KIND CONTRIBUTIONS In-kind funding for services and materials requires deciding on what kinds of support you need from each person or group to enhance a specific project or program. Specific needs should be listed by all the involved stakeholders. Be careful to identify what you really need and accept only that assistance. For example, avoid taking someone's old books just because you think you might need them in the future. Someone else's hand-me-downs can become a storage nightmare (like the garage that has "really important stuff" piled to the ceiling and unused for the last 20 years). Equally frustrating is promising a business or community agency that you will use their new curriculum and allow them to train teachers to use it, when it doesn't fit within any program guidelines. Students and teachers should receive some benefit from the in-kind donation and have identified it as a true need.

One example of in-kind services and materials that our school has sought is related to the enhancement of our Health Careers Academy. The Health Careers Academy wanted to add another career path in nursing. We had the opportunity to apply for a Regional Occupation Program (ROP) Teacher to teach a Certified Nursing Assistant Program on our campus. This would be an in-kind donation of four periods of teacher time paid by Adult Education. However, in order to qualify for this ROP teacher, certain requirements had to be met. We needed to provide a classroom that contained running water, medical terminology books, stethoscopes, blood pressure measurement devices, and a hospital bed. We did not have a classroom available with running water, and we did not have any general or grant funds to pay for the books or medical equipment.

The only answer to this dilemma was to seek in-kind donations. We looked first to our formal partners, Kaiser Sunset Hospital, Los Angeles Trade Technical College, and Los Angeles Community College. They came through. Kaiser Sunset Hospital supplied a classroom at the hospital site. Adult Education agreed to the classroom, and even supplied the bus to get the students to and from the hospital for the class. Kaiser couldn't supply the hospital bed, but they called a contact at Children's Hospital Los Angeles who was able to supply and deliver the bed to the classroom at Kaiser. Los Angeles Trade College supplied the medical terminology books, and Los Angeles Community College offered stethoscopes and blood pressure devices. Voila!— one great new career pathway at no cost to our school.

The donation of persons to provide services to a school is another type of in-kind donation. The Constitutional Rights Foundation provided our school with one of their AmeriCorps Members. She assisted us with our Youth Task Force service-learning club, and helped classroom teachers to implement service-learning projects in the classroom.

For example, one classroom was interested in dealing with issues of racial violence as part of a service-learning grant investigating types of violence and implementing projects to combat violence. Our AmeriCorps member contacted a nonprofit organization supported by the federal government that had created a curriculum that teaches students to facilitate conversations on racism and prejudice. This agency not only supplied curriculum frameworks for the teacher and every student in the class, but also provided for full training sessions for all the students. The students who have been trained are now facilitating these conversations in other classrooms on our campus and at other local schools. The experience became a real win-win situation for all involved.

Draw up a long range plan that projects goals at least five years ahead.

The Marshall Career Academy wanted to provide us with six computers that could be used by students to research careers and write career-related papers. We had $2,000 allocated for computer equipment in our Tech Prep Grant. At best we would only be able to purchase two computers with the money. Therefore, we went to KABC, a local affiliate of the television network, ABC. We knew that KABC regularly updates their computer equipment. We asked if the next time they were going to dispose of some outdated computers, they might be willing to donate them to us. It turned out that they were in the process of getting rid of eight 386 personal computers. They said we could have them, if we came to pick them up. We knew that it could cost approximately $250 to upgrade a 386 PC to a Pentium PC. To upgrade eight would cost approximately $2,000. This was a great way to make our money go much further to serve more students' needs.

As with grant seeking, we have found seven factors to be essential in securing in-kind funding:

1. Look at all business/community agencies for support. Don't look at one partner for everything; spread the need to as many partners as possible.

2. Compile an informational data base of potential goods and services that can be donated from local businesses/community agencies. Update and add to this list on a continual basis.

3. Contact businesses/community agencies to explain what role they can play in providing needed goods and services to your school. They are not mind readers. If they know your needs, then they may call when they have goods or services they know you need.

4. Trade out goods and services with other schools. Often they have things your school needs, and you have things their school needs.

5. Network! Network! Network! Attend community functions as often as possible.

6. Read as many educational periodicals as possible. Often, they are filled with free information on in-kind donations of goods and services. Other times, they have free samples of materials that can be secured by sending in a response card.

7. Check the Internet and list your needs on a bulletin board. Other people are almost always willing to help you meet your program/project needs.

FIVE RULES OF FUNDRAISING

1. In writing for grant funding or asking for in-kind donations of goods and services, always identify the end goals. How will the additional funds or goods fit into and enhance your school's current or projected programs or projects?

2. In seeking commitments of time and money from businesses and community agencies, know that an equal commitment of time, intelligence, and coordination must be made by all school personnel, not just you, to insure successful school use and implementation.

3. I have found that positive, optimistic people excel in accessing funding and in-kind donations for their schools. They do not easily give up. Show patience and know that grant writing and in-kind donations can't be accomplished overnight.

4. Dovetail the funding for as many programs or projects as possible to assure that the same teachers and much needed funding are not spread too thin trying to implement too many programs or projects at the same time.

5. While financial funding from grants and in-kind donations is important, it is never the essential reason I seek them. Fundraising should not become a goal for its own sake. Funding

and in-kind donations are only a viable means to enhance an existing program or to free up school personnel, provide focused training seminars, and help prompt the teachers who implement our programs to pursue creative learning experiences for their students.

Janis Fries-Martinez is Coordinator of the Technology Academy and the Health Careers Academy at John Marshall High School in Los Angeles, California. She was a Fellow in NSEE's Leadership Development Program, funded by the DeWitt Wallace-Reader's Digest Fund.

INNOVATIVE FUNDRAISING

by Andrew E. Fisher

As the 1996 academic year begins, hundreds of new schools nationwide will open their doors for the first time. But very few can claim service-learning as a core curriculum ingredient. And even fewer can claim such innovative fundraising as New Technology High in Napa, California.

New Technology will open this fall, with service-learning as a requirement for students to graduate. The main obstacle the organizers face is shared by most service-learning programs —finding the resources to support their innovative approach to teaching and learning.

The money to fund the building itself came from a reallocation of district money. (It had previously been earmarked for portable classrooms.) The start-up money for equipment and teacher training, two of the key factors in starting a service-learning program, was raised independently over five years. A half million dollars was raised during that time. Napa Valley is not a wealthy district. It is of average wealth in a state that ranks 42nd out of 50 nationally in spending per pupil.

What enabled New Technology High to succeed was a novel approach to fundraising. Robert Nolan, director of New Technology High School, and his team of organizers, included service-learning school projects in all of their grant proposals. Adding service-learning made their proposals stand out and may have been the deciding factor in receiving funding. A portion of those funds was channeled into the service-learning start-up fund.

Nolan's group involved businesses from the beginning, asking for their input on what today's students need. The response from the business community was clear: students need to be in the community, acquiring work experience, and contributing needed, meaningful service. These businesses were eager to contribute to the school, and as soon as the first few jumped on board, word spread and everybody wanted to be associated with the project. In addition to monetary donations, the school has received important in-kind donations. A local high technology company made sure other businesses were aware of the project, advertised that it was a great idea, and actually helped with the building design— all for no charge.

In return for giving the school money, equipment, or expertise, the school provides different avenues of public relations for the businesses. For example, if a business wants to buy a computer for the school, the company's name will appear on it. There will also be "walls of donors" and other highly public lists of people who have contributed significant amounts to the school. The team is also considering collegiate-style fundraising. This plan involves naming a building or classroom after major contributors.

The day-to-day operations of the school are supported by regular tax money. The burden of finding start-up money was handled over a five-year period that involved creative fundraising and community effort. Nolan's team was able to raise a huge amount of money in unlikely economic territory simply by looking differently at what they had to work with.

Evaluation Helps Programs Function Better

WHENEVER PARENTS ASK WHY A SERVICE-LEARNING PROJECT MIGHT BENEFIT THEIR SON OR DAUGHTER, IT HELPS TO BE ABLE TO SAY, "Based on our evaluation of the impact of this program, your child is likely to benefit in one or more of the following areas...." A carefully designed evaluation plan can give you the information you need to answer parents' concerns.

BY L. RICHARD BRADLEY

An evaluation can also help address questions from administrators about the educational benefits of this program versus the costs of implementing it. Teachers want to know about the program's impact on student academic performance, attitudes, and behaviors. Community groups need to know what service-learning has to do with education, what it will do for students and the community, and whether it is worth the trouble. An evaluation plan may also be required by your funding agency. The basic question for all these constituencies is: "How do we know if it works?"

The first step in answering this question is to articulate and build a consensus around the goals and outcomes of the evaluation process. An initial stumbling block for many schools is the fact that the term "evaluation" means different things to different people. A person trained in this type of research distinguishes between "qualitative" and "quantitative" approaches, between "process" measures and "outcome" evaluations. The science of evaluation involves many potential tools that can be useful. But they need to be put into a language that teachers and other stakeholders can understand and that are specific to each situation. The charts at the end of this article summarize the main evaluation approaches useful for service-learning programs.

After deciding on the various evaluation approaches that might be used, a program has to decide on what overall strategy will work best. Several basic questions can guide you in this process:

- What do you want or need to evaluate? What questions would you like to be able to answer?

- What is the purpose of your evaluation? To satisfy the requirements of funders? To help you make decisions about whether and how to continue a program?

- Will the results be shared publicly or are they primarily for your own use?

- What resources do you need to conduct your evaluation?

Relationships between these questions and various evaluation strategies are summarized in the charts.

Another decision is whether the evaluation is done by someone outside or inside your organization. To the extent that the results

Evaluation should flow naturally from the curriculum and from the service experience.

of your evaluation are to be made public, it may be to your advantage to hire a non-biased outsider whose presence will lend greater credibility to the results. Chief disadvantages to this "external" evaluation are cost and availability of a qualified person in your area. An "internal" evaluation, typically done by someone within your organization who has the necessary expertise, is less expensive and allows for familiarity with unique aspects of your program. But the findings of an internal evaluation may not be as widely accepted, no matter how objective your evaluator is.

WHERE TO BEGIN For the past 10 years I have been working with a consortium of four suburban school districts in Columbus, Ohio, helping teachers design service-learning programs funded by various state and federal grants, and then doing program evaluations. During the 1994–95 school year, there were 57 service-learning projects in 58 schools (32 elementary, 15 middle, and 11 high schools), involving some 30,000 students. One of every five students was involved, providing 27,650 hours of service to the environment and to about 4,100 senior citizens, other students, and poor or handicapped people. Funded by Learn and Serve America, the projects collaborated with 30 community agencies.

In thinking about evaluation of service-learning, three guideposts have been useful for us:
1. start small,
2. involve teachers in planning the evaluation, and
3. build evaluation into your program design.

Focus on one or two key outcomes the first time around. Ask yourself, "For this program to be viewed as successful in the eyes of school administrators, parents, and community partners, what information will they need to see?" Think about the resources you have available to help you with evaluation. Will you be doing it on your own or can you enlist the help of graduate students or others?

Evaluation should flow naturally from the curriculum and from the service experience. Our strategy is to ask teachers what they would like to know about their students and the program when it is completed. For example, we ask them to think about evaluating the success or failure of the project and to tell us the questions *they* think we should ask. Then we have them answer the questions that they generate. What information will they need to make a "go/no-go" decision on the project next year? How can we help them obtain this information in a way that does not interfere with the things they already have to do?

We've learned that collecting only the information and data we intend to use is the best approach. Teachers are busy enough teaching. They don't need (or want) to be filling out lots of unnecessary forms. Basic information is needed for all projects on the number of students involved, their grade level(s) and ethnic background, the number of hours of service they performed, beneficiaries of this service, the number of beneficiaries, and how the program is connected to the curriculum. Two forms can be used for this—a *pre-project report form* that asks for estimates and tentative project plans, and a *post-project report form* that asks for actual project data. We distribute both forms to teachers before their projects begin.

For selected projects, we use various evaluation tools to gather other information on the program's impact on students' knowledge and skills, on students' attitudes and behaviors, on teachers, and on the community. As we focus on these four specific areas, we also keep in mind factors that might affect an overall program, potentially undermining it. We call this "listening to the environment." A new administrator who is not supportive of service-learning might arrive or a school could change its mission. Policies could change regarding students being out of class for their service. In some cases, our schools have had a hard time finding a community partner willing to work with them.

Sometimes teachers say they really wanted to try service-learning in their classrooms, but they just couldn't figure out how to do it. Here the failure is not in the program itself, but rather in providing the necessary assistance to launch it. When this happens, we ask teachers to identify the specific obstacles they faced in trying to implement service-learning, how they tried to overcome the obstacles, and what additional assistance might have helped them be successful?

Below are examples of specific evaluation projects and tools we have used, focusing on students, teachers, and the community. The impact on students can sometimes be clearly distinguished between knowledge/skills and attitude/behaviors, but some evaluation tools tend to blur this line between knowledge and attitude.

IMPACT ON STUDENT KNOWLEDGE AND SKILLS Often, we set specific goals for a project in terms of knowledge and measure whether the project accomplished that goal. We use various surveys to gather quantitative data that can show increased knowledge or shifts in attitudes as a result of new information. We also use self-reflective instruments to assess expected student outcomes such as personal development and citizenship. Some changes can also be assessed by comparing test scores before and after service activities.

Quantitative surveys can work in many situations. For example, a 7th-grade social studies class sought to increase student awareness of the causes of homelessness as part of a unit on the Great Depression. We assessed student knowledge and attitudes towards homelessness before and after service activities, using a questionnaire designed by the teacher and the director of the Open Shelter, where the students did their service. Quantitative results showed increased awareness of how and why people become homeless and a decrease in negative attitudes towards the homeless. Another middle school project had similar results using a survey on "Aging and the Mentally Retarded Person," designed by the teacher and the agency's volunteer coordinator.

In a school-wide elementary project to develop a wetlands on school property, we assessed students' knowledge about a wetland before and after the project using tests designed by teachers. Teachers also monitored student math and writing skills during the project period. A middle school science project sought to heighten awareness among teens (and their parents) of the need for organ donors. Students wrote and illustrated an information brochure for their peers. After several revisions by the students, the brochure was accepted by the director for use in the Life-Line of Ohio Organ Donor Project.

At the completion of their service activity, students can use a self-reflective instrument called the Checklist of Personal Gains. This instrument is designed to assess expected student outcomes suggested by Conrad and Hedin and others. The instructions ask students to "check all items which are true for them as a result of their participation in this project."

Under the category "self-esteem/personal development," for example, students can say if they feel more self-confident and have a sense of competence, feel a greater sense of usefulness in relation to their community, believe more strongly that they can make a difference in their schools and community, and are more assertive and independent. A category on citizenship/social and interpersonal development allows answers indicating more concern about the well-being of others, working effectively with others, more positive attitudes towards other people, and putting into practice beliefs and values that a student finds important.

Some of the checklist categories involve academic and cognitive development and career development. Students can indicate if they feel more motivated to learn and participate in school, have improved communication skills, can better use what they have learned in school and in life to solve problems, and can better gather and analyze information. They can also express if they have more realistic ideas about the world of work and possible career choices.

We've learned that collecting only the information and data we intend to use is the best approach.

IMPACT ON STUDENT ATTITUDES AND BEHAVIORS Assessing attitude and behavior changes can be done in various ways. Teachers or other school personnel can observe and record student behaviors such as attendance, disciplinary referrals, and dropout rates before, during, and after service activities. Changes in attitudes such as assumptions about the poor can be assessed quantitatively by giving an instrument such as the one used in the homelessness project, which assessed both *knowledge of* and *attitudes toward* the poor.

Student journals and/or reflection can also be used to gather qualitative information on how service-learning affected attitudes and behaviors. Teachers can pose such questions for reflection as: What were your first impressions of the service site? In what ways was the service experience the same (or different) from what you expected? In what ways has your participation in this service activity changed your perspective on the issue(s) involved? What did you do at your service site? What was most challenging to you? What is the most important thing you learned about yourself as a result of your participation in this project? What will you do differently next time? How would you rate the overall quality of your service experience? If you could change one thing about your service site, what would it be?

These journals often reflect more positive attitudes about learning, school, and the self as a learner. As one student wrote, "Once I saw the connection between what we were learning in school and what these people needed, I couldn't wait to learn more!"

IMPACT ON TEACHERS AND COMMUNITY The impact on teachers falls generally into four broad areas: increase in instructional time devoted to service-learning, changes in teaching methods, changes in emphasis within a subject area, and changes in teacher attitudes towards students. Assessment is done by asking teachers to respond to questions such as: How did the service-learning approach differ from how you taught this material in the past? What is the most important thing you learned in doing this project? Are your attitudes toward your students after doing this project different than they were before it? If so, in what specific ways?

Because we are also interested in being able to transfer these projects to other schools, we also ask teachers what they would do differently, being as specific as possible, and how another teacher could replicate this project. These types of questions are on the post-project report form distributed at the beginning of the project.

Qualitative information can be gathered by asking all participants, including on-site supervisors, such questions as: What happened that probably would not have happened without the involvement of students? Was the project designed to meet real community needs? If so, how and by whom were these needs determined? If not, why not? Were students and agency staff significantly involved in planning the project? If so, in what ways? If not, why not? Was the service performed by the students *meaningful* to them and to the agency and its clients? If so, in what ways? If not, what things need to changed next time? Did the school and the agency work well together? If so, in what ways? If not, what problems arose? What could be done to prevent these problems from arising next time? What were the tangible costs and benefits to the agency as a result of participating in this project, being as specific as possible?

QUALITATIVE AND QUANTITATIVE RESEARCH COMPARED

QUALITATIVE is usually conducted to explore problems about which little is known	**QUANTITATIVE** is usually conducted to study concrete phenomena that have been examined to the point where they can be measured
begins by examining observations and reports of phenomena as they occur in everyday life	begins by examining pertinent knowledge from previous research to build an argument that answers a specific question
is primarily concerned with developing models (theories) which accurately describe observed phenomena	is primarily concerned with increasing knowledge about the adequacy of a given theory
emphasizes the *construction* of theory research	emphasizes the *testing* of hypotheses
is understood as a process that builds theory *inductively* over a period of time, step-by-step	research is understood as a process that builds knowledge *deductively* over a period of time, step-by-step

COMPARISONS OF EVALUATION STRATEGIES

FORMATIVE EVALUATION—QUANTITATIVE OR QUALITATIVE

QUESTIONS YOU WANT ANSWERED	WAYS TO ANSWER YOUR QUESTIONS
Are you doing what you said you were going to do in your proposal or program description? Is your program operating efficiently and in a timely manner?	process observation of programs/operations interviews with program staff, administrators, students, parents, other stakeholders questionnaires for stakeholders minutes of meetings

SUMMATIVE EVALUATION—QUANTITATIVE OR QUALITATIVE

QUESTIONS YOU WANT ANSWERED	WAYS TO ANSWER YOUR QUESTIONS
How well were your program goals and objective met? What impact has your service-learning program had on student skills and attitudes? What decisions do you want to make about your program?	checklists of goals and objectives surveys observation self-reflective tools such as journals pre-/post-service assessments on key indicators, such as GPA, behaviors, and attitudes statistical analysis

REFERENCES AND SUGGESTIONS FOR FURTHER READING

Conrad, Don, and Diane Hedin. *Youth Service: A Guidebook for Developing and Operating Effective Programs.* Washington, DC: Independent Sector, 1987.

Gub, Egon, and Yvonna Lincoln. *Fourth Generation Evaluation.* Newbury Park, CA: Sage Publications, 1989.

Osborne, David, and Ted Gaebler. *Reinventing Government.* New York: Penguin Press, 1993.

Dr. L. Richard Bradley is an Adjunct Assistant Professor in the College of Education at Ohio State University in Columbus. Since 1988, he has also served as Program Design and Evaluation Consultant for the Four-District Consortium in Columbus, Ohio.

Curriculum Integration

issue 4

For service-learning to transcend volunteerism or community service, it must be integrated into the curriculum. Only then will teachers, administrators, policy makers, parents, and students recognize service-learning as a legitimate and effective teaching method.

DENNIS BRUNTON recounts how service-learning transformed teaching and learning across the curriculum in the Springfield, Massachusetts, school district.

HELEN FINKEN suggests ways to integrate service-learning into a particular course.

TERRY DEAL REYNOLDS follows with ideas for forming interdisciplinary connections through service-learning.

MARILYNN CUNNINGHAM connects assessment of student learning through service-learning to the design of the curriculum.

WAYNE HARVEY demystifies reflection as the critical component that transforms community service experiences into learning.

AUDREY WELLS emphasizes the importance of celebration and closure for service-learning experiences.

Integrating Service-Learning Across the Curriculum

IN 1987, CONGRESSMAN RICHARD NEAL, THEN THE MAYOR OF SPRINGFIELD, MASSACHUSETTS, READ *HABITS OF THE HEART* BY ROBERT BELLAH, which convinced him that the Springfield Public Schools should begin a community service-learning program. He believed it was an essential step in Springfield's future. A medium-sized urban community, Springfield faces many of America's urban problems, such as increasing high school dropout rates, violence, teenage pregnancy, and lack of hope for the future.

BY **DENNIS BRUNTON**

Soon after, Dr. Peter Negroni was named superintendent of the Springfield school system, which has 41 schools and 24,000 racially diverse K–12 students. He was a strong supporter of community service-learning (CSL) and saw it as a vehicle to promote school reform. He began several school reform efforts, with the basic premise that all students can and will learn, and will meet the highest of standards. This meant changing how we did business, moving from a top-down management system to one that involved and valued the community, parents, teachers, administrators, and students. These constituencies were included on school-centered decision-making teams at each of the 41 schools. The teams identified needs, set improvement goals, and developed the school's mission and vision, which the administration agreed to help implement.

In addition, each school developed partnerships with businesses, community agencies, and parents under a program called Springfield School Volunteers. Also, a formalized professional development process provided seven days per school year for retraining all the teachers in the system in the new school approach, including a new learner-outcome-based curriculum. Curriculum supervisors, administrators, and teachers began examining what each student should have learned in a holistic manner at the end of grades 2, 5, 8, and 12.

Meanwhile, the Commonwealth of Massachusetts began a similar reform process two years after Springfield. This resulted in the creation of core curriculum frameworks to be implemented statewide and a policy that requires students to spend a definitive amount of time learning in each of the core curriculum areas.

In Springfield, we had the context of multiple reform efforts to develop a service-learning program that was an integral part of the curriculum. We also had the challenge of doing this in individual schools, while working through a district-wide process.

AN EVOLVING PROCESS The new professional development program set in motion the process that led to what is now CSL in our school system. This evolution occurred in part by purpose, in part by reaction, but mostly because it was needed. The system

As we began, we did not know if CSL was an entity, a methodology, a philosophy, or a combination of these.

began working with a core group of teachers, mostly at the elementary and middle school levels. We attempted to involve students in identifying community needs. They sought to find connections to the curriculum and implement service projects to meet community needs.

As we began, we did not know if CSL was an entity, a methodology, a philosophy, or a combination of these. We knew community service-learning involved community, but we hadn't defined what "community" was. We knew it involved service and learning. But we hadn't answered, "learning what?" For CSL to be integrated into the system's curriculum, we knew we needed to be part of the larger school reform process.

This core group of teachers became strong supporters of CSL. Under the guidance of Dr. Carol Kinsley, the group wrote a K–8 curriculum called "Whole Learning Through Service," which described service-learning project ideas and suggested ways of connecting them to the curriculum. Through this initiative we began to understand how CSL projects can and should involve planning, preparation, implementation, reflection, evaluation, and celebration. While this group was working, Springfield Public Schools (SPS) began several initiatives designed for community service-learning specifically.

First, SPS appointed part-time CSL teachers in many of our schools, which actually delayed the integration of service-learning into the curriculum. After these teachers were appointed, whenever CSL was mentioned in a school, the response was, "Oh, CSL, that is so and so's job." This initiative also deepened the confusion as to whether CSL was a separate entity or a methodology of teaching for anyone. The separate-teacher approach was dropped after one year. This experience reminded the central office staff that teacher perception was a key element in the development of the CSL program, as well as the other reform initiatives.

A far more successful initiative was when the superintendent convened a task force comprised of core curriculum supervisors, school administrators, teachers, students, and community members. It clarified many of the issues and questions we had about CSL and provided a sense of direction and structure for the future of CSL in our school system. The task force made the following recommendations:

- connect CSL to curriculum so teachers would see it as co-curricular, not extra-curricular or an add-on;
- create CSL facilitation teams so teachers would not see it as a one-person job;
- define community to include family, extended family, classroom, school grounds, neighbors, neighborhoods, and the PTA, so teachers would realize that CSL did not require that they leave the building;
- develop a clear definition of CSL;
- recognize that schools need resources and control of those resources for CSL to work, and that the programs should be decentralized and school driven; and
- identify the schools' need for the central office to help facilitate projects, provide staff development, and secure and assist in accessing resources—but not mandate programs.

Another major step occurred when the central office CSL facilitator, a position I assumed shortly thereafter, was added to the Core Curriculum Committee. Having the CSL facilitator as a part of this key committee was an important factor in determining how SPS would eventually define CSL. This committee provided an essential forum to discuss how CSL did and should fit with the core curriculum content areas. In the early stages, the core curriculum supervisors were supportive but still very possessive of classroom time, which continually presented scheduling nightmares for projects and programs.

CLEAR DEFINITION As SPS continued with its professional development plan and worked through the learner-outcome-based curriculum development process, a clear definition of CSL evolved: CSL is a philosophical approach to learning and a highly motivational methodology of delivering curriculum.

This process of defining CSL has been a major factor in the core curriculum supervisors moving from passive support to active participation in integrating CSL into their core curriculum frameworks and setting examples throughout their own professional development workshops. Also, teachers are seeing that, by integrating multiple learner outcomes, they gain greater flexibility and control of scheduling and curriculum delivery.

In the early stages of CSL development within the system, teachers noted consistent effects on student development. Early on they referred to these effects as "unexpected outcomes." After completing research over a two-year period and observing the consistency of these effects, we realized these were CSL learner outcomes that result from using the CSL process as a methodology of curriculum delivery.

Besides developing learner outcomes, CSL meshed with other school reforms that were underway. It provided a perfect opportunity for businesses, agencies, and parents to become active participants in curriculum development and implementation instead of being passive observers. In addition, the professional development process introduced hundreds of teachers to CSL. This helped to eliminate the perception that CSL was an add-on.

The curriculum planning group incorporated service-learning into its process. In the plan, all graduating seniors must demonstrate that they can contribute to the school, local, and global community; have acquired skills to be self-directed learners; and can effectively explain and defend the need, purpose, development, and evaluation of their CSL project and the academic skills it enhanced. The earlier grades have very similar requirements to demonstrate competency. The 8th graders, for example, must "discuss" rather than "defend" their CSL project.

PUT UP OR SHUT UP The planning process for integrating CSL into the curriculum had gone extremely well, with the context of school reform helping to pave the way. But still, we were not actually integrating CSL into all of the schools. In 1994, we received a Learn and Serve K–12 grant based on a three-year plan. At this time we felt that after the extensive training and discussion that had occurred, it was time to put up or shut up. The first year was for demonstration and implementation. The second year, the schools used CSL to achieve a school improvement plan goal.

Integrating service-learning into a school's curriculum needs to be part of the larger process of experiential education and education reform.

This gave us the opportunity to utilize the fruits of school reform. We formed an Advisory Board of experienced teacher practitioners, administrators, community members, parents, and students. We also developed a management team that included two core curriculum supervisors, the district CSL facilitator, Supervisor of School Volunteers, and a cooperating consultant. This group developed an individual school grant proposal that required each school to create a CSL facilitation team composed of teachers, administrators, students, parents, and partners to function as a subcommittee of the school-centered decision-making team. It would manage, implement, and document the grant. The school could use the broad definition of community described earlier, and students and partners/parents should be involved in all phases of projects. Core curriculum learner outcomes and CSL learner outcomes must be clearly addressed. Finally, projects and programs must be documented using a simple teacher-created documentation form. The individual school awards ranged from $500 to $3,000 based on school enrollment.

The overall management team, with input from various groups, evaluated these proposals, highlighting strong points and making suggestions. This process increased involvement and incorporated many of the aspects of school reform. This also enhanced the core curriculum framework instead of competing for time with it.

We're still in the process of "putting up." We begin the third year of the grant in the fall of 1996, with a goal of each school moving toward program sustainability. Over a five-year period, all 41 schools should have completed the process of integrating service-learning into the curriculum. There is much left to do. For example, the school system is currently working on the assessment process that corresponds with the CSL learner outcomes and is beginning to test the validity of this outcome-based curriculum.

Integrating service-learning into a school's curriculum needs to be part of the larger process of experiential education and education reform. We have learned in our process to be flexible, reflective, and persistent. As various schools seek to integrate service-learning with the curriculum, in varying situations and circumstances, I hope the lessons we have learned can be of some assistance:

1. Focus on all involved but especially on your teaching staff.

2. When working with groups, stress CSL as an entry point for parents and corporate partners to become involved in curriculum development and delivery so they cease to be only observers.

3. Allow the individual schools to integrate CSL into the curriculum in a way that meets their own needs, plans, and vision. This has resulted in a variety of valid models within the Springfield Public Schools.

4. Allow schools to dream big. Help them define their visions and assist them in creating the necessary partnerships.

5. Allow schools to make mistakes. They learn from them. Explain this is a minimum three-year process.

6. Take advantage of every opportunity to give examples of how staff can integrate CSL into curriculum. Have lots of examples.

7. Connect with other reform efforts—school-to-work, mediation, anti-violence, school volunteers, etc. These initiatives will also have to integrate with curriculum.

Good luck in your efforts. This is a process with attainable goals.

Dennis Brunton is the Community Service Learning Facilitator with the Springfield Public Schools in Massachusetts. Previously, he was a teacher and service-learning coordinator at Putnum Vocational Technical High School in Springfield. Dennis was a key liaison for NSEE's Pilot Project, supported by The Hitachi Foundation, to strengthen and sustain high school service-learning programs.

Under Construction: Knowledgeable, Committed, and Active Citizens

SOCIAL STUDIES TEACHERS ARE CHARGED WITH THE RESPONSIBILITY TO PREPARE STUDENTS TO BE GOOD CITIZENS. Courses in history, economics, and government are required for high school graduation because they provide a knowledge base for effective citizenship. It has been assumed that by taking these courses, students will also be inspired to perform their civic responsibilities as adults. However, low voter turnouts, lack of confidence in government's or an individual's ability to serve the common good, and increasingly disturbing societal problems at all levels indicate that citizenship requires more than *knowing*. It requires *practice* through active involvement.

BY **HELEN A. FINKEN**

We learn to build houses by building houses; to play the harp by playing the harp; to be just by doing just acts.

— Aristotle

The Iowa City High School social studies department decided to design and implement a course which could give students a greater sense of civic empowerment and responsibility. We hoped that by linking civic learning with civic participation, our students would develop the life skills, knowledge, and desire requisite for active citizenship.

We wanted a course which would help students see the impact of federal government policies at the local level, as Matt did when helping with flood relief work at his local church. His new-found awareness that people "have fallen between the cracks of federal aid" put him face-to-face with the impact of the Federal Emergency Management Act. We also wanted students to experience personal growth, as Katie did when she said, "I have never enjoyed calling strangers on the phone. I had to do that in order to find a place to volunteer. This class helped me get over that fear." And, we wanted students to understand that solutions to social problems are not simple, as Adam did when he worked in the local elder care center. His realization that elderly patients did not recognize him from one time to the next, that others would walk away without notice unless they were equipped with an electronic armband, and that very few patients had relatives who made frequent visits, gave Adam a broader perspective on the problems of the aged.

Furthermore, we wanted students to realize that individual Americans, like the students themselves, are confronting social issues daily, trying to make improvements in the quality of people's lives. We wanted students to understand that the cliché, "*You* can make a difference," is actually true. Elissa realized that her volunteer work at a day care program was important on a larger scale. "It has made me happy that this day care program exists," she reported. "When I went to grade school, I was a latch-key kid, and I would have to walk home everyday and go to an empty home. I'm glad that I can help kids have an enjoyable and safe place to be."

GETTING STARTED The hardest part was creating a course structure that could support our goals. For the greater part of two years, we read journals, visited magnet schools, attended social studies conferences, and brainstormed with other teachers. In the process, we came across many people who were integrating service-learning into their curricula. Though most of these programs were designed for elementary or junior high school students, we were convinced that service-learning could and should be a critical part of our new course.

We designed several activities to help students attain the goals for the course. During the class, students would research contemporary world problems (such as apartheid), the change agents who were trying to solve the problems (such as Nelson Mandela, Desmond Tutu, Stephen Biko), the power structures which limited change (such as governments, social classes), the strategies which change agents utilized to implement changes (such as non-violent resistance), and the impact of the change agents' work (such as independence from colonial rule). Following these academic activities, students were to become change agents themselves by choosing a local problem, designing a way to solve the problem, completing a service-learning project, and writing reflectively about their experiences. Students would measure their learning through authentic assessments—photo essays, journals, posters, presentations, and papers—to show what they learned.

Global Portraits of Change has become our new trimester-long social studies elective. It relies heavily upon student research, seminars, teacher-student conferences, guest speakers, group work, and cooperation. Community activists, volunteer agency representatives, and former students speak to the class about possible service projects. Students use two weeks of class time to investigate community needs, locate service agencies, identify existing programs, and brainstorm new ideas. Students post their service-learning plans, advertise for helpers on projects, plan all-class projects, and use class time to contact community groups. The classroom becomes a hub of activity as e-mail messages are sent, letters and phone calls are made, and reports of successful experiences are shared.

To meet their service-learning requirement students have conducted a wide range of projects. They have held neighborhood canvasses for the Ronald McDonald House, helped with flood relief efforts, sacked potatoes for the food bank, tutored children at a nearby elementary school, presented AIDS education lectures, performed with a musical group at a senior center, made greeting cards for the home-bound, collected wheel chairs for Third World countries, and served meals at the Free Lunch Program. Their knowledge of the community has increased, their sense of connection has grown, and their appreciation for people's struggles has deepened.

UNDERWAY To implement Global Portraits of Change, we followed several steps. First, our department received approval for our proposed course from the school and district curriculum councils as well as the Board of Education. Following approval, students were invited to enroll. We prepared a special flyer about the course, which the counselors gave to students during registration assemblies. Social studies teachers explained the course to students and other faculty. The first time we offered the class our enrollment was better than we anticipated: over 55 students signed up!

We realize that the long-term evaluation of our course will be the quality and extent of students' civic participation as adults.

Our next step was to write course objectives, design activities, identify materials, and determine assessment tools. We obtained curriculum writing funds for the two social studies teachers and the media specialist who would develop the course and purchased a wide-range of trade books and documentaries for the library collection to support course lessons. Funding for the materials came from the school district's new course fund ($2,500), the social studies department ($1,000), and the media center (over $500). The media center and social studies department expand the Global Portraits of Change collection each year. Our local regional educational center purchases films which complement the course curriculum.

We also received two grants. US West awarded $2,500 to establish a Global Portraits of Change Foundation. This student-run foundation awards small grants to class members who find matching funds to address community needs that they identify in the course of their service-learning project. One grant for $75 matched a donation from Procter and Gamble to purchase children's video programs for the Ronald McDonald House. A vice president of a local bank serves as an advisor to the Foundation Board. The Foundation provides students with the opportunity to make economic decisions, an important component of citizenship training.

The second grant, a $1,000 ComServ Grant from the Iowa Department of Education, enabled a member of the social studies department to write a unit about types of service, rationales for serving, the history of civic participation in the United States, the benefits of service, and activist models from throughout the world.

STILL BUILDING As Global Portraits of Change enters its fourth year in 1997, it is still "under construction." We have learned that current classes benefit from previous students' reflective writing about their service-learning, their photo essays, and videotapes of their presentations. We hope to publish a student-designed pamphlet to introduce Global Portraits of Change to students, service supervisors, and parents. We recognize that students' short-term and long-term planning skills need constant practice and refinement so that academic and service-learning commitments can be completed in a timely manner.

Have we accomplished our initial goals? Enrollment remains steady and teacher enthusiasm is high. Students write positively about their service-learning experiences and the academic content of the course. Class members research extensively, often reading the change agents' publications or memoirs. (As one student commented on a midterm self-evaluation, "I have researched to perfection.") Students are inspired by the excellent work of their peers. And, encouragingly, students often continue their service beyond the school year.

Community service agencies appreciate the contributions of class members and are quick to support student efforts. When the executive director of the Ronald McDonald House saw the photo essay documenting the "Wish List" supplies campaign, he asked the three student organizers of the project if he could take their portfolios to Ronald McDonald Headquarters in Chicago. Class members' enthusiasm for their service-learning projects has had a nice ripple effect. Many students not enrolled in the course join class members in completing community projects!

We realize that the long-term evaluation of our course will be the quality and extent of students' civic participation as adults. We are confident that adding Global Portraits of Change to the social studies curriculum has been a step forward in our ability to develop active, compassionate, and informed citizens. The class has provided worthwhile academic and service-learning experiences which have strengthened students' understanding of, and commitment to, active community participation. We hope that students will continue to build upon their Global Portraits of Change experiences and view community service as a necessary ingredient for constructing a fulfilling life.

Helen A. Finken is a social studies teacher and department chair at Iowa City High School in Iowa.

SERVICE-LEARNING AND DEVELOPMENTALLY HANDICAPPED STUDENTS
by Andrew E. Fisher

Many educators believe that service-learning's hands-on style allows developmentally handicapped students to learn more and to tap the self-esteem necessary to function in the real world. But service-learning does more than build confidence in these students. According to Gwen Martino and J. Lisa Bennett, teachers at Warren Western Reserve Junior High in Warren, Ohio, service-learning connects classroom learning to a real-life setting and teaches developmentally handicapped students applicable job skills.

The relevant link between academics and the service activities is clear. In one project, the students cook for a variety of people, including school staff members, parents, senior citizens, two local homeless shelters, two soup kitchens, and a battered women's shelter. In this context, students are able to apply their math and science skills. They must differentiate between measurements such as teaspoons and tablespoons, and they learn about different physical properties of substances. For example, they learned that low-fat margarine cannot be used when making fudge. (The end result, they indeed found through using the low-fat stuff, is an undesirable product, which they ate with a spoon.)

Other activities include making refrigerator magnets and writing letters to Veterans. The students help the elderly, hold canned food drives to fill the pantry of a local senior citizens center, and do monthly shopping for shut-ins. The students also write and publish a newsletter which is distributed to parents, school administrators, and board members.

Their biggest accomplishment by far may be their efforts for children. In addition to having made and donated over 300 quarts of spaghetti sauce to the local Ronald McDonald House and other agencies, the students have made children's books for the last three years. They created number books for pre-schoolers. Denim covers each book, and the pages are made of calico and filled with felt dots and numbers. Children can count the dots and then look and touch the right number. This year, the students are planning to make alphabet books.

With each of these activities, students associate what they see on a chalk board with what they see outside their windows. The community benefits from the projects and learns more about the developmentally handicapped. The students at Warren Western Reserve Junior High learn valuable job skills. They learn to follow both written and oral directions and to seek help if they do not understand something themselves. They learn not to waste materials. They learn respect for authority. And most importantly, they learn how to cooperate with their peers.

SERVICE-LEARNING AND LEADERSHIP DEVELOPMENT

by Andrew E. Fisher

As the year 2000 approaches, leaders of the next century must be well rounded and adept at handling a variety of dynamic issues within school, government, corporate, and community settings. Good leadership will make the difference between an idea becoming a reality and a thought that withers. At Field Middle School in Northbrook, Illinois, students are learning this lesson about leadership while serving as leaders themselves through service-learning.

The activities students engage in are very hands-on, according to Barbara Kurth, the school's Advisory Coordinator. For example, 7th-grade language arts students teach senior citizens how to use computers. During "senior day," students ask the seniors questions about history, then compare the responses to the "facts" presented in the textbooks. The 7th graders use their math skills to graph demographics, and also interview the seniors as they study World War II and the Depression.

In these examples, and all service-learning at Field Middle School, the students are developing their leadership skills. The key to the program, says Kurth, is to involve students as much as possible in every stage of planning and implementation. The students generate the ideas and make decisions. For example, after their work with the senior citizens, the students inquired with local businesses about senior citizen discounts. They compiled a list, then created a "senior citizen discount booklet" with over 90 pages of coupons, and distributed over 300 copies to local seniors.

Through the service-learning projects, students learn empathy as well as the "nuts and bolts" of leadership. They discover that conflict is inevitable, but that compromise is necessary for effective leadership. They learn that having a good idea is useless unless it is followed through with careful planning, good time management, and total commitment—even when things get tough.

Creating Interdisciplinary Connections

WHEN TEACHERS WORK TOGETHER TO DEVELOP INTERDISCIPLINARY UNITS INVOLVING LOCAL ISSUES, STUDENTS HAVE THE OPPORTUNITY TO INVESTIGATE A PROBLEM FROM MANY PERSPECTIVES. They gain scientific and technical knowledge through experimentation and observation, can apply computation skills to analyze and solve problems, and learn about local governments and how politics influence decisions. They also can research and write about the impact that these decisions have on individuals in a community. Most importantly, through participation in a project that involves service to their community, these students are on the road to becoming responsible and informed citizens.

BY **TERRY DEAL REYNOLDS**

Don't forget that teacher interest is just as important as students'.

Giving students the opportunity to explore community issues with real-life consequences as an integrated part of their school curriculum is service-learning at its best. Young people acquire not only the skills necessary to progress through school, but they also begin to realize that learning is a never-ending process.

"We never consider a unit of study completed," says Debbie Brown, 6th-grade science and math teacher at Carolina Day School in Asheville, North Carolina. "It is always evolving and changing in order to meet the needs of the students. It requires commitment and time. You must force yourself to make that time to talk specifically about how you are integrating the curriculum."

WHY INTERDISCIPLINARY? Students and teachers benefit from a chance to pool resources, ideas, and energy. Parents, administrators, and community members might also catch the excitement of service-based learning and work together toward creating positive solutions to the dilemmas of our times.

Teachers can develop interdisciplinary projects in various ways. In my work with Brown and the other middle school teachers at Carolina Day School, we have found that a valuable approach is to focus on a local issue, often one that is controversial. This gives students the opportunity to investigate a problem from many perspectives. The topic is not decided in advance, although the skills covered remain constant. For instance, goals of the environmental unit might be to develop spelling and vocabulary lists, write a research paper based upon in-depth study of both past and current implications, develop interview techniques and journalistic writing, collect scientific data in the field to be used by the school laboratory, develop historical time lines, and use mathematical graphs and calculations to problem solve and record information.

With these goals in mind, the teachers

involve the students in the selection of a topic. Students seek to determine what is timely in the community by reading the newspapers and listening to the local news broadcasts. With teacher input, students can make a list of interesting topics. The team of participating teachers makes the final decision for the unit of study based upon availability of resources and accessibility to the site. They brainstorm to determine which topic will most easily lend itself to accomplish the goals set forth in the curriculum development. Don't forget that teacher interest is just as important as students'. It is much easier for a unit to be successful when teachers are engaged, active participants in the learning process.

Once a topic is agreed upon through team meetings and the involvement of the students, teachers must find time to work together to develop the interdisciplinary units. This may be the most difficult obstacle of all. In the busy day-to-day schedules of teaching, planning, evaluating, and the many other duties of our lives, we all can feel that there is no time for anything else. But finding a common meeting time is crucial. It may be as little as one hour a week, or ideally, a shorter daily update. A supportive administration can create scheduling that will allow interdisciplinary meetings. Convincing the skeptics is worth the work.

"Creating interdisciplinary units requires administrative support and partners committed to making it work," says Kathy Kline, 6th-grade English and history teacher at Carolina Day School. "We meet on a weekly basis plus some extra hours to revise the curriculum. We are continually breaking it down, cleaning it up, making sure that it all makes sense. Touching base regularly is critical, ideally one and one-half hours a week."

It may be wise to start small. When our middle school resolved to adopt an interdisciplinary, thematic approach to learning, the teachers were given the task of re-writing the entire curriculum. In theory, it was a wonderful opportunity to incorporate a desire for integrated learning with fresh ideas involving the particular needs and environmental treasures of our community. We were able to accomplish significant changes in a relatively short time. But this approach felt like learning to swim in deep water. It was an overwhelming task, and in hindsight, I would limit the changes to one or two units a year. An interdisciplinary project may work best the first year when one teacher decides to begin by working with only one other teacher.

THE LOCAL LANDFILL The day our 6th graders decided to explore a local controversial issue concerning the future site of a county landfill, they were familiar only with what they had read in the newspaper or heard on the evening news. The topic was timely, involving both social and environmental consequences. The students selected the topic from a list of possibilities generated by class discussions. The teacher team decided it would meet the goals of the curriculum and knew that the controversy about the project would make it an interesting topic.

As part of the classroom activities, the students set up interviews with people living near the site and with public officials involved. They also conducted research in the community library files for a full day before visiting the current landfill site. We consulted the librarians ahead of time, and they created a file of both archival and recent articles. With specific tasks assigned, the students poured through microfiche, used computer on-line resources, and took extensive notes. They learned about sanitary waste management, studied ground water contamination, and created a time line of historical events. County and state officials also came to our classes at school, helping the students to explore the different options for dealing with solid waste. With an understanding of the events leading up to the proposed landfill, the students were then able to prepare thoughtful interview questions and personally contact government officials, politicians, environmentalists, county planners, and residents near the landfill.

The issue really came to life for the students when they got out into the rural community and talked with the residents who might either lose their homes to the landfill or face the prospect of living beside the landfill. "We traveled up an old dirt road to the house of Reverend Ball," wrote Jonathan, a 6th grader, in his journal. "The Reverend was an older man whose eyes had faded with time. He had trouble hearing, which also showed how time had taken its toll. He was wearing what looked like a new pair of overalls that still had a crispy blue tint to them. Reverend Ball spoke of how the country representatives had informed him that his property would become part of the new landfill. He didn't take the news very well.... This visit helped me realize that it is hard for people on both sides of the issue.

"Reverend Ball has lived in the area for 46 years now and can't re-locate because of health problems," Jonathan wrote in his journal. "It has made me realize how important it is to look on both sides of a problem before making a final judgment." Early participation in regional issues can plant the seeds of understanding that will grow and mature in the future leaders of a community. The benefits of getting students to write about a local controversial issue helps them to see that no problem is as simple or one-sided as it might appear. Real situations with no easy solutions affect real people.

With the landfill project, we adapted the curriculum to a working syllabus. A syllabus helps to keep parents and students informed and gives concrete deadlines for assignments, research, and projects. It also ensures that all teachers are working toward the same goals. At Carolina Day School, teachers may be granted a professional leave day in order to accomplish the initial brainstorming and planning process. The team also meets regularly to determine where they are, where they are going, and how the process is working. Ideally, all of the teachers in a grade—including art, music, and other areas often not considered "basic subjects"—participate in the planning and implementation of the unit.

As with any collaborative effort, we have differences of opinion about various aspects of the projects. Support from the administrators and overall faculty can help reluctant faculty members to jump into something new. However, it is possible to coordinate efforts with just one or two other teachers when you don't have the full support of your colleagues. The important thing to remember for planning and implementing a successful unit is to schedule a regular meeting time to touch base with your partners.

Evaluation of interdisciplinary projects is very important. It can be presented in an informative event for students, parents, teachers, and members of the community. With the landfill unit, we presented a "press conference" where the students probed a panel of experts representing varying interests. When a topic is timely, the local media can also be involved. Students can record audio sound bites to be aired on the local public radio station or have their ideas featured in the newspaper or community television broadcasts. Allowing the students to present their results in creative, interdisciplinary ways enhances the overall effort.

If ways can be found to participate in some solutions to the problem explored, even integrating them into community actions, the overall process of connecting to the real world becomes even more concrete. After looking at the complexities of the landfill issue, our 6th graders decided to use their knowledge to develop a "Comprehensive Waste Management Proposal" for the county. Local officials recognized the quality of the work. This problem-solving exercise culminated in the design of home and school recycling programs.

STONE SOUP PHILOSOPHY The landfill project is just one example of an interdisciplinary unit that grew from a desire to incorporate math, science, social studies, and language arts into a meaningful learning experience. We have also studied the impact of pollution from a local paper mill on river quality, the effects of acid rain at Mt. Mitchell State Park, the cultural and historical celebrations of the people of Appalachia, mining and minerals in the mountains, and the great forests of the southern Appalachian mountains. The ideas unique to the economic concerns, social dynamics, and environmental treasures of a particular area are endless.

The "stone soup" philosophy guides us in designing interdisciplinary units involving theme-based community service. Each participating teacher has something valuable to contribute, and without the input of everyone involved—including the students—the resulting "broth" would not have so many rich flavors. This pot of soup is consumed as a whole, not separated out by ingredients. We don't put the learning process into narrow compartments. Students are the beneficiaries. They are exposed to a variety of skills and presented problem-solving opportunities that encourage higher-level thinking.

When such units are developed, students acquire competency skills while also gaining an understanding and insight into their community. Such understandings cannot be measured by a letter grade. The students are able to identify with a problem in a personal way with far-reaching, concrete consequences. The benefits of service-learning projects based on social and environmental issues unique to a community are immeasurable. These are lessons carried into adulthood that create concerned leaders and empathetic decision makers.

Support from the administrators and overall faculty can help reluctant faculty members to jump into something new.

Terry Deal Reynolds is a teacher at Carolina Day School in Asheville, North Carolina. Her educational background in English and environmental studies, along with experience working with children in outdoor settings, combine to support her experiential approach to teaching and learning.

Assessment—An Integral Part of Experience and Learning

FOR 20 YEARS, I HAVE BEEN FOCUSING ON THE ASSESSMENT OF EXPERIENTIAL LEARNING. From the beginning, education leaders have asked, "How do we grade it?" After a decade of work establishing a format to connect the experienced-based community learning to academic credit and grades, the back-to-basics movement of the 1980s called our program into question. Much like a transplanted heart, the experienced-based learning model seemed always under threat of being rejected by the academic body. To avoid rejection, we had to "prove it."

BY MARILYNN CUNNINGHAM

To consider assessment alone promotes isolation instead of connection.

Academic validity of service-learning is critical for having this learning approach integrated into curriculum. I had tried to establish this validity working as Communications Coordinator of the Experience Based Career Education (EBCE) program in the Fayette County school system, which serves greater Lexington, Kentucky. Faced with this new attack in the 1980s, I felt we had to prove the tools we had developed. How can we validate experiential learning as it becomes more integrated into a school's curriculum?

I decided to try to answer these questions working directly with students. I asked to be moved from the central office to a high school teaching position. I was an add-on, working half-time at a school that already had a full-time experience-based learning coordinator. My students were juniors or seniors who showed up on the first day to register. One-third of them had dropped out the previous year. It was hard leaving the comfortable environment of meeting around conference tables and reflecting on process and procedures with colleagues. But I was also losing energy in that sterile environment. I knew I needed my own assessment of experiential learning with real students. And, I got it.

One by one, I saw lives transformed and empowered as these students came alive while serving and learning. The assessment was rigorous. We used a system of building student portfolios that contained assessments of their learning, covering content, process, and context. They were involved in the creation of their learning and wanted to share their portfolios, performing for anyone who would listen. Their other three traditional classrooms were often the audience. Because the teachers knew the history of the students, they were impressed, and so was I. This assessment system was contributing to the learning itself. But could it work with the serious challenges that some students presented, such as those of a student I'll call Scott?

"Mrs. Cunningham, I know I am failing," Scott said one day, near the end of the semester. He had dropped out the year before as a senior and only needed four semester hours to graduate. "I told my mother I would come to school and go through the motions to please her. But I haven't turned in any work up to now, and I am not changing. You will have to flunk me."

Scott was reporting to his community placement and doing what he was told. On calls and visits to his community placements, his advisors usually complained about his sloppy dress and bad language. But they also said he was able to get along with others and most of the time followed through. "He does not cause any trouble," said one advisor. Could the assessment system we had developed work with a student like Scott?

ASSESSMENT AS A PART OF LEARNING To consider assessment alone promotes isolation instead of connection. Assessment needs to be viewed in a larger context of educational goals. This requires a vocabulary that is understood and accepted by both experiential educators and traditional classroom educators. The traditional education platform rests on three primary elements: the written curriculum, classroom instruction, and evaluation through student testing. In contrast, the three primary elements of experiential education are experience, learning, and assessment.

In traditional or experiential education, communication and connections among the three elements are needed. For either model, it is helpful to think of a three-legged stool, with the key elements supporting the educational goals. This stool requires that each "leg" have equal distribution for good balance. For an efficient and effective service-learning course, there needs to be equal distribution of experience (service), learning (reflection), and assessment (documentation).

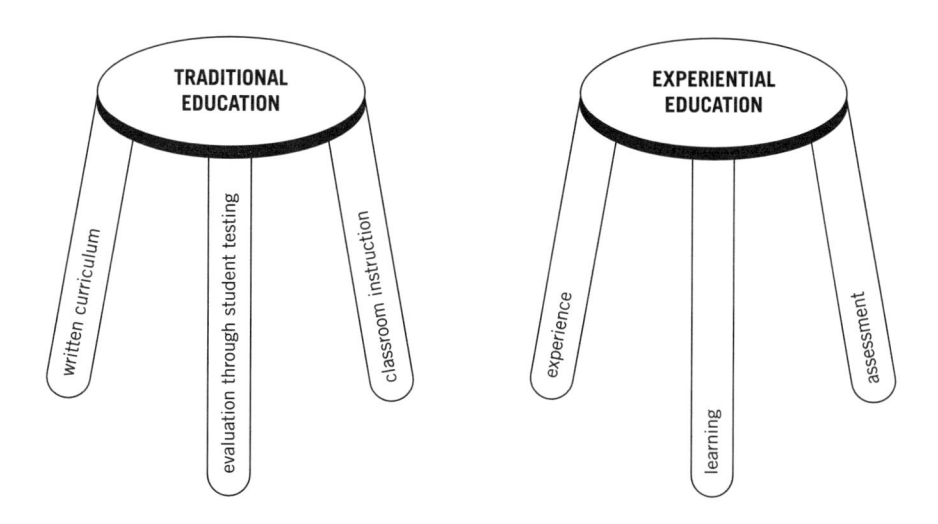

In traditional education, testing is done on subject material presented in the classroom, from texts and other resources, usually isolated to a specific subject area. In the model we developed in Fayette County, the setting for the learning is transferred from the classroom to the community. The textbooks or written curriculum become what we call the "activity sheet." Students develop their activity sheets by gathering the resource materials while engaged in the internship or service-learning project and reporting it to the learning coordinator.

Assessment is an integral part of the learning and encourages documentation of what students learn. This shows what students know rather than what they do not know. This is critical, since new information must be meaningfully connected to prior knowledge if it is to be learned.

THREE-PART ASSESSMENT Good assessment of service-learning hinges on a well developed system for placing students in the right community setting. In our model, students develop their own curriculum for the service-learning course using a grid system to match interests with course area concepts (English, social studies, etc.) and sub-concepts (research, writing, etc.). The method for presentation of learning to be assessed is mutually agreed upon between the student and coordinator. Through this activity sheet, the curriculum, activities, and assessment are developed at one time. The activity sheets are individualized to reflect each student's experience.

Four days a week, for two to four hours a day, students are placed with community resource people at community sites. They can rotate community experiences every four weeks, or they can extend one placement up to 14 weeks. With a longer placement, a mentorship relationship usually occurs. The learning coordinator meets weekly with each student, collecting the weekly activity sheets. These sheets are the reference points for assessments. The curriculum the students develop through the activity sheets and an overall "student program guide" are kept in each student's working portfolio.

At the weekly conference after Scott said he was resigned to failing, I opened his student program guide. His top match on the interest grid was "educational services." So far during the year, his placements had been the police department and recreational department. I looked at the community openings under the category of educational services and saw that a child abuse center was available. Bingo! It was a match that might work. Scott's courses were leadership and literature. No learning was documented thus far. "Scott, let's let your assessment grid drive your next placement and place you at the child abuse center," I said.

"No, Mrs. Cunningham," he said, "I don't want to work with kids and I don't want to work at all. Let me stay in-house [in school] for the rest of the semester, and then I will drop out."

There was a long silence. He had told me in previous conferences that he was tired, tired of trying to make it work. He had lost his dad in a car accident and had taken out his feelings of loss in delinquent activities. This had caused problems for his mother and brothers. He did not have the energy to do the work of school and was resigned to the path of least resistance, to quit caring. But I insisted he go through the motions of his last rotation and be placed at the preschool for abused children. He reluctantly agreed. His classmates chuckled when told of his next placement and ribbed him. Scott's face turned red with embarrassment, but he went.

With Scott, as with all the students, the assessment model involves a thorough set of tools looking at *content, process, and context.* These tools allow assessment of different learning styles, varied interests, multi-intelligence levels, and integrated knowledge. They focus on what students can do with what they know. During the reflection process, the student addresses questions to uncover the significant learning occurring while serving in a community placement. How? Why? Where? What? For what? So what? Now what? These questions promote learning, as applied to the changes within the student and within the community setting.

CONTENT LEARNING To assess the content learned in service-learning, students select their favorite method of documentation, using written, verbal, or audiovisual approaches. Written formats can be reports, charts, graphs, logs, journals, research papers, essays, and others. Verbal approaches can include discussions, oral reports, speeches, seminars, speak outs, and town meetings. Audiovisuals can be slides, charts, pictures, photographs, posters, audio tapes, video tapes, and simulations. Other types of reports may also work.

We award points based on content, using criteria based on reasonable expectations for that particular student or on externally established proficiency levels. The scoring guide is mutually developed between the student and learning coordinator. Criteria include completeness of data, clarity of presentation, application of logic, clarity of organization, thoughtfulness of conclusions, accuracy of information, extent of detail, neatness, sentence structure, and many others.

PROCESS LEARNING Process skills are also an essential part of assessment, involving five inquiry steps, shown below with the elements of a student's ability being assessed:

1. **state learning objective or problem**—identify a specific objective, problem, or outcome;
2. **gather data**—identify appropriate sources, utilize the sources, and assess their validity;
3. **analyze data**—organize data and evaluate its relevance to learning;
4. **generalize or infer**—understand meaning of data, determine trends, or draw conclusions; and
5. **communicate**—articulate conclusion clearly and produce specified product.

CONTEXT LEARNING Through descriptions, checklists, rating scales, and time sheets, this area of assessment measures the mutuality of the experience. It is designed to monitor the common good of the learning experience, for the student as well as the community site. Measures of context learning are objective as well as subjective. Objective measures include time sheets. Subjective measures include evaluation forms completed by site supervisors and self-evaluations completed by students. We ask students the questions: "Who am I?" "What is a need of the community site?" "How can I best meet the community's need and my need at the same time?"

CAN IT WORK? Scott came to the first conference after going to the child abuse center with a journal. "I am bored watching the class," he wrote, "so I thought I would write some things down." We looked at the journal and talked about the connection between observations and research. It was a beginning.

Later in the week, he began to talk more about his experiences. "I hold them up to the water fountain and wipe their noses. They like me." I overheard him talking to his classmates about the children. Scott was getting engaged. But I still wasn't prepared for the next weekly conference.

Assessment is an integral part of the learning and encourages documentation of what students learn.

Scott presented a report based on his observations and some readings found in the library about child abuse—and a poem he had written. By anybody's standards, the poem and the report deserved an A. They were just the beginning of the work that Scott completed that semester. During the next two months, Scott read his own works to anybody who would listen. He read anything he could find about the subject of child abuse, and the center director mentored him for the rest of the year. Scott completed school and walked with his classmates at graduation. He pursued his studies in college, eventually becoming a child psychologist.

Meanwhile, I returned to the central office, re-energized by my own learning experience and the satisfaction that assessment is an integral and successful part of service-learning. I work now to assure community leaders and school leaders that student-centered learning works. Every year it is a little easier. Every year, there are more success stories like Scott in our Experience Based Career Education program.

Marilynn Cunningham is the Professional Development Specialist with the Fayette County Public Schools in Lexington, Kentucky. Previously, she was the district's Communications Coordinator of the Experience Based Career Education Program. Marilynn has been a Mentor in NSEE's Leadership Development Program and a Consultant with NSEE's National Initiative, funded by the DeWitt Wallace-Reader's Digest Fund.

ACTIVITY SHEET

STUDENT	AREAS	NATURAL SCIENCE	MATH	SOCIAL STUDIES	CAREER EDUCATION	ENGLISH	OTHER	OTHER
LEARNING COORDINATOR (LC)	CONCEPTS	X		X		X		

EXPERIENCE SITE

START

ESTIMATED STOP

ACTUAL STOP

ACTUAL NUMBER OF DAYS TO COMPLETE ACTIVITY SHEET

SUB-CONCEPTS
ecology, research

SITE INFORMATION
State Department of Agriculture

CODE
1 define problem
2 gather data
3 analyze data
4 generalize
5 communicate

ASSESSMENT
5 excellent
4 commendable
3 satisfactory
2 improving
1 needs to improve

PROJECT
The student will be able to rationally and knowledgeably exemplify, document, and verbally present one aspect of man's impact on ecological balance through systematic research into the advantages and disadvantages of DDT as a control agent for insects harmful to one type of agricultural crop.

ACTIVITIES

	code
1. With your RP and appropriate research materials, identify the primary agricultural uses of DDT in the past, including: the insects used against, the crops affected, and the main geographic areas affected.	2
2. Research, document, and summarize the major evidence which establishes the harmful effects of a large scale use of DDT.	2 3 4 5
3. Select one crop and one insect as a "case study," and identify: the impact of the insect on the crop, the alternative forms of control and their outcomes, and the impact of DDT on the insect. Contrast, in writing, the advantages and disadvantages of each method, in terms both of ecology and of economics.	3 4 5
4. Determine which alternative control form is now most prevalent since the ban on DDT. Using your RP and his contacts, estimate the statewide agricultural impact of the ban on the case study crop and insect (e.g., increased crop losses, increased prevention costs, etc.).	4
5. Summarize the economic impact of the ban on DDT with the case study crop and the ecological impact of continued use of DDT.	4
6. State whether you think the ban was justified. Why or why not (be sure to cite your personal values, where appropriate)?	4
7. Prepare and give a seminar-type presentation to your RP and LC, using pictures, charts, tables, major point outlines, and other visual, and having all your research data, analyses, and conclusions as backup. Evaluation will be on: clarity, organization, and completeness of presentation; reasonableness of conclusions; quality and variety of visuals; extent of research; and thoroughness of documentation.	5

(columns: code, assessment by others, self assessment)

Assessment Comments (criteria determined by LC and student):

Distribution: copy to LC, site supervisor, and student

Adapted from the Fayette County Public Schools Experience Based Career Education program.

STUDENT EVALUATION FORM Completed by Site Supervisor

This form was developed because of the difficulty encountered in accurately assessing a student's performance using the traditional grading system. Therefore, we are asking you to fill out this form after the student finishes his/her assignments at your site. Please mail your form back to the Learning Coordinator as soon as possible. Thank you for your assistance and cooperation.

STUDENT   EMPLOYER SITE

Brief Description of Experiences

PERSONAL QUALITIES	EXCELLENT	ABOVE AVERAGE	AVERAGE	BELOW AVERAGE	POOR	NOT APPLICABLE
Accepts and understands the needs, feelings, and faults of others						
Accepts and fulfills responsibilities						
Exercises good judgement						
Is friendly and courteous						
Has a sense of humor						
Is accepted well by other employees						
Is dependable						
Is willing to accept suggestions						
Is conscientious in fulfilling assignments						
Follows directions						
Work is neat and accurate						
Is honest and sincere						
Asks appropriate questions						
Reports to site on time						
Is cooperative and industrious						

SPECIAL COMMENTS (student strengths, weaknesses, or unique projects)

Signature of Resource Person

This form is only used in conference between student and Learning Coordinator. It is not used in grading.

Adapted from the Fayette County Public Schools Experience Based Career Education program.

Reflection Leads to Real Learning

FOR 23 YEARS THE LINWORTH ALTERNATIVE PROGRAM HAS PROMOTED EXPERIENTIAL EDUCATION AND THE REFLECTION WHICH IS NECESSARY TO AUGMENT THAT LEARNING PROCESS. The school is an optional program for 180 high school students of the Worthington City Schools, a suburb of Columbus, Ohio. The community is upper middle class and largely professional and supportive of the 11,000-student school system. The school accommodates a full range of academic options for students who choose it rather than one of the two 1,300-student traditional high schools in the system. The program emphasizes student choice, student responsibility, and experiential education.

BY **WAYNE HARVEY**

Reflection at Linworth is not viewed as an add-on element, especially in the area of experiential education. Reflection is viewed as part of the educational process, a necessity that is as important as the experiences and knowledge gained through education. This is an area of learning that goes beyond the mere accumulation of facts and experiences.

Reflection contextualizes information and experiences. It places a personal meaning on what is learned by relating it back to the individual's own thoughts and experiences and sense of the universe. It causes the learner to create a relationship with the information and experiences rather than merely storing it away. Through the reflective process, people relate new experiences and information to themselves, to other information and experiences they already hold. Reflection serves the paradoxical purpose of creating both a more personal meaning to what is learned and also a greater global context for what is learned.

At Linworth, reflection is enculturated. It becomes one of those terms to which students respond in a comparable fashion to hearing certain things at home. "Don't let the door slam." "Wipe your feet before you come in." At Linworth, it is "Be reflective with your learning." Both in the classroom and out, the staff promotes the idea of reflection because of the culture that has developed at the school. For almost any action students take, they know they may be asked certain questions such as: "Whom does this affect? What does it say about you? How does this reflect on the Linworth Program? How does it fit into the Big Picture of what you are trying to do?"

We push our students and each other to look beyond ourselves and reflect on who and what may live in the consequences of our actions. We want to lead students to view the suggestions they make and actions they take beyond the length of their arms. They may want to paint a wall mural of this week's hot movie, such as *Bill and Ted's Excellent Adventure*. Our job is to get students to

...the reflective process creates unusual learning circumstances.

think about the potential ramifications of having the school perpetually tied to this movie because that is what the students wish to paint today.

Several elements of the Linworth Program add to this enculturation of reflection. Many of our classes are based on discussion. Several elements of the reflective process are brought into play through discussion. First of all, to be effective in the class discussion a student must have completed work prior to class in order to participate. Having completed the work before class, that experience is in the student's brain with the potential of being recalled and contextualized before class. This promotes more thought and reflection than the "I didn't read the book, but hum a few bars of the theme and I'll tell you what I think about it" attitude that teachers often get in a question/response approach in the classroom. As different individuals in the class express opinions in the course of discussion, different contexts are presented for the students to consider after class. Further reflection and contextualization of information is promoted through this process.

Eventually, students realize that opinions from the tops of their heads may not carry the weight of others who have studied and thought about the topic at hand. There comes a time when a student is asked in a discussion to justify a limited viewpoint in light of the argument an author put forth on page 27 of an article. The student smiles in resignation because he knows that he can't. He hasn't read it and accepts that he has no position because he has not prepared. A student once told me, "It took me two years in classes like this to concede that John Muir's experience probably gives him a better basis to form an opinion than what I am manufacturing in my head." This approach to reflection is pervasive in our school and extends beyond the classroom.

Our school runs on a Town Meeting style of government. Once a week, the students and staff meet in the Big Room for a discussion of issues, proposals for new programs, and ideas for the school. It is a forum for complaints and resolutions to problems. Each person has the opportunity to express ideas and to be responded to by the remainder of the assembled Linworth community. When 190 persons have the opportunity and tendency to voice ideas, many different perspectives and viewpoints and interpretations are put forth. Each of these perspectives provides another point of context for thought and experience.

It is not uncommon for a student to present a proposal with an air of consummate confidence, knowing that she will be supported by others and can fend off all attacks on her proposal. Almost as often, one of the students will ask a question that obviously has not been considered by the author of the proposal. As the series of waves of realization pass over her face—I never thought of that; that is totally outside of anything I have considered; I don't have an answer; that's a point worth considering—the author will face her audience and say, "I don't know. I hadn't thought of it that way." Not only does the enculturation of reflective thought allow this student to go through this in front of the whole school, it also means the community responds not with catcalls or surprise, but with a reserved recognition that not all perspectives may be seen from one vantage point.

Anything said in Town Meeting may very well be embraced or attacked by other members of the community. Discussion classes call for work to be completed before class and be considered before the discussion begins. These approaches promote intentional thought. "Being intentional" at Linworth is in the category of "being reflective" and "wipe your feet before you come in." Our students get a bit weary of hearing it, but it is part of the culture. Intentional thought brings in another part of reflection—pre-flection. It calls for students to anticipate and think about what is coming, what they are going to experience, and to hold that expectation loosely enough to grasp it without having an unchangeable death hold on it. It promotes the idea of thinking in advance to prepare oneself for the experience that is about to come. Students can then relate what is being learned and experienced to the vast reservoir of personal experiences they already possess.

In areas of experiential education, we usually allow students to walk through the process of reflection so that they can become more intentional about it. Usually this entails starting with merely narrating what they have experienced in a lesson or through reading or in some experiential setting. Beyond recounting the experience through different senses and through different levels, this narration encourages students to start to make comparisons. In many instances these comparisons are personal; they establish how this particular experience relates to others the individual has had. As time goes on, these comparisons range wider and include how this experience I have had relates to the one you had and how they both relate to what happened to my older brother and how that relates to what happened with the Inuits in 1919.

The next level we push students toward is through a series of "Why?" questions "Why do you remember this experience? Why is it important to you?" These two questions usually prompt students to analyze what is memorable about an experience and how it stacks up with other experiences they have had. "Why is it important to anyone else?" This question leads students toward the idea of their experiences in the context of other people. Why is it that anyone should care about what they have experienced or learned or thought? The final question places this in an even larger context. "Why (and how) does this relate to the big picture?" This encourages thinking about this experience in terms much larger than themselves or the single experience—their current goals, their long range goals, the school, society, the world, the universe. The "Why's" are very difficult to wrestle with and create great frustration at times. But they definitely start to put students on a different level of learning.

In order to capture all this reflection, we encourage students to keep journals, which provide two very basic elements for reflection. First, journal writing captures the experience. While this may seem relatively inconsequential, and more like a diary, it is an important and elementary step. Second, the journal leaves behind a record which can be reviewed and looked upon as a point of comparison. It allows students to see where they were last week, last month, or last year with an idea or a similar experience. They can look at growth or patterns or other surprises that may occur from reviewing that record.

Journal writing also slows down the mind a bit. It creates a situation which "causes the pauses" that allow the mind to get out of its normal racing mode and slow a little to see things differently. In this state, students tend to develop deeper thought connections, more sincere connections between and among experiences they have had. This depth of thought and the connections stimulate a broader context than what the students usually have. Consistent journal writing over

We have discovered that putting information and experiences into a broader context gives tremendous personal meaning to what is learned.

a period of time develops the capacity for this intentional, reflective thought.

The most important element of this is the process—the thought mode and mental machinations necessary to be reflective. We have discovered some students don't do well with the written journal because of their aversion to writing or the circumstances in which the students are working. In such cases, the Linworth staff looks for alternatives that can still incorporate the mental process of reflection. One effective option has been the use of audio tape, speaking into a tape recorder as opposed to writing in a journal. A second, though time-consuming, option is the personal interview. Some staff have had great success by sitting down over lunch once or twice a week and having a reflective conversation/interview with a student who is having difficulty with the written journal. In some instances we look for areas of student strength and go with those strengths. An artistically talented student was encouraged to do reflective sketches and cartoons to activate reflection. Any option which captures the experience, leaves a record, and promotes reflection should be explored.

Through the years of promoting and enculturating reflection at Linworth, our experience has taught us many lessons. What we have experienced is that reflection is a learned process that can be enhanced through practice and that in all probability, very few of us take enough time to reflect on our current experiences. We have discovered that putting information and experiences into a broader context gives tremendous personal meaning to what is learned. Reflection takes the learning process to a personal depth far beyond simply accumulating information and experiences.

Promoting reflection is almost always difficult. In a world geared more and more to immediate gratification, taking the time to reflect is not an instinctive activity for most students. Frustration can get incredibly high for both students who are being pushed to reflect and staff who are trying to take students in that direction. However, when connections are made, when insight is found, when the reflective process works, the benefit of what is learned far outweighs any of the problems encountered along the way.

A final lesson we have learned is that the reflective process creates unusual learning circumstances. Flashes of insight fall from the sky at unpredictable moments and unforeseen places. The greatest moments of learning may not occur in the classroom or while doing homework or at the experiential placement. They may happen while doing the dishes or taking a shower or waiting at a lunch counter. For example, a student once told me the most important thing he learned in an experiential placement was the importance of choosing an occupation that he would enjoy. When asked, he said he came to that realization by looking at the faces of other drivers while commuting to his placement daily and seeing so few people who seemed to be happy to be on their way to work. Some lessons cannot be planned.

Wayne Harvey is Director of the Linworth Alternative Program in Worthington, Ohio. He also has experience as a classroom teacher. Wayne was a Fellow in NSEE's Leadership Development Program, funded by the DeWitt Wallace-Reader's Digest Fund.

REFLECTION WRITING

by Deborah Genzer
Director, Community Service Learning
San Francisco University High School

Journals

Students need to be taught how to keep a journal. It helps if the teacher is having students keep journals during other units or in their other courses. Teachers also need to define the purpose of the journal, for example, how they see it fitting into students' understanding of writing skills.

Students need clear guidelines on how the journal will be responded to and evaluated. How will the journal be figured into the grade? Will the teacher mark grammar and spelling? What exactly is the teacher looking for.

Students need to know who the audience will be. A related issue, however, is that students sometimes write what they think their audience wants to hear. One strategy for getting more honest responses from students is to have them write stories rather than answer questions directly. Other alternative modes of expression for entries in the journal can include poetry, pictures, or quantitative analysis.

Let students choose the notebook in which they keep their journals. This sounds like a small issue, but students will take more pride and ownership in their writing if they choose the notebooks in which to write.

Essays

Essays are not just the final product. The journal can be a useful source from which students can draw ideas for their essay at any point in the process.

Publish and distribute student writing (with their permission). These essays are often well suited for sharing with agencies.

Consider writing to the agency. This begins a dialogue that can result in new creative roles for students.

Consider using peer editing. Students like seeing what other students have to say, and they can learn from each other about grammar and essay composition.

The Grand Reflection: How to Bring Closure to an Open-Ended Service-Learning Course

"I WAS AN IDEALIST AT THE BEGINNING OF THIS COURSE, BUT NOW I AM A REALIST. The problem is now that I understand the vast complexities of social problems, I often feel defeated, discouraged, and depressed. I expected to save the world, but didn't."

BY **AUDREY WELLS**

Students deserve an audience and will find great motivation knowing they will be facing one.

We were surprised to hear such dismaying yet frank words as these from our students at the end of the school year. The seniors in our elective, team-taught course had done important community service work and had matured noticeably. We had repeatedly offered praise, encouragement, and reflection opportunities throughout the course. Most students had been informally, if not formally, recognized by those with whom they had worked. In journals, students recorded delightful moments of triumph and understanding. Nonetheless, many expressed self-deprecating comments at the end of the course such as feeling "defeated, discouraged, and depressed."

We wondered, "Why couldn't they see and accept the value of their work? How could we help them learn to appreciate their own efforts and their new-found knowledge? How could we forge their youthful zest with their emerging adulthood and galvanize them into a forward-looking, confident, optimistic position? How could we leave them hopeful?"

FIRST TRY AT CLOSURE Social Advocacy: History, Theory, and Practice is a senior-level elective course at University Laboratory High School on the University of Illinois campus in Urbana. Developed in 1985 by Barbara Wysocki, a social studies teacher, and me, an English teacher, the course continues to be team taught and modified. In the course, students serve weekly as volunteers in various community agencies such as tutoring programs, homeless shelters, and nursing homes. Class time involves writing and discussion, readings, guest speakers, films and videos, special assignments, and field trips.

Social Advocacy is a course that encourages self-exploration. The interests, concerns, and experiences of the students enrolled in any given year determine the course in part. When designing it, we knew we needed some way to define the boundaries and direction so that it would not flood uncontrollably or lie stagnant.

Our solution for imposing an order on the curriculum that would not too tightly restrict the free flow was to create a set of core questions, replete with subquestions, around which and from which the course would follow. Accordingly, we present our students with large questions, questions thinking adults ask repeatedly throughout life, questions so large there is no one answer. In brief, we ask, "What is society? What is a healthy society? What is a social problem? Who defines a situation as problematic? Who are you and how has your identity, behavior, value system, and self-esteem been shaped by this society? How do you affect the shape of your society? How does the media affect our lives? What does it take to remedy social ills?" As students discuss and write on these questions, so do we as teachers, modeling the values of reflection and open-mindedness.

After a few weeks into the course, students come to trust and enjoy the role of teacher as facilitator and the candid classroom exchanges. The core questions serve to provide direction through the semester. How to end such an open-ended experience in a way that most benefits the students is more of a challenge. We know we do not want students writing, "I often feel defeated, discouraged, and depressed."

Initially, we decided to end the course by combining reflection with presentation and recognition. Parents, volunteer coordinators from the various sites where students worked, and school administrators were invited to our End-of-the-Year Course Symposium. The Symposium opened with students presenting, in pairs, their final reflections on the core course questions. After these speeches, audience members commented and discussion followed. This audience engagement was uplifting for students and audience alike. Discussion was followed by a recognition ceremony for students, appropriate thank-you's, and refreshments.

Bringing the key players together to celebrate was a good idea. Students received recognition not only for volunteer work but also for intellectual growth. We liked this ending with one exception: It was somewhat dull, dry, and as a result, a bit cold. It didn't seem to bring out students' personal and social accomplishments. The rather stodgy academic format took the sparkle out of the experience. Most importantly, it did not help the students incorporate their service as positive, valuable experiences for themselves and the community.

LOOKING FORWARD BY LOOKING BACK *Close your eyes. Imagine it is the year 2006. Where do you live? How do you spend your time? Imagine that you open up the newspaper one evening and on the front page or on page three, or perhaps back on page nine there is a story that features you. Why? Because you have helped to do something wonderful, challenging, and notable for our society. What is it you have done?*

By the third year of our course, we decided to discard the core-question speeches for the Symposium and try something more creative. We began by reviewing with students all the topics discussed, places visited, and people heard from during the year. Then, we led them through the exercise italicized above, which they took to joyfully, and thus introduced what we call the "Poster Project."

The Poster Project asks students to work alone or in pairs and to illustrate a hypothetical advocacy project for the future. Students let their dreams fly because the ideas are hypothetical, yet we require them to dream in detail which leads students to plausible ideas. The assignment has four requirements:

1. Give your project a name.
2. Explain who it will serve, what need it addresses, and how it will function.

3. Explain your role in the project and why this role is appropriate for you.
4. Acknowledge any major obstacles.

During the last two weeks of class, students discover and develop their ideas, sometimes by finding inspiration reading through our growing file of newspaper clippings concerning innovative, real advocacy projects, and by seeing past student posters. After clarifying their ideas, students make their posters (we provide markers, scissors, glue, stencils, and lots of old magazines for pictures) and rehearse short presentations.

These presentations have two parts. The first asks students to share with the audience a brief description of the volunteer work they did and a summary statement of what they learned. The second part of the presentation is an explanation of the ideas illustrated on their posters.

Students have often surprised and impressed us with the ingenuity and direction of their advocacy ideas for the year 2006. One advertised volunteer opportunities on the local television news with on-location stories. Another designed youth theater groups or summer camps that would bridge racial, economic, and geographic boundaries. Other projects included: providing a traveling birth control information van for rural communities; starting orchestras at Boys and Girls Clubs; publishing a magazine for teens that would feature real people who have a variety of body types; and designing systems, both public and private, to help people on welfare save money and gain financial independence.

Our End-of-the-Year Symposium has evolved into a gala event. We hold it in a new building on campus which immediately gives it status over our tired, old school building. In addition, we send out printed invitations and invite not only parents, administrators, and volunteer supervisors, but also local politicians, members of United Way, university professors, and others from the volunteer sites besides supervisors. The display of student posters adds color and vitality. The event includes student presentations, accolades, expressions of gratitude, a certificate-awarding ceremony, a question and answer exchange, a photo session, and refreshments. The adults in the room enjoy meeting with each other and can't help but be charmed by the students. The students blossom from seeing everyone together and from getting such strong feedback on their ideas. Without fail, this event puts a smile on everyone's face.

LEAVE 'EM SMILING Lesson number one we have learned is not to underestimate students' ability to underestimate themselves. It is often difficult to measure the worth of service work. Even students who have loved their volunteer work and who received lots of positive feedback throughout the year may be secretly harboring the thought "Well, my efforts didn't really matter that much because anyone could have done what I did."

There are a few essential steps and ingredients to the recipe for successful closure to a service-learning experience:

Review and Discover. As with good literature, an old photo, or a strong memory, when we recall or recreate past experiences, we learn something new each time we allow ourselves to linger, ponder, and reconsider meanings. Establish a time, place, and method that accommodates your students' need to review their service experiences and discover new meaning.

Encapsulate and Decorate. A goal should be to somehow make students' conclusions concrete. In our case, the posters serve to encapsulate students' past experiences and future visions. There are, of course, many possibilities such as creating theater, visual art, or a publication. The key element is to solidify ideas in a format that encourages students to dwell on their work. Having to decorate something, so to speak, encourages nurturance and development.

Vocalize and Enlighten. Students deserve an audience and will find great motivation knowing they will be facing one. Having a real audience will help students feel responsible for the ideas they express. Real audiences can be reached in a variety of ways. Public speaking is one way, but using radio, television, newspapers, personal letters, or the Internet are some others.

Memorialize and Project. Closure for a service-learning experience should be much like a commencement which honors both past achievements and future enterprises. An effect of the experience should be to sweeten memories while stimulating aspirations. Accordingly, include formal recognition along with jovial celebration.

Students thrive on having some creative control.

Above all, stay alert to difficulties and maintain the creative flexibility to adjust. Work openly with students and together take ownership for the approach. A problem we encounter is how to schedule our closing event so most people can attend. It makes a big difference to students if the folks they know from volunteering show up, but unfortunately, not all can get away from their jobs during the day. In the future, we may design an evening event and expand it into a dinner. Students who have experience with athletic banquets suggested this alternative. Looking at ways other activities, such as athletics, are revered is a good method for finding inspiration. The Poster Project idea came from seeing how research scientists proudly display their findings in the corridors of university laboratory buildings.

Students thrive on having some creative control. While our students were putting together their posters, they decided to bring in music. Each student assumed a day when he or she would bring in the music. This small touch lightened the atmosphere and helped ease the way.

Bringing closure to an open-ended service-learning course is a tricky assignment requiring those involved to look back with wisdom and, at the same time, look forward with promise. We have had great success with our approach. The End-of-the-Year Symposium illuminates the past efforts and future dreams of students. No matter how tired students may be at the end of the year, facing a real audience provides a boost. The natural charm of their young adulthood shines through impressively as they sincerely present their ideas for the future and fuse their idealism with real possibilities.

While cleaning up after the symposium and saying goodbye, we often hear our students say, "Thank you. This event was a lot more fun than I thought it would be. Listening to my classmates share their feelings about volunteering and their advocacy ideas made me proud. My worries about sounding corny vanished when I realized how much the audience enjoyed what we had to say. You know what would be cool? To plan a reunion for the year 2006 and see what our futures became...."

Audrey Wells is Executive Teacher in English at University High School, a laboratory school on the Urbana campus of the University of Illinois. She teaches English classes, a course in film study, and Social Advocacy: History, Theory, and Practice. Audrey was a Mentor in NSEE's Leadership Development Program, funded by the DeWitt Wallace-Reader's Digest Fund.

Faculty Involvement

issue 5

Often, it takes one dedicated and innovative individual to initiate service-learning. But educators cannot sustain themselves and their programs without the support and assistance of their colleagues. Faculty who are involved in service-learning can enhance their own professional and leadership development while helping to ensure long-term success for the program.

LINDA KNICELY describes the process for recruiting peers as allies for service-learning.

ROSALIND CHIVIS follows with perspectives on rewards for faculty who participate in service-learning.

ELIZABETH GIBBS outlines successful strategies for training faculty in service-learning principles and practice.

DEBORAH GENZER tackles the complexities of training faculty to facilitate reflection.

PAULA ROWE suggests the importance of forming effective faculty committees.

A Grassroots Approach for Enlisting Faculty Support for Service-Learning

A DAY IN THE LIFE OF A CANAL WINCHESTER HIGH SCHOOL STUDENT BEGINS WITH FINDING ONE'S OWN WAY TO SCHOOL. The elimination of high school busing is one in a long list of cuts enacted by the local school board as it faces a school funding crisis of epidemic proportions. School districts across Ohio grapple with an archaic and inequitable school funding system currently under challenge in the Ohio Supreme Court. Voters in Canal Winchester, a fast-growing suburb of Columbus, have rejected six requests for new operating funds in the last two and a half years.

BY LINDA KNICELY

In my opinion, bribery works better than blackmail.

The student mentioned above is probably Caucasian, of European origin, since 98 percent of the high school student body is white, non-Hispanic. The first class she enters has probably been growing larger with each passing day. The little village of Canal Winchester has finally been "discovered." Gone are the years when the graduating class picture reflected, almost in its entirety, the kindergarten class profile. Residents, old and new alike, are predominantly well educated and middle to upper-middle class. Low-income neighborhoods virtually do not exist here. Security guards, student IDs, metal detectors, and weapons in schools are, as yet, foreign. As class begins and the student gazes out the window, a village truck lumbers past, proudly proclaiming Canal Winchester a "safe, clean, conservative community."

Given this socio-cultural picture, one operating principle for the district that might be observed is "If it ain't broke, don't fix it." Community members, parents, board members, administrators, and teachers view the school system as successful by such indicators as standardized test scores and scholarship monies awarded. The district is only peripherally involved in most of the school reform and restructuring initiatives sweeping the nation, and espouses a traditional approach to education. For example, block scheduling, which can certainly facilitate service-learning implementation, has not yet been introduced at Canal Winchester High School.

A second operating principle might be defined as the occasional reluctance among the teaching faculty to embrace and act eagerly upon directives that are issued "top-down." This was especially true with the administrative leader in place when the school district's service-learning program was initiated. Therein lay a dilemma of getting faculty to buy into service-learning in a meaningful way.

The origins of service-learning at the high school are rooted in a year-long peer helping/service-learning course for credit begun in the late 1980s. I am the guidance counselor for grades 9 to 12, with more than 400 students. The principal (himself, a former counselor) and I trained 20 to 25 students in the course in communication skills within a teen issues-based curriculum for nine weeks. Then we got them involved in student-selected individual and group activities and experiences through which they could practice and reinforce those skills. Eventually, the course focus fell more and more on community service with emphasis on preparation and reflection through teaching others and each other. What a great idea, we finally figured out! But how to provide this type of experience for more students school-wide than just the handful vying each year for those competitive slots? The solution seemed obvious—to sell other teachers on the idea.

MIGHTY OAKS FROM LITTLE ACORNS GROW Our effort to involve more faculty began with a ten-minute spiel outlining the basic elements of service-learning at the end of an after-school teachers' meeting. One might expect a less-than-enthusiastic audience, but by the end of that meeting, I had eight teachers willing to give service-learning a try. Attracted by the intrinsic benefits of service-learning to faculty members, my likely looking pilot staff included a senior government teacher, two English teachers, a biology teacher, a home economics teacher, an industrial technology teacher, a teacher of developmentally handicapped (DH) students, and one of students with learning disabilities (LD). For program credibility, I had hoped to attract educators representing a wide spectrum of core academic and vocational/elective disciplines who interacted with differently abled as well as high-achieving students on a daily basis, and to this end I was happily successful.

Food is, not only for students but also for teachers, a powerful motivator.

This group was enticed with a day away from their students in the spring. With substitutes in charge, we met at a local church to munch on bagels for breakfast and subs for lunch while we listened and talked and learned and developed a common definition of service-learning and what it was to mean in Canal Winchester schools. We supported the day and other such trainings with mini-grant funds available to us since I was a participant in NSEE's Leadership Development Program, funded by the DeWitt Wallace-Reader's Digest Fund.

The following fall, business people, ministers, social service representatives, parents, and school board members joined the team and developed a broader vision by engaging in a community needs assessment and action planning session. By the end of that school year, LD students were writing newsletter articles for a local historical farm metro park, and DH Life Skills students were partnering with senior citizens in and outside of their homes on projects. Reading students had developed puppet shows and reading activities for a local pre-school, and industrial technology and advanced biology students were involved in units connected to construction and sport in physiology, respectively, by designing an exercise course for the community. These were just some of the initial projects.

By the time the next school year began, other high school teachers, as well as elementary and middle school teachers, had begun to take note and were asking how they might become involved. Over the next two years, approximately one third to one half of the teaching staffs at all three building levels have requested and received initial training in service-learning. A wide variety of service-learning activities are now on-going—from individual classroom studies/projects to an environmentally themed interdisciplinary unit involving four grade levels at the elementary school last spring. What happened? How did teachers get "hooked"? In other words, how was faculty support enlisted? Following is a series of strategies, some intentional, some unintentional, that seem to have worked.

Don't just take my word for it. Faculty support for service-learning is strong because it is, and always has been, a grassroots movement here. A few brave souls tested the waters and then convinced other teachers to give it a try, not with words, but by *utilizing* the methodology to show them it could and would work. In all cases, it was important to recruit allies carefully. I encouraged not only a cross-section of teachers representing a variety of disciplines to get involved, but worked with those, initially, with whom I had an already-established relationship, those who were vested, not necessarily with formal authority in the power hierarchy, but with the respect of their colleagues, and those who not only had the best of intentions when turned on by a new concept, but who also had the staying power to organize and see a project proposal through to a satisfactory conclusion.

Another helping of carrots, please. In my opinion, bribery works better than blackmail. In other words, come up with as many "carrots" to offer teachers as possible. While the intrinsic benefits are many, we all realize that implementing service-learning can take extra time and effort, especially in the beginning. It also involves a certain element of risk taking and, at times, discomfort on the teachers' part as they "try on" a new teaching style. Provide tangible and intangible rewards for their dedication, commitment, and indeed, bravery.

Funds from the NSEE mini-grant and three consecutive Learn and Serve America grants have provided the means to facilitate and support teacher planning and implementation efforts. In a district starved for financial resources, money for substitutes allowed faculty time for training and planning as well as for supervision of off-campus service-learning activities. It has also covered buses, field trips, and consumable supplies used in carrying out service-learning projects. Many times this type of support has only been available to teachers involved in the program.

End-of-the-year celebrations have recognized teacher, student, and community involvement with plaques, books, and dessert buffets. Food is, not only for students but also for teachers, a powerful motivator. Holding team planning meetings or in-service trainings while providing breakfast and/or lunch makes them palatable in more ways than one.

A few faculty have been able to attend the National Service-Learning Conferences in Albuquerque, Philadelphia, and Detroit where they have reveled in the opportunities to learn from and be inspired by the national leaders in the field.

That which is old is new again. The premise, if not the terminology, of service-learning, is a familiar one to many veteran educators, particularly those in vocational education and special education where students have long been encouraged to apply what they learn in real-life settings. I always acknowledge that fact up front, to sidestep any resentment which might be directed toward this "fresh upstart" as well as to reinforce the concept that we *all* have areas of expertise and should draw on each other as resources. Partnerships in these areas are some of our strongest in the district.

A little nudge. Developing an infrastructure that will provide logistical and inspirational support to the faculty involved on a continuous basis is probably the most important, and at the same time, most difficult, goal to achieve. In our district there are no assistant principals, no curriculum supervisors, no central office staff to help facilitate the planning/implementation process. A full-time, or even part-time, service-learning coordinator? Forget it! I quickly learned that unless someone was around to jostle, prod, nudge, or harass, even the most passionate service-learning advocate can quickly get sidetracked, buried beneath papers to grade and lesson plans to complete.

The need for ongoing program support became even more critical for us when our program expanded to the other two building levels. Luckily, I have been able to convince enthusiastic and energetic coordinators in the elementary and middle schools to take on supervisory responsibilities in addition to implementing their own service-learning units. We strive valiantly to stay in touch with each other, get answers to teachers' questions, forward project proposals, and, in general, stay on the same page. A service-learning consultant, available to us through grant monies for a three hours per week, is a tremendous help as a trainer, resource person, building and community liaison, and (my favorite), completer of endless federal grant reports! Time, in this instance, is a more precious commodity than money.

A shot of adrenaline now and then. When an outside consultant gave the keynote at a teacher in-service last year and described the potential role of service-learning in overall school reform and restructuring initiatives, she re-directed attention toward the program. Timely doses of these types of opportunities are important in keeping faculty moving in the right direction. If teachers are convinced that utilizing service-learning methodologies can help them, individually and as a member of the district educational team, in making headway toward broader goals and objectives, it can become a win-win situation.

Straight from the horse's mouth. To help encourage teachers who might be reluctant to get involved or might not yet be convinced (despite our best efforts) that student reaction would be positive, I went straight to the horses' mouths. I developed a student questionnaire that almost every high school student completed. One of the questions asked students to identify three subject areas in which they would like to see service-learning methodologies incorporated. Armed with effective weaponry in the form of a computer base of expressed interest, I then shared this information with the reluctant teaching staff, gaining more new converts.

A one dollar sticker.... I have heard my new high school principal, a former football coach, tell of how hard football players would work, in practice and on game day, for those one dollar (in our case, "tomahawk") stickers for their helmets that represent a tackle or block made, a pass intercepted, or some other example of outstanding individual performance. It's not the monetary value of the sticker, but the respect, the recognition of the hard work behind it that is important to those young athletes. In the teaching profession, it is much the same. In a society where respect and admiration for any occupation seem to correlate directly with high salaries, teachers suffer by comparison in the public eye, especially with their counterparts in Asian and European schools. They yearn, too often in vain, for recognition of their dedication to young people and the hard work that they invest in their jobs.

At every turn, I try to be as demonstrative as possible in expressing my appreciation to the faculty members involved with service-learning—encouraging them as innovators and risk takers, on the cutting edge of school change, and as leaders within their own educational setting. When visitors from out of state fly in to observe the program, they talk to the teachers, not me. When grant applications are re-approved, it is because the teachers are providing proof of program credibility in their classrooms and in the community. I reinforce the value of the teachers' leadership in as many ways as I can, both tangibly and intangibly, because I firmly believe that it can never happen too often, and because it's the truth. I think it makes a difference. My most personally and professionally rewarding collegial connections have been made through service-learning, and I am warmed and constantly encouraged by the enthusiasm I see on the faces and hear in the voices of those who work with me in these efforts.

CHALLENGES AHEAD There is a unified emphasis in the Canal Winchester service-learning program on curriculum integration, complete with project proposal formats detailing graded course of study goals and objectives achieved through each activity. All faculty members interested in accessing grant funds for service-learning must complete a minimum one-day training experience in which adherence to high standards of quality in service-learning programming is promoted. Teachers are encouraged to brainstorm project ideas, curricular connections, and solutions to potential difficulties, drawing on the resources and creativity of the group to forge ahead. This approach is empowering and gives novices the self-confidence to shift a little in their teaching styles and make room for service-learning on their plate of teaching techniques.

At every turn, I try to be as demonstrative as possible in expressing my appreciation....

While I am greatly encouraged by the growth of the program in terms of the numbers of teachers involved, it is still lacking in depth. Most practitioners seem to have become comfortable with including one or two service-learning projects/units at some time in the school year, often in the spring, when classrooms are feeling claustrophobic. I hope, in the future, to see more meaningful paradigm shifts where teachers are willing to restructure greater portions of their course instruction by using this or other alternative methods. At present, they seem to be keeping each other company perched on a very large plateau. I believe movement from this plateau will require close attention to greater leadership development issues within faculty bodies, and may only come when the district, as a whole, makes a commitment to a wider-ranging school reform platform. The reality that has dictated that our service-learning program be wholly supported by grant funds has tremendously impeded the institutionalization process. A district's commitment to the philosophy of service-learning is far more substantial in those locales where it is a line item in the budgeting of local funds.

My other personal frustrations center around the pro's and con's of my "de facto" service-learning coordinator position. I have never wished to be an administrator. Yet, here I am, coordinating a program which leaves me much less time for the direct involvement with students in service-learning that drew me in the first place. I've also needed to learn to give up control at times, to stifle the desire to step in and fix or rescue, instead trusting that individuals need to succeed, or fail, as the case may be, on their own, and that I can not do everything that I would like.

But I am not bemoaning my role in this entirely. I am more than compensated by the numbers of teachers and students who have received a tantalizing taste of service-learning thus far and by the community connections that have been forged. Yet, my greatest rewards have been serendipitous: The computer technology teacher who, while not formally trained in service-learning or a sub-grantee of funds, nonetheless wrote service-learning applications into his advanced topics course description; the art teacher who, during her Board of Education presentation on the high school art curriculum, focused on her "Helping Creative Hands" project which draws advanced design students and multi-handicapped students together; the middle school teacher and high school teacher who are developing their master's theses on the foundation of service-learning; the rifts that begin to heal when elementary, middle, and high school teachers, who often approach educational issues from very different perspectives, gather around a table to build inter-building alliances with students at the center. These types of experiences make teaching not just a place to report to between paychecks, but a wondrous adventure, and service-learning such an exciting and rewarding field!

Linda Knicely is a Guidance Counselor in Canal Winchester High School in Ohio. She was a Fellow and a Mentor in NSEE's Leadership Development Program, funded by the DeWitt Wallace-Reader's Digest Fund.

Rewards for Faculty

ADMINISTRATORS OR PRINCIPALS OFTEN HAVE INNOVATIVE IDEAS THAT THEY WOULD LIKE TO INTEGRATE INTO THEIR SCHOOLS. Too often, they lack financial incentives to get teachers to try a new approach, and without such obvious rewards as a salary increase, the teachers may not be interested. Likewise, teachers may have ideas they would like to pursue but need some kind of incentive to get started or to keep going, especially when risking a new, unpredictable approach. For a service-learning approach to work in an ongoing way, programs must find ways to offer incentives and rewards to faculty for their efforts.

BY **ROSALIND CHIVIS**

Most service-learning programs emphasize rewards for students. Celebrations and closure are emphasized as ways to connect the students' work with the community and achieve recognition for the students' efforts. Community groups often receive recognition as well. Too often, however, the faculty members' efforts to initiate and sustain the service-learning program do not get the same extra attention in terms of incentives or rewards.

Teachers are usually overworked, and initially, most service-learning projects involve extra tasks. There are community people to contact, logistics to work out, different approaches to curriculum content to sort through, and grading adjustments to be made. Incentives are needed for faculty members to be open minded, to be flexible, to re-think their approaches to teaching. They need to be willing to take a risk, which usually requires some kind of incentive to leave the standard, everyday practice. After taking the risk, rewards are needed to keep faculty involved. These can range from tangible rewards, such as new opportunities for professional development, to intangible rewards, such as recognition, new connections with colleagues, and satisfactions for a job well done.

TANGIBLE INCENTIVES AND REWARDS
Financial incentives are nice but are not always possible. Salary increases are usually not tied to a new teaching approach such as service-learning. Many schools, however, have sought and received grants for implementing service-learning projects, including curriculum planning grants and other types of training stipends. These may provide some financial assistance, often during the summer months, to develop service-learning projects and courses. Sometimes, grants through community organizations are available as well, as community groups increasingly are interested in school reform efforts. Stipends for new types of teaching approaches can be an important incentive for teachers.

Professional development opportunities are another tangible incentive and reward. As faculty members invest time and interest in

Service-learning requires teachers to network and break out of an isolation mode.

service-learning approaches, they may be able to attend national and regional conferences and training sessions in the field. This is an opportunity to explore new ideas with people from around the country and get re-energized for teaching.

Occasionally, teachers may receive tangible rewards from community organizations. Community partners that offer services, such as a museum or zoo, often allow faculty members to visit free of charge, to keep interest strong in the program.

INTANGIBLE INCENTIVES AND REWARDS Often, intangible rewards motivate a faculty member to try out and continue to use a service-learning approach. Intangible rewards can come in small, daily ways or at major end-of-the year celebrations. Sometimes, the rewards aren't even clear immediately, but may settle into a person's consciousness when reflecting about the parts of the school year that were meaningful and important to her or him as a teacher.

One important intangible reward is recognition. Recognition is valuable for anyone, for small jobs done in the family to large, complex efforts completed on the job. People naturally thrive on recognition whether they're willing to admit it or not. It can be as elaborate as a banquet or as simple as a word of praise. Praise is an excellent source of recognition. It is inexpensive, very powerful, and you can use it as much as you like or need to. Some types of recognition that are helpful for faculty members include:

- bulletin boards focusing on staff members and the program,
- acknowledgments on the school's message board,
- announcements on the loud speaker,
- sending staff to other schools to discuss the program,
- letter of commendation from the principal with copy to the superintendent,
- nomination for teaching award,
- recognition dinner,
- newspaper articles or other media coverage, and
- recognition in assemblies.

Another essential intangible reward is the connection that faculty members make with other teachers, community members, and students. Service-learning requires teachers to network and break out of an isolation mode. Partnerships have to be created with others. An interdependence automatically develops among teachers, staff, community agencies, and students. A networking mode quickly replaces the isolation model so deeply ingrained in teacher preparation. Staff begin to look at colleagues as resources instead of crew members stuck in the same boat with different areas of expertise. We don't live in isolation. Why should we teach in isolation? If a science teacher wants to involve students in testing the water in a nearby creek, or take radon readings in the homes of community members, why not involve the math teacher to pick up the math piece and the English teacher to work with the writing assignments. Suddenly, the teacher has partners to work with. The "I" becomes "we." The "we" encompasses staff, students, parents, and the community.

A home economics teacher, for example, developed a project that provided homeless people living in a shelter with a nourishing meal one day each week. The students raised funds, solicited surplus grocery items from supermarkets, prepared and served the food. Parents helped too. What began in the home economics department later involved history, economics, math, English, and social studies teachers. Because this teacher engaged so many other staff members and community partners, the program now practically runs on its on.

SATISFACTION IN TEACHING Often, teachers become frustrated fighting feelings of inadequacy. Why can't I get through to these kids? How can I make a difference? How can I make learning more interesting? These are the kinds of questions many teachers ask themselves.

The most powerful and lasting reward for faculty members involved with service-learning is watching the growth in students, particularly how students connect the curriculum with real-life situations. Involving the students in the initial planning promotes an investment in the project on the part of the student. This makes it easier for the teacher to step out of the role of conveyer of information and into the role of facilitator of learning. The walls of the classroom are broken down, as the school building and the larger community become the classroom.

After participating in service-learning projects, you can hear students say things like, "I never knew how important little things that I take for granted every day mean to old folks." Or, "It makes me feel good to be appreciated and needed." Hearing such comments, teachers become curious. When teachers hear a community person describe one of their socially challenging students with marvelous praise, the teachers become more than curious. They have difficulty believing that the same students whose behavior is such a challenge in the classroom are so productive and well behaved on the field placement. These types of testimonials send powerful messages to teachers. They also serve to encourage more participation from staff and students.

One student wrote, "Without even realizing my community service time was dwindling down to a few precious hours, I knew this was where I wanted to be—but how? I approached Linda and requested to stay even after my hours were served. She agreed. I have been at the Center since September and I love every minute of the time I spend there. My children have become a part of my life. There is nothing more satisfying than hearing the words, 'Miss Colleen, can you help me?' I have learned that children are probably the most honest people in the world. They love to laugh and they love to learn. What's more important is that they teach me to love and learn."

Sometimes the satisfaction is also tangible, such as when a proposal you have written is funded, or when the principal earmarks funds from the operating budget for your program. Then there's the sense of accomplishment and enthusiasm that comes with actions taken, the satisfaction that comes with a contribution towards the shaping of minds and the examination of value systems. You have strengthened communities and community partnerships and helped develop a generation of caring citizens.

Service-learning is somewhat frightening to a newcomer who doesn't understand the rationale for it. As you mentor staff and teachers to get them involved, encourage them to mentor someone

The most powerful and lasting reward for faculty members involved with service-learning is watching the growth in students....

else. Eventually, using this strategy, you will achieve systemic change. Along the way, praise teachers as often as possible for jobs well done. Take every opportunity presented to showcase your program and the staff who administer it, being careful not to alienate other staff in the process. In the end, what really matters is that service-learning programs maintain the interest and commitment of the people involved, recognize efforts and achievements, and engage students in meaningful learning.

> *Rosalind Chivis was appointed Assistant Principal of Central High School in Philadelphia, Pennsylvania, in 1993. She is currently on special assignment in the School District of Philadelphia as the administrative assistant to the Assistant Superintendent in the Office for Senior High Schools. Rosalind serves on the Advisory Board for the Pennsylvania Department of Education's Learn and Serve Program, and she was a Mentor in NSEE's Leadership Development Program, funded by the DeWitt Wallace-Reader's Digest Fund.*

Training Faculty in the Principles and Practice of Service-Learning

APPROACHED WITH YET ANOTHER "NOVEL" IDEA OR TECHNIQUE REQUIRING A WORKSHOP OR TRAINING SESSION, MANY EDUCATORS CRINGE. Many teachers already feel that too much is "dumped" upon them and may resent the request of their presence at a mandatory training. While the majority of teachers are open to perfecting their classroom techniques for the sake of improving students' learning, these same teachers are not necessarily willing to give up their classroom time and attend a three-day introductory workshop on service-learning.

BY **ELIZABETH GIBBS**

We knew that this would be the case even in the Bloomfield Hills School District, in the Detroit, Michigan, metropolitan area. Our district consistently encourages teachers to attend conferences and workshops on improving student performance, and for the last decade has required 40 hours of community service in order to graduate. Even so, the idea of service-learning was new to our district. As community service coordinator for the district, I had the challenge of trying to institutionalize service-learning in the school district. I knew that involving faculty at the outset was essential for this process. We had to think creatively about training faculty, thinking more broadly than traditional workshops.

Service-learning may not be a totally new concept to all of your faculty members. However, even those "seasoned" educators still need to participate in service-learning training. Service-learning represents a paradigm shift in the way many of us teach. While the emphasis in high school classroom instruction may still be predominately on the lecture format, hands-on experiences become extremely critical in keeping and generating students' interest, in transferring classroom skills to real-life applications, and in retaining information for a longer duration. Ideally, every teacher and administrator who has direct contact with students should receive some kind of instruction in service-learning. Because not every teacher is going to see this in the same way, offering a choice for participating in service-learning training will probably work better than an administrative mandate.

GETTING STARTED In order to get a sense of our staff climate as well as to assess their prior knowledge and experience on the topic of service-learning, we developed a survey for all the high school teachers in the district. This is a good initial tool, and the simpler the survey, the more likely it is to be returned. We asked: "Are you familiar with service-learning as a teaching method?" "Have your students had any service-learning experiences in your classrooms and would you describe these?" "Are you interested in learning more about service-learning and would you be willing to attend a workshop or training in this area?" We had an 80 percent response and got a lot of information that helped us with the next steps in training.

...some of our teachers had included service projects as a part of their classroom experiences for years.

We discovered that some of our teachers had included service projects as a part of their classroom experiences for years. The survey also helped us identify those who might want to participate in the first steps toward faculty training in service-learning. From the survey respondents, we created a list of potential participants who would be willing to share their lunch hour in discussion with their colleagues about every six weeks. We were fortunate to be selected as a site for NSEE's Pilot Project, supported by The Hitachi Foundation, to strengthen and sustain high school service-learning programs, and that project provided us access to outside consultants. They helped us create this lunchtime structure, called a "Learning Circle," as a means of sharing these experiences in service-learning. High schools are structured, for the most part, to segregate teachers into specific discipline areas, which rarely allow teachers to converse with colleagues outside their content areas.

...by using the tools themselves, the faculty were learning techniques for their classrooms.

The Learning Circle was unlike any other advisory board in the school. It was a networking opportunity and a chance for professional development. This was done in an atmosphere of trust, openness, and collegiality. As a former teacher, I realized that teachers tend to keep their best teaching secrets to themselves. For the Learning Circle to work, a supportive atmosphere must be encouraged. Also, some logistical problems may need attention. Our teachers ate lunch in two different periods, which prevented a shared meeting. With the support of our administration, we managed to get teachers released for both lunch periods occasionally, and the Learning Circle was highly successful.

REAL-LIFE TRAINING Our Learning Circle participants recommended that we proceed with service-learning workshops and conferences. Many teachers needed examples of service-learning projects as well as time to develop their own projects. To continue, we needed more funds, to send our Learning Circle participants to workshops, and to purchase resource materials on service-learning. Fortunately, we received a grant from Michigan's Learn and Serve Grant Program. We made faculty training a priority for the first year of the grant, believing this would eventually help us institutionalize service-learning in the district.

All school districts are not going to apply for or receive such grants. Other ways of funding staff training must be researched. Many school districts have a staff development budget. A more inexpensive way to train faculty in service-learning might be to send two or three staff members to an intensive training in service-learning and then have them facilitate training for the rest of the faculty. Instead of taking teachers out of the classrooms during the school day and having to pay for substitutes, faculty training could take place during the summer or after school, with a stipend or curriculum pay offered to teachers who participate.

We used our grant money to bring in a team of service-learning trainers for a three-day workshop at the beginning of the school year. To offset some of the cost, the district invited other local school districts to send one or two teachers to attend the training. The workshop included 24 of our district's high school teachers and approximately 10 teachers from other districts. It was important to have a good cross section of teachers from various disciplines in this initial training, and we also invited some middle school teachers. Some of these teachers had some previous personal experience with community service while others had not. By setting up the training over a three-day period of time, we were able to get the participants involved in a service project for one morning. It was important for the teachers to experience what we envisioned our students experiencing.

We organized the training around three of the basic phases of service—preparation, meaningful service experiences, and reflection. Our first day of training included learning the basic concepts, philosophy, and methods included in service-learning. There was always ample time for the staff to share and teach each other, drawing from their own service-learning experiences. On the second day, we actually engaged in a service project, going through the steps we would expect to do with the students. Just as the choice of a project is important for students to have a good experience, so it was for this workshop, along with preparation for the sites. The teachers chose placements in nursing homes, soup kitchens, child-care programs, and schools. We spent the afternoon reflecting upon the service experiences, using a variety of reflection techniques and tools. Thus, by using the tools themselves, the faculty were learning techniques for their classrooms. By the third day, the teachers were ready to develop some service-learning projects for their own classes. They also had the opportunity to share these project ideas with the other participants and to receive feedback.

INTO THE CLASSROOM Now came the hard part—implementing these projects. We had at least 24 out of about 120 teachers from the two high schools in our district who were excited about using service-learning and were willing to go back to their classrooms and try it out. Then hopefully, these activities would get other students and staff members curious enough about service-learning to want to learn more. This was the process that we used and it worked!

The grant money continued to be a help with this spreading of the word. Not only did it provide the means for sending teachers and students to additional service-learning training, but it also gave us credibility for what we were trying to do within our school district. Many of the other staff members began to take notice of what was happening in service-learning due to the positive publicity the district received because of the grants.

The greatest satisfaction came from watching the teachers develop new projects and share their successes in the Learning Circle. There were teachers experienced with this kind of project and those who had never tried it before. For some who had been teaching for years and were near retirement, service-learning sparked their excitement about the prospects of teaching again. For example, our Spanish teacher worked with her upper level students in an elementary school. The high school students constructed elementary books in Spanish and then took them over to the elementary school with a significant Hispanic population and read them. Afterwards, they directed the young children through an art project reflecting the general themes of the books they had been reading. It didn't take long for other high school students to begin talking about the neat projects that were taking place in Mrs. Chasco's Spanish class and to ask their other teachers if they could try something similar.

Successes appeared in many types of classrooms. A high school special education class became involved in service-learning. Once a week for one semester, the special education class spent time at a nearby elementary school teaching basic math skills and reading to a special education first grade class. For most of the high school students, this was one of the first times they had the opportunity to be role models and leaders for other students. It was a profoundly moving experience for all those involved.

We found many resources useful to help teachers develop ideas such as these two projects. Books that were particularly helpful were two volumes of *Combining Service and Learning*, published by the National Society for Experiential Education, and *Growing Hope* and other materials from the National Youth Leadership Council. While such resource guides are useful in helping teachers get started in service-learning, the most important element is what teachers and students bring to the projects together. Faculty need to realize that students must have a vested interest in the project.

We are still learning and growing through our experiences as we seek to integrate service-learning into our curriculum. Service-learning has become part of our district mission statement. "In our multicultural world it is important to foster awareness of the needs of others and a willingness to fulfill social and civic responsibilities," the mission states. "It is our intent to encourage students to be sensitive to the rights of others, to understand the dangers of prejudice, and to be active participants in the democratic process."

Service-learning is the tool that we can use to achieve our goals in our mission statement. More and more teachers have attended various workshops and conferences in service-learning and are now at the point to disseminate information and share their experiences with others. As we continue to search for ways to expand our efforts, we will continue our Learning Circle. We will be publishing a district-wide service-learning and experiential education newsletter that will highlight projects. Hopefully, such efforts will continue to break down the notion that educators do not want to share their best kept secrets, and will nurture a cooperative spirit. In this collaborative approach, we can help students see their potential and responsibility in being active citizens within their communities.

Elizabeth Gibbs is Coordinator of Community Service in the Bloomfield Hills Public Schools in Michigan. She has been a Mentor in NSEE's Leadership Development Program and a Consultant with NSEE's National Initiative, funded by the DeWitt Wallace-Reader's Digest Fund. Beth was also a key liaison for NSEE's Pilot Project, supported by The Hitachi Foundation, to strengthen and sustain high school service-learning programs.

Involving Faculty in Reflection

SERVICE-LEARNING SHOULD IDEALLY BE AN EXCHANGE BETWEEN TWO PARTIES, THE STUDENT AND PLACE WHERE THE STUDENT ENGAGES IN THE SERVICE. Both parties are learners and both are servers. Service-learning is a partnership where people work together toward a common goal and value all those involved in the process. As coordinator of the service-learning program for 9th to 12th grades at a small, private urban high school in San Francisco, I have the challenge of helping to make this ideal exchange become a reality. This is a lofty goal, even at our school, which has a decade of experience at this and has numerous resources on which to draw.

BY **DEBORAH GENZER** WITH **WILLIAM FINGER**

How can this ambitious goal be reached? One of the most critical elements is to instill the value of reflection among our faculty. In terms of service-learning, reflection can help with preparation, the service itself, and learning from the service. This is a difficult concept to teach. When I have taught pre-service teachers, those getting credentials for teaching, I have stressed the importance of reflection. But saying it's important is not enough. They need to see it in action. What they want to know is how the kids are going to react.

Teachers are experiential learners by definition. They learn their craft by trial and error and naturally use reflection in the process. Yet learning to apply reflection to the curriculum is a process that takes time. Even so, every teacher or service-learning coordinator can rely on some guideposts while experimenting. Every guidepost will not apply to every faculty member at the same time. People are always on different points of a learning cycle, ready to hear certain things at certain times. The guideposts discussed below, gleaned from my work as a service-learning coordinator at San Francisco University High School and as a consultant and trainer in other settings, can be useful, even as faculty and service-learning coordinators learn to use reflection in their own unique ways.

GUIDEPOST 1 *Teachers often start with the assumption that service and the curriculum will enrich each other automatically, and they do not think an explicit effort (e.g., reflection) is needed to make this connection.*

In the mid-1980s, during a special summer planning session, teachers of English and history at our high school created an integrated 9th-grade curriculum with the overarching theme of community and culture. The plan was to teach students facts and concepts about specific cultures such as China and India, while also helping students learn the skills of cross-cultural understanding. Encouraged by our school mission statement, which says in part that we strive to take advantage of and contribute to our city, faculty decided that students would learn the cross-cultural skills by providing

Teachers are experiential learners by definition.

service to an ethnic neighborhood in our city. However, the curriculum made no plan for making connections during class between the experience and the curriculum. It was assumed that the connections were so obvious that students would see them naturally.

To implement this plan, the school hired me to place students in cross-cultural settings. I had not been part of the planning committee that summer, and I did not have expertise in linking service to the curriculum. Few high schools had tried that by the mid-1980s. Given my background, I did not feel in a position to question whether the students would learn all that we hoped. But I was experienced at matching student volunteers to agency needs, and I knew that we had to at least check in with students about their progress. I knew I needed to express this to the group but I was hesitant because I didn't want to create more work for teachers who were clearly already working hard enough.

GUIDEPOST 2 *It is critical that the coordinator of service projects be part of the group that plans and reflects on curriculum.*

A tragedy gave me the resolve to bring the issue to the group and to take my place "at the table" as an equal with the teachers. One of our students was serving as a tutor at an elementary school. The day before he went to the school, one of the teachers there had committed suicide. In the frenzy of handling the crisis, the school had forgotten to call our high school. Our student tutor entered a classroom in chaos. When he returned, he didn't know where to turn for support. I only heard about the incident through the grapevine. Upon hearing the story, the freshman curriculum committee was persuaded that we needed to be more responsible for providing a designated way for students to discuss what was happening in their service projects.

Often, the service-learning coordinator or community resource person is not officially part of the academic department. This can be a strategic disadvantage on many levels. You may not be aware of basic information. Not being an equal at the planning table affects interpersonal relationships. You might be viewed as a person who merely implements what others conceptualize and plan. People with a strict academic orientation may see a resource coordinator as not having proper qualifications to be an equal in the planning process, not a clear stakeholder in the service-learning process. For all of these reasons, it is essential for the service-learning coordinator to be an equal in the planning and design process.

GUIDEPOST 3 *Teachers need a forum to discuss reflection strategies with each other. They need a way to exchange ideas and actually reflect on their methodology.*

At our bi-weekly freshman curriculum committee meeting, we reflected on our first approach to reflection—lunch-time discussion groups—and decided to stop them and try student journals instead. The faculty reasoned that journal assignments could be given instead of other homework for that night and therefore would not be an add-on. It also would not take away from class time, which was a key faculty concern.

Teachers need to time to reflect. The bi-weekly meeting gave us one forum in which to make changes. The forum for such discussions should be in keeping with the culture of the school, such as regular department meetings, an existing service-learning committee meeting, or a teacher workday. Discussions that involve teacher reflection can lead to significant program improvements. That is exactly what happened with our shift from lunch discussions to journals.

GUIDEPOST 4 *Journals can be an excellent starting technique for faculty new to reflection.*

The journal writing had many benefits. Students had practice writing, which was certainly a curricular aim in English and history. And the writing itself was thoughtful, raising important questions such as "How do I handle the discipline with the children—I don't agree with the agency's approach?"

The teachers brainstormed about a set of questions that would further enhance student reflection. What we were really encouraging was critical thinking. Posing questions such as "In what ways are you crossing cultural lines?" or "What are the implicit rules of this agency and how do you know?" helped students to demonstrate comprehension, analysis, and synthesis. These are habits of mind greatly valued by teachers. The teachers also valued getting to know the students in new ways and being able to guide student learning in a personal, non-threatening but effective way, through comments in their journals. The writing also gave the teachers something they could evaluate.

Enthusiasm for journal reflection was high, which led faculty to seek other opportunities for written reflection. When we added a computer literacy requirement to the freshman curriculum, for example, the faculty had students write personal essays about their service experiences in the word processing unit. On the down side, however, some students just could not communicate well in written form. Teachers were frustrated with entries like, "Today I went and nothing much happened." A new dimension needed to be added to the curriculum.

GUIDEPOST 5 *Teachers must have a central role in creating the service-learning and reflection curriculum, and must learn to plan the reflection activities.*

To help students connect with their community placement, a faculty member and I brought a proposal to the curriculum committee. After the students had been at the placement for a month or so, and they were beginning to understand the culture, we could have the students reflect on ways in which they could make a personal contribution. The journal would be the place to formulate the ideas, and the students would then communicate their ideas in written proposal form to the agency. The agency could then reflect on the proposal with the student and together they would create a place for the activity, including any training that might be needed.

The faculty liked the idea a great deal because it enhanced the curriculum, furthering the skills of crossing cultural lines, and could provide a real audience for student writing. It could also increase the students' engagement; students were happier and a great increase in the number of creative and meaningful projects resulted. For example, students who had complained about visiting senior citizens moved beyond the obvious cross-cultural barriers of ethnic origin and age.

The students discovered that the elders were feeling out of touch with youth culture and wanted an education about modern issues such as AIDS, which was a high-profile concern in San Francisco. Teachers and staff helped our students prepare a culturally sensitive and age-appropriate presentation that was well received. This led us to using different styles of reflection for different phases of the service-learning process: preparation, training, service activity, and evaluation.

This experience helped faculty further their skills of planning reflection activities. Planning and implementation are two different things. Incorporating reflection into the planned curriculum is a good starting point. But until it is built into specific lesson plans or structured in some other concrete way, reflection may be a good intention but not get done because of too little time. Using reflection to adjust the service experience itself, as we did, incorporated reflection as an integral part of the curriculum.

Ideally, reflection would involve agency people in the planning, implementation, and exchange of reflection tools....

GUIDEPOST 6 *Faculty will value reflection if they see that it will better enable their students to understand the curriculum.*

Even with successes such as the senior citizen AIDS presentation, there were still varying levels of faculty buy-in to incorporating service-learning into the 9th-grade curriculum. All teachers were required to agree on what service component would happen, which meant that some teachers could not go as far with their ideas as they wished. This changed dramatically when teachers divided themselves into teaching teams, which allowed more freedom to branch out. For example, one team linked up with a local elementary school to develop and teach a cultural storytelling unit. The 9th graders developed the lesson plans to teach elements of a story, while the 4th and 5th graders shared and created stories from their own cultures. Joint reflection happened throughout the project, among all the grade levels.

The English teacher who spearheaded the idea had a strong commitment to service, while the history teacher was more skeptical of the project. The experience brought the history teacher into the elementary school and in ongoing dialogue with her students about cross-cultural issues. As she saw her students become more engaged with the curriculum material through these elementary students' stories, she transformed her perspective to being more supportive and intrigued by service-learning.

GUIDEPOST 7 *Broad faculty consensus is helpful for institutionalizing reflection and service-learning.*

Tell colleagues about your students' accomplishments to generate support for service-learning becoming an essential part of the curriculum. Recently, we have compiled a two-volume set of our 9th graders' personal essays about their service experience. We have placed copies in the library, community service office, and other reference centers. We took this book to the curriculum committee for the school. After seeing this product of the students' reflection, they have given us even more support for service-learning.

GUIDEPOST 8 *Agency involvement in reflection has multiple rewards—from enhancing the service experience for all involved to enhancing a partnership rather than a one-sided giver and receiver relationship.*

Ideally, reflection would involve agency people in the planning, implementation, and exchange of reflection tools, such as discussions, journals, presentations, and celebrations. We have been able to involve agency people in some cases, such as the supervisor at the senior center and the elementary teachers. But this guidepost has been a challenge for us, and we are struggling with it now. There are logistical problems and challenges in being ready to hear each other. A lot of groundwork has to be laid.

Instilling reflection as a teaching tool among faculty is a pivotal part of moving toward this true partnership. Usually, an invitation to an agency for using reflection comes from the faculty member, or perhaps from the student with the faculty member's support. Some agencies are beginning to build reflection into their service projects regularly, whether a school is involved or not, so some initiative can also come from the agency side of the partnership. For example, a soup kitchen here now requires volunteers to stay an hour after serving to reflect on the process of service.

Moving towards a true partnership from the educational institution requires faculty members to embrace reflection as an essential learning tool. Moving the reflection to the time and place where the service is being done is a challenge. But as faculty see the value this gives to students, they embrace it all the more, and understand that reflection is the key to both student and faculty learning.

Deborah Genzer is Director of Community Service Learning at San Francisco University High School in California. She has been a Consultant with NSEE's National Initiative, funded by the DeWitt Wallace-Reader's Digest Fund.

The Faculty Committee—An Essential Ally

LENNY MOYER WAS IN HIS 27TH YEAR OF TEACHING AND FRANKLY, HE SAYS, "I WAS STALE. I LOVE TO TEACH, BUT NEEDED SOMETHING FRESH. I had been the golf coach, had led the ski club. I was stale there too." Mr. Moyer taught advanced placement political science and other social studies classes in the large suburban high school in Maryland, near Washington, D.C. But it was a conversation with a science teacher, not a politician, that renewed his interest in teaching. And, in the process, he assumed a pivotal role in institutionalizing an innovative service-learning project in a school and state already committed to experiential education.

BY **PAULA ROWE** WITH **WILLIAM FINGER**

As I've begun to think of myself as a CEO, I've been able to think of the faculty committees as resources to help me run my corporation.

Faculty committees can be a critical part of launching and sustaining a service-learning project. In my experience at Springbrook High School in Silver Spring, Maryland, we could not have institutionalized our service-based class without the help of my colleagues who, like Lenny Moyer, serve as teaching assistants in the class, and others who serve on our Faculty Advisory Committee. Most teachers are not trained to administer or direct programs. I am no exception! As a science teacher, I had experience with research and with guiding student science projects, but I was definitely not prepared for all of the administrative challenges of our service-learning project.

For the last two years, I have been the designated teacher for a service-learning pilot project, the Technology and Research Partnership (TARP) class. In this course, highly motivated students utilize state-of-the-art technology and the scientific methods to conduct research on authentic problems for government agencies and private corporations. I have thought a lot about what this job has been like and have concluded that I function like a CEO of a small corporation, with a small budget and many action items. Administering, directing, and coordinating requires me to identify needs, assemble the resources to meet the needs, continually observe and evaluate the results, and make appropriate adjustments as necessary.

Faculty committees can assist with all of these steps. Two general guideposts have been particularly useful to me in working with my colleagues at Springbrook High. First, faculty members need to be enthusiastic supporters of the project, while coming from a variety of disciplines. Because our project focuses on technology and research in all disciplines, and because we need teachers with a variety of skills, we involve teachers from many departments—English, math, social studies, and the media center. Second, faculty members can be involved in just about every aspect of a service-learning project if the duties can be broken down into small parts and adequately defined and communicated in a timely fashion. As I've begun to think of myself as a CEO, I've been able to think of the faculty committees as resources to help me run my corporation.

TARP STRUCTURE Service-learning projects vary enormously in structure, purpose, design, numbers of students involved, and community placements. At Springbrook, in addition to my work with TARP, we have two part-time staff, one serving as our newly added service-learning coordinator and the other as the supervisor of our long-standing internship program. At the district level, we have a director for the Executive Internship Program. All of these people have been very helpful to me. Community service is a statewide requirement for high schoolers in Maryland.

Planning for TARP at the district level began in the fall of 1993 when it was decided that schools would be recruited to develop and pilot an interdisciplinary class designed to give juniors and seniors an opportunity to use organizational and technological skills in partnership with community-based businesses or public agencies. In the spring of 1994, Springbrook's principal formed a committee and chose me to teach the new course. The committee included the assistant principal in charge of curriculum and scheduling, a media specialist, a science resource teacher, a technology resource teacher, and myself. We were given the freedom to create our unique model for TARP.

The initial committee evolved into a Faculty Advisory Committee, which helped recruit students for the first year, create a positive image of the program, and contact the parents. Twenty days of summer pay were made available to divide between me and various committee members. Our duties included finding community placements, refining our model for TARP, and developing the technical writing and statistics portion of the curriculum. I was given two teaching periods for the first experimental year of TARP.

In the spring of 1995, we prepared to move the experimental first-year project into the second year of the pilot phase. The administration did not feel that two teaching periods could be allocated for so few students. In addition, I had felt overwhelmed by so many different duties. So the faculty committee agreed that we would form a second committee, the "TARP teaching assistants." At Springbrook High, each teacher has an IRA ("instructionally related activity") period, which varies from study halls to tutoring students prior to state functional tests. I sought out faculty colleagues who would be willing to be TARP teaching assistants during their IRA periods.

The enthusiasm of the faculty was heartening. One of the teachers I talked with was Lenny Moyer. "This was appealing to me," says Mr. Moyer. "In our regular classroom, we're talking to 32 students at once. This was a chance to work more one-on-one, to give more direct advice."

Two science teachers and a math teacher joined the team, along with Mr. Moyer and myself. To prepare for the second year, I received 10 days of work time from the county during the summer to plan the expanded curriculum with the teaching team, and to determine the new community placements. I was also able to arrange for one day of pay for each of the TARP teaching assistants for planning the course during a day-long workshop. The assumption in

June was that as the TARP teacher (coordinator), I would be given one teaching period and one IRA period if the enrollment went up to 18 students. The enrollment did indeed rise to 18, but in August I found that I did not have the teaching period. I turned to my faculty committees for help.

"I had known the principal for many years," says Mr. Moyer. "I taught advanced placement political science. It didn't take a genius to figure out what we needed to do. I went to see the principal. I was the point man for presenting our case. He had a lot of competing priorities, but when I made our case, he agreed that the coordinator needed the teaching period."

Politics is part of every school, and having the right faculty supporters at this crucial stage of TARP was essential. Without the firm stand taken by Mr. Moyer and without his political skills, the program would not exist as it does today. Now that I had a teaching period, along with my IRA period, for TARP's second year, I was ready to begin functioning like a CEO.

ENTHUSIASM AND SKILLS The competencies associated with instruction and administration of the TARP course require more skills than any one teacher usually possesses. The TARP teaching assistants filled the voids. For example, the curriculum includes instruction in using computers for data analysis, literature searches, and slide show presentations; in studying ethics and management issues in the workplace; in developing personal skills in interviewing and presenting a résumé; and in reading and writing technical papers.

The teaching assistants come to class for one period every other day, providing personalized instruction as well as general skills. Each of the TARP teaching assistants has had different experiences in these areas. For example, one had more computer skills to share, and the math teacher provided special assistance to students involved in mathematics research.

"All of the teachers have given me a lot of support," says Eva, one of the TARP students this year. "The biology teacher has been a big help in analyzing my data. And the English teacher helped us get things just right and taught us how to make our presentations look professional."

The direct contact with the students gives the teaching assistants opportunities to stretch themselves. For example, Mr. Moyer has taught the students how to use a software package called ASTOUND, which allows students to make scientific slide presentations directly from the computer, something that is new even for many of the professional sites.

Eva is working on a project involving plant genetics. While she has broad interests, in musical theater, for example, she has enjoyed the challenge of a sophisticated science research project. She is working in a laboratory at a U.S. Department of Agriculture center studying desired effects of alfalfa. "Mr. Moyer is my preceptor," she says. "He is very strict. You have to earn his respect. He's demanding but he's nice. I've worked hard and applied all of what he's said to my work. He's been a tremendous help to me."

On a Friday afternoon, administering a makeup test for a handful of students, Mr. Moyer discussed

TARP and its satisfactions. Told of Eva's words, he was quiet, obviously moved. "We don't get many compliments in this business. It's different in TARP than in my other classes."

HELPING THE CEO Unlike the TARP teaching assistants, the Faculty Advisory Committee does not have direct contact with the students. Their input has to be nurtured in other ways. In the initial planning stages, the Advisory Committee recognized the importance of the class being interdisciplinary and began calling it the "research arm of the school." They had a vision for the program, which was invaluable to me as I added this new project to my regular teaching load. The Advisory Committee had a vested interest in the project's success; they wanted to add a new "signature program" to the high school. An award-winning school, Springbrook strives for innovative ways to attract outstanding students. The Advisory Committee saw TARP as having that potential.

During the first year, the Faculty Advisory Committee only met twice. Finding meeting times when all of us could attend was too difficult; everyone was very busy with various duties. So I found ways to work with each member on an individual basis, calling on their assistance in numerous ways. The media specialist developed lesson material and conducted training sessions with the students and me on the technology available in the media center. The English teacher was always available for the students, proofing papers and providing guidelines on technical writing. The list could go on with each member of the committee.

The first year, working only with the Advisory Committee, was challenging. It was difficult to anticipate and define duties that could be carried out by others. Working through the experimental first year enabled me to draw more efficiently on the TARP teaching assistants the next year. One example of knowing how to tap their expertise was the process we used for the final evening seminar and receptions. The teaching assistants and members of the Advisory Committee helped with scores of details: preparing a guest list and sending invitations, coordinating the food, setting up the lobby area with tables displaying the student posters, arranging for photographs, and coordinating an evaluation of the event, among other duties.

The Faculty Committee and teaching assistants are essential resources in all aspects of the program, from planning the curriculum to the final celebration. They help establish community contacts for the students, prepare publicity for TARP within the school, recruit students, and plan special events. Once these duties are clearly defined, they can be coordinated by members of the teaching staff rather than by the program coordinator. If I can think of myself as a CEO, my teaching assistants become a group of vice presidents, all invested in the success of the project.

The most important strategy in getting broad faculty committee support was to make the program interdisciplinary and involve faculty and students from throughout the school. TARP is not a science department program in competition with other departments for resources. It is a school-wide effort to give students the opportunity to use their skills solving real problems. Eva is working on a research issue that the Department of Agriculture has not yet solved. She's contributing her enthusiasm and skill, with the help of Lenny Moyer and our other faculty.

> *...my teaching assistants become a group of vice presidents, all invested in the success of the project.*

For me, the Faculty Advisory Committee and the TARP teaching assistants have been essential human resources, in the skills they have brought and in their broad knowledge and enthusiastic participation. They help identify needs and resources, assist with the continuous evaluation, and provide insights about future adjustments.

"I get more contact with the kids this way," says Mr. Moyer. It's late Friday afternoon, when any teacher is worn out from the week. But he smiles and adds, "That's why I do it."

Paula Rowe is a teacher and Director of the Technology and Research Partnership project at Springbrook High School in Silver Spring, Maryland. She was a Fellow in NSEE's Leadership Development Program, funded by the DeWitt Wallace-Reader's Digest Fund.

Student Involvement

issue 6

Student learning is at the heart of the educational process and teachers' work. Service-learning allows students a unique opportunity to take a more active role in their own learning, while making meaningful contributions to their communities.

LANA BORDERS HOLLINGER provides an overview of the principles of student leadership, relative to service-learning.

LORI EBBIGHAUSEN AND **JENNIFER BATSON** discuss recruitment issues and diversity.

BRENDA COWAN suggests strategies for gaining parental support.

STEVE ZIMMER explores the dynamics of student preparation for service-learning activities.

ANNE PURDY shares effective strategies for assessment of student learning.

MARIANNA MCKEOWN offers ideas for recognizing and rewarding student participation in service-learning.

Coaching Students to Be Leaders

"REMEMBER, THE REASON YOU WERE ASKED IS THAT THE AUDIENCE WANTS TO HEAR FROM YOU." Countless times, I've said this to students as they prepare to speak, write, or inform others about their service involvements through our community service-learning program. Students often lack the confidence or knowledge of how to be a leader and how to have the courage to speak about their experiences.

BY **LANA BORDERS HOLLINGER**

Developing student leadership is a key element to service-learning. Student leadership can and should be nurtured in every student. Taking initiative, becoming motivated to act, and following through on a service project all require leadership within oneself.

In order to address issues about student leadership, we must first think about what leadership is to each of us, personally. Is it getting others to follow us or to join us? Does it mean involving others or being a model for others? Exploring possibilities together or handing out duties? Figuring out our own skills or waiting for others to identify them for us? Getting things done or showing what's possible? Taking the heat or passing the buck? Acting on our beliefs or waiting for others to establish a path? Understanding our own leadership style helps us understand what kind of student leadership qualities we are trying to nurture.

For me, student leadership development has been an outgrowth of my desire to involve students in all facets of their learning. Service-learning creates an environment which allows risk taking for students without penalty or fear of failure. The service-learning program with which I am affiliated has successfully modeled that students are integral to any project plan being pursued for the benefit of students. Student involvement is not an afterthought. Students act as coordinators of service projects and speak at conferences where they are frequently invited to present. They work as equals in work sessions with teachers and adults from the community and have opportunities to illustrate to local government leaders and residents that they are resources to be included in plans for community action. Students work with adults as we develop resources for implementing school-based community service projects.

In a specific example, a student coordinates our mini-grant project, which puts recycling profits back into innovative school-based community service projects. For two years he has led the grant-writing process, the recipient selection committee, and public relations efforts, while also mentoring a younger student to assume this position.

Community service provides opportunities to promote a broadened view of student achievement. It reduces passivity as we collectively learn how to shape school experiences that promote active citizenship and an attitude of caring for our human family and for the environment that we share.

Service-learning creates an environment which allows risk taking for students without penalty or fear of failure.

But how and where does this development take place? If you are like me, you are busy running a very demanding service program. In the middle of all the planning, organizing, driving, telling, talking, calling, fighting political battles, and trying to have a life, where do you find the time to train leaders?

COACHING EVERY DAY The leaders of tomorrow's service programs and activities cannot rely on rules laid down today. They need to be people who have caught the spirit of someone in action. An apprenticeship can help mold the kind of person who doesn't just step into tomorrow's leadership role in service but creates and shapes the leadership role itself. You can teach all the rules in the world and miss the most important ingredient to leadership. As Maya Angelou puts it, "The greatest virtue is courage."

But how can we teach courage as part of leadership development? A person learns courage by being placed on the firing line of life. We learn courage by going into life side-by-side with someone who shows us that we can be scared and still go on. We learn courage when we see it in others, especially in our mentors.

To get this kind of leader, you don't *train* students, but rather you *coach* them. You find people who think and act in the world with a philosophy of service and you coach them. Coaching is a thing you can do in those cracks of time left after all the other details of your program have eaten up the big chunks. Coaching is an art you can carry in your hat wherever you go. You can coach that student beside you in a car or on a plane going to a conference. You can talk to students in a deep and meaningful way. You find and develop opportunities to stand beside students as a doer and point the directions that can bring them success both today and tomorrow.

Coaching requires that the students do the learning activity themselves. You can say "here's how," "you try it," and "try again," but in the end the student has to do the job. You can talk with a boy or girl about how to get ready to make a presentation to the Board of Education, but the words, feelings, and experiences that they bring to that presentation must be their own.

Business and local government leaders also help coach our students. I connect community leaders in actual service delivery with students, and businesses provide some of the service sites for students. They meet with teachers to define ways in which students can link up with business in innovative ways to serve community needs. Students learn the value of networking by doing networking alongside their adult coaches.

STUDENTS HAVE POWER Four years ago our program encouraged Emily, a bright but unfocused 9th grader, to submit a proposal during a service-learning project that resulted in her designing and painting a mural for the exterior wall of her school's Service-Learning/Recycling Center. The Center was created through a school/community partnership. "The mural portrays a message of community unity through service with others and the environment," says Emily. "It instills the sense that there is still hope for a better world.... It brings life to the Center and displays the connection and involvement between school, community, and environmental improvement." The mural gave Emily the opportunity "to take action on my dreams."

With leadership coaching, Emily has developed a strong ethic of service in responding to needs which exist in the community. She just completed a semester as an intern at the local AIDS Task Force office. With this background, she led a week of AIDS awareness-building activities for the entire student body of her school. She served for two years as the district's student recycling coordinator, starred with a well-known local newscaster in an instructional video on recycling, and was selected to be a summer recycling intern responsible for developing educational displays for school and community use. She has spoken at Chamber of Commerce luncheons and school board meetings, and met with State Department educators, student leaders from around the country, and national PTA leaders. She has helped shape the agenda for national conferences, sharing leadership with adults and other students.

Emily has found a way to integrate her knowledge, artistic talents, and concern for the well-being of others and the environment. A critical component in this development of leadership was working side by side with a mentor, who worked to help her be successful even when she was really scared to leap into unknown territory. As a graduating senior this year, she has received a full scholarship to a private university based largely on her ability to articulate the meanings of her school-based service to her daily life.

Our program has coached another senior, Sara, for many years. As an 8th grader, when Ohio legislators began considering their first service-learning legislation, Sara gave eloquent testimony to the power of service in changing her life and the lives of several of her peers. She has spoken at several national youth leadership conferences on how students can influence public policy. For example, she helped change a school policy on absenteeism.

Several students were concerned that they were being penalized for attending local, state, or national meetings regarding service-learning. Even though they were contributing to the meetings, they were being counted as absent from school. Valuable learning occurs when students are asked to prepare for speeches, exhibits, and presentations, or to assume leadership roles with their peers and adults, Sara explained. "There is no absence of learning only an absence from traditional classroom attendance," Sara told the school board at a meeting. "In fact, the student's learning has been facilitated by the school through its service-learning program on the one hand, and on the other, the student has been penalized by the system through its outdated and inconsistent policy." Sara helped the Assistant Superintendent develop a procedure that would treat service-learning experiences as valid field experience. She developed the form and procedure that the Board of Education adopted and is used by students now.

Developing student leadership goes much further than such obvious success stories as Sara and Emily. The Community Service Learning/LINK Program, where I work, has an office in each of five school buildings in Groveport, Ohio. Hundreds of people from the schools and community make this program work. Young people are partners in the solution to problems at the same time that they are applying their academic and critical thinking skills.

Our students are leaders of community recycling efforts, working in collaboration with the local government and Ohio Department of Natural Resources. LINK participants, both students and

Young people are partners in the solution to problems at the same time that they are applying their academic and critical thinking skills.

community members, regularly serve at the Community Kitchen, Groveport Recycling Center, Mid-Ohio Food Bank, a wetlands site, local government offices, composting and other environmental facilities, and the Franklin County Animal Shelter. LINK initiated a daily school lunch delivery to local homebound senior citizens, where more than 4,300 lunches have been delivered. Senior citizens look to LINK as a source of enthusiastic young people who can assist them with chores, meals, transportation, and the need for social and mental stimulation. We have conducted a community-wide recycling program for five years and are working with environmental groups and state agencies to establish a WetWatch education program on 70 acres of school-owned wetlands. Students respond to local community crises and annually work with the area Adopt-a-Family program. In eight years, more than 2,250 students have pursued academic and personal growth while making a difference in their local and global communities.

LEADERSHIP: A DEMOCRATIC IDEAL Community service-learning brings schools, families, and communities together, recasting the roles of student, teacher, school, and community. It encourages at-risk students to stay connected to school and nurtures all students in developing a spirit of caring, compassion, and tolerance for a lifetime. It encourages students to take action to address social injustice, using academic skills. The challenge is for all students to have successful school careers that prepare them for an enriching life. The notion of incorporating leadership skills is essential for this process to work.

A holistic view of each student's developmental needs includes citizenship training and character development. These are not easily taught through abstractions. These concepts become more clear with direct application in the real world rather than study in a theoretical sense. The opportunity to reflect upon one's actions and to use those reflections to inform one's future actions is especially beneficial. Reflection activities are essential to well managed service opportunities.

Schools need to become places that nourish all children out of passivity and into action. Our Community Service Learning/LINK program asks students to address human, educational, environmental, safety, and poverty issues in their schools and throughout our community. When they do this, first with coaching and then on their own, with support as needed, they demonstrate that leadership development has worked. This learning is not like a date they forget or a math process that slips away. Leadership skills are with them forever, so long as they are used and sharpened, as with all skills that have lasting value.

Lana Borders Hollinger coordinates the Community Service Learning/LINK Program in the Groveport Madison Schools in Groveport, Ohio. She was a Mentor in NSEE's Leadership Development Program, funded by the DeWitt Wallace-Reader's Digest Fund.

STUDENT-DRIVEN PROJECTS THRIVE
by Andrew E. Fisher

Despite the talk about today's students becoming increasingly apathetic towards education, students want to have some input into how and what they learn. When students are intimately connected with curriculum decisions, the overall learning experience is enhanced. They have invested a part of themselves in the curriculum choice and therefore want to learn from it. They connect learning with meaning. A prime example of this attitude can be seen at Orono High School in Orono, Maine.

At Orono High, service-learning is a graduation requirement. It is a three-year process that involves 9th, 10th, and 11th graders. As students progress from grade to grade, they gain more responsibility for their service-learning projects. Teachers are available, but students are trusted to make more key decisions as they move to the next grade. They emerge with a better understanding of themselves and their community.

In the 9th grade, teachers expose students to a curriculum that applies the skills and knowledge learned in the classroom to solving problems faced by the communities in which they live. For example, math students may help the town with recycling, English students may teach poetry to elementary students, or science students may work on a community garden project. It is here that the service-learning seeds are planted.

In the 10th grade, students participate in seminars and become better acquainted with issues that impact their community. They also become aware of various needs of the community. There is even a Student Advisory Council of 10 students whose purpose is to represent students' concerns regarding service-learning.

At the end of their sophomore year, every student is paired with a mentor, usually a civic-minded adult from the community. They plan a service-learning project that benefits the community and has an academic connection. The students have until the middle of their junior year to complete the 30-hour project. At that time, the students make one formal presentation to the agency where they worked, their mentor, a teacher of their choice, and their parents. They explain how they identified a need and the change they personally brought about because of their involvement.

Seniors are not left out of the picture. Many continue to help out in a mentor-like role. Since they have already completed the program, their advice is helpful to the younger students.

Connie Carter, Service-Learning Coordinator at Orono High, realizes the importance of student involvement in such curriculum choices. By exposing students to this type of curriculum, educators are allowing them to make important career or educational choices. Carter believes that the two biggest lessons the students learn are the importance of responsibility and care for others. "Students are an under-tapped community resource. They have energy and talents and appreciate being expected to share them," she states. "If you expect more, you get more."

RETHINKING STUDENTS' ROLE IN EDUCATION
by Andrew E. Fisher

Students must be actively involved in their education. They need a proactive mind set, not a reactive one. They should have a lot of say in what and how they learn. Service-learning provides the ideal vehicle for students to accomplish this goal. An example of this is the High/Scope Educational Research Foundation's Institute for IDEAS in Ypsilanti, Michigan.

John Weiss, Director of the Adolescent Division at High/Scope, runs the four-week educational program, which includes a very diverse group of students from around the country and the world. Students engage in hands-on activities in the arts and sciences. Service-learning is a required component for all students, but they have a great deal of latitude in making specific choices about their projects.

According to Weiss, the latitude in student choice enables the students to take more ownership of their learning. This is not educational anarchy; there is a structured daily routine that intentionally guides students through a number of large- and small-group activities throughout the day. But within these guidelines, students are constantly making choices. As a result of this student initiative, the "traditional" roles of students and teachers change. Teachers, instead of being viewed in an omnipotent, sometimes intimidating role, are seen as facilitators who are trained to ask open-ended questions, empowering the students to think and evaluate situations for themselves.

During the last week of the IDEAS program, students discuss ways they can continue to be involved in their home communities. The students leave with a great sense of community and the contributions they can make while learning.

There are even more tangible results about this type of student-directed service-learning. A five-year longitudinal study, *Challenging the Potential*, shows impressive figures. Seventy-three percent of those students who attended the program went on to post-secondary education, versus 55 percent of the comparison group. Of those students with low to moderate achievement in high school, 65 percent of those who attended the Institute went on to college versus 29 percent of the comparison group. Most impressively, regardless of the various obstacles they faced—problem behavior in high school, low parental expectations or encouragement for academic achievement, economic difficulties, or early marriage after high school—the majority of Institute students, by age 21, had chosen to attend college, were persistent in pursuing their college educations, and had plans to complete college. The study concluded that the Institute achieved its impact by providing students alternative role models and influential experiences, including service-learning. (Copies of the report are available from High/Scope, 313-485-2000.)

Weiss believes that, with some modifications, similar student-driven service-learning programs could be adapted to any classroom or school. He says the crucial element is trust. If we encourage more student-driven projects, service-learning can stretch the parameters of the classroom and enhance students' learning and growth.

Recruitment and Diversity

SINCE 1979, THE NASSAU COUNTY YOUTH BOARD'S YOUTH/ADULT PARTICIPATION PROJECT HAS BEEN TRAINING YOUNG PEOPLE, 14 TO 21 YEARS OF AGE, TO TAKE A LEADERSHIP ROLE IN THEIR COMMUNITIES. The focus of the year-long training program is youth empowerment, youth-adult partnership, experiential education, appreciation of diversity, and community service-learning. Each year 40 to 50 teenagers participate in the county-wide projects, and an additional 50 young people participate in our school-based service-learning program. These youth volunteers represent various racial, ethnic, religious, and socio-economic backgrounds. Because our organization has made a commitment to recognizing the leadership potential in all youth, we strive to be inclusive in our recruitment efforts. This means establishing clear criteria for participation and success and extensive outreach to all possible referral sources for youth volunteers.

BY LORI EBBIGHAUSEN AND JENNIFER BATSON

The Nassau County Youth Board's focus is positive youth development, meaning we are proactive rather than reactive in our programming. We strive to engage youth volunteers before they get into trouble. We expose youth volunteers to positive options in an effort to keep them from dropping out of school, becoming teen parents, or becoming involved with the juvenile justice system. We believe that every youth is at risk and that every youth has the potential to grow and develop. We also recognize that, as a county, Nassau is segregated. There is little diversity from community to community—people in a town tend to look like one another and to share similar backgrounds, values, and experiences. This split is magnified further in individual schools, where students tend to segregate themselves not only by race and economic status, but by age and social status as well.

One of the benefits that we seek for our volunteers, whether in the county-wide or school-based programs, is exposure to other ideas, experiences, and value systems. We ask the youth volunteers to make the commitment to develop their individual leadership skills with the underlying premise that an effective leader must be successful working in a group.

CAPACITY FOR DIVERSITY The more diverse the participants, the greater the potential for learning—and the greater the challenge. Beginning with honest dialogue among staff is essential to creating an atmosphere where youth volunteers feel comfortable with each other. At the Nassau County Youth Board, the staff explored how we tend to group people by how they look, where they come from, and what they call themselves. We addressed how our values, attitudes, and beliefs affect how we work with others, regardless of how we identify ourselves. Even if we look alike or call ourselves by the

It is important that the methods for reflection and evaluation be as diverse as the participants themselves.

same label—Jewish, African-American, White, Latino—we can have very different definitions of what the label means. Each individual has his/her own special qualities, talents, and personality. We stress that differences are positive and should be celebrated.

Having explored the impact of diversity on the staff, we had to consider what this meant to our program. We considered the age, gender, and race of our target population. Middle school students are developmentally different from high school students. Their maturity levels, ability to grasp the abstract issues, and ability to process information and tasks are different. Because the approach staff takes in working with a group should reflect these considerations, we found it more rewarding for participants to be grouped by age.

We also considered the richness of diversity that is possible among program participants. Gender, race, ethnicity, religious, and socio-economic backgrounds are important. We had to be careful that the representation was balanced—not too many males versus females, European Americans versus African Americans versus Latinos versus Asian Americans. It is important for youth to feel that they are adequately represented and supported.

Our staff and organization delineated certain structures and expectations to create a supportive environment. This was challenging, especially since the focus of our recruitment was to engage diverse youth. We invested considerable time in establishing our vision and working with the staff of our organization on roles and responsibilities for supporting our vision. In our weekly staff meetings and our year-end staff evaluations, we constantly revisit our mission and how our activities relate to our goals.

We also knew that opportunities for reflection and evaluation are important to build into the program for our youth volunteers. Reflection is especially important for our service-learning program because we face many challenges in maintaining the diversity of our target population. It is important that the methods for reflection and evaluation be as diverse as the participants themselves. Some youth volunteers feel more comfortable expressing themselves in writing; others in small group discussions. Establishing a routine for reflection and evaluation also creates a sense of openness and program ownership for youth volunteers. They begin to feel more comfortable expressing themselves, even outside regularly scheduled reflection sessions. This process facilitates youth volunteers learning who they are as individuals so they can better appreciate the differences in other people.

Reflection and evaluation also ensure that the program constantly changes to respond to the needs of the new youth volunteers. At the end of every year, the youth volunteers evaluate the training and program activities they have participated in throughout the year. We reflect on how these training and activities have enhanced not only the personal growth and development of each youth, but also the success of the group. Staff use this input and feedback to better plan for the new program year.

Reflection and evaluation reinforce the maintenance of a positive environment that supports volunteers expressing their inherent power, developing their individual strengths, and appreciating their diversity. We facilitate a process of doing *with* the youth volunteers and not for them. The youth volunteers are responsible for choosing the issues and implementing the community service-learning projects. These projects, and the training that prepare the youth volunteers to achieve their goals, provide opportunities for the group to continuously explore the diversity of their ideas, experiences, and values.

In the past, youth volunteers have designed county-wide conferences and speak-outs on teen pregnancy, suicide, stress, and other real life issues. They have worked with state legislators to draft and pass legislation enabling 16- and 17-year-olds to comprise up to one half of a working quorum on Boards of Directors of nonprofit organizations that address youth development, recreation, and delinquency prevention. The group has done a rap music video on diversity and documentaries on discrimination and violence. They have traveled to schools and agencies throughout the county to give workshops on such topics as diversity and leadership. Their community service is not your traditional volunteering in nursing homes or at soup kitchens. The young people are encouraged to choose an issue, take a step back to research the larger impact, and develop a social action community service-learning project to address their concerns. One of the main goals of the project is to prepare young people to take on policy-making positions— to have a role in the planning, implementation, and delivery of youth services in Nassau County.

In 1991, the Project partnered with a local school district to adapt the principles of the county-wide program to the high-school setting. Three years of working in partnership with the students and staff of the high school, supported by Learn and Serve America funding, culminated in the institutionalization of service-learning in a two-credit social studies course, "A Practicum in Social Issues," co-facilitated by a social studies teacher and local community-based agency staff. The Youth Board has expanded its efforts to two other communities that are vastly different in their demographics. In addition to duplicating the process of institutionalizing the social studies course, these districts are participating in a multi-community exchange designed to break down the barriers of race and ethnicity.

RECRUITMENT TAKES EFFORT All of our community service-learning programs require a minimum of a year commitment on the part of the youth volunteers. While it is not possible to think of everything that can occur that might interfere with program participation or turn off youth volunteers, it is important that time be invested in exploring these issues in the front-end, before the outreach for volunteers begins.

There were a number of possible barriers to participation that we needed to look at in order to support youth volunteers effectively throughout the project. Staff became aware of our limitations, as an organization, to address these barriers and issues. For some youth volunteers, transportation was an issue. Could we reimburse for public transportation? Other youth volunteers have child care responsibilities, extracurricular clubs, sports, and part-time jobs. Could we hold meetings in the evening to accommodate youth volunteers who were not available immediately after school?

We established a clear calender of meetings/events and requirements for successful participation

...youth volunteers have consistently identified the opportunity to work with youth of different backgrounds as being the most attractive and rewarding aspect of the program.

in the group. We needed to be clear about what we were asking the youth volunteers to commit to. We established learning contracts to reinforce in writing what the expectations were for both staff and volunteers. While it is important for youth volunteers to buy into the program, we also worked to involve parents/guardians in this process, because families are a primary source of support. We felt it was important that they knew what we were asking for their child/ward. This resulted in annual parent/guardian orientations.

Once staff capacity, program methodology, and organization limitations are addressed, recruitment of diverse youth can begin. It is time to think of yourself as a salesperson. Networking is important! You have a program to market not only to youth volunteers but to all the possible referral sources for youth—parents, schools (social workers, administrators, guidance counselors, teachers, coaches), agencies, libraries, probation departments, pregnancy and parenting programs, newspapers. The list is endless. Whether you are operating in the school or community setting, there are a number of ways to advertise the program,

The Youth/Adult Participation Project staff have found it beneficial to have written information to distribute upon demand. This ranges from simple one-page synopses and brochures to full packages about the Project and how it fits in with the Nassau County Youth Board's overall mission and purpose. The presentation changes depending upon our audience. Youth volunteers may be attracted by a colorful brochure that outlines more specific aspects of the program, while parents/guardians and school personnel might want to know more about the organization and staff. They need to make sure we are legitimate and can be entrusted with their children and students.

This written information can be used to advertise your program through many different mediums. This may include press releases to local newspapers, television stations, and radio stations, and mailings to schools, community agencies, and libraries. It is helpful to follow up mailings in person, making a call or stopping by to make sure they received and understood your information. Volunteer to give presentations at schools, agencies, local community events, and service fairs. The more you are out there, the more you are remembered and become established as a group that works with youth. It takes time to establish relationships and a reputation. You may not see results immediately, but year after year you will begin to build a strong presence in the community you serve.

Once the program is established, the youth volunteers with whom you work are your best resources. Youth volunteers can do presentations about the program with your staff. What better advertisement than to hear first-hand how the project has affected a volunteer? Word of mouth is a valuable recruitment tool, and it is free. So encourage youth volunteers to tell their friends about their experience.

Special outreach efforts are necessary if you truly want a diverse group. We target certain agencies specifically because we know they work with youth in need. We reach out to residential group homes and agencies in the youth development system. This outreach should be aggressive. This may mean making two or three phone calls and personal visits to show that you are truly interested in working with their young people. Keep in mind, however, the barriers to participation. Transportation issues must be resolved before you engage young people who may already have experienced enough let downs in their life. All appropriate resources must be in place. It is a grave disservice to youth to get them excited about participating in the program only to have them unable to keep the commitment because of something like transportation.

We had a young man who lived in a group home quite a distance from the weekly meeting and Saturday training sites. We thought we had covered all the bases and that the student would be able to take the public bus back and forth. We soon discovered that the bus did not run late enough to get him back to the group home after our evening meetings. We explored all the possibilities with the young person, the group home staff, and with our staff. We made the commitment to reimburse for taxi transportation to get the young man home. In order to get to the meetings, the group home's social worker either dropped the young man off or he took the bus. A benefit of this process was that the young person had the experience of becoming more independent and had the opportunity to learn how to negotiate and compromise when faced with difficult situations. It also demonstrated to the young person that we valued his contributions to the group and to our organization.

In our literature and our presentations we stress the fact that we recruit a cross section of young people from across the county, or, in the case of our school-based initiatives, across the school. Throughout the years, youth volunteers have consistently identified the opportunity to work with youth of different backgrounds as being the most attractive and rewarding aspect of the program. Every year now, the youth choose to plan and implement a service-learning project for their peers called, "Appreciating Diversity Workshops."

Recruitment and diversity are two challenging aspects of any community service-learning initiative, whether based in schools or communities. Our experiences have shown us that before we even open our doors, we as an organization have to know what our goals, expectations, and limitations are. Once we have a solid sense of our vision, *then* recruitment begins. Consistency in message, aggressive outreach, and follow up are vital to the continued success of the program. After getting over the hurdle of that first year, you begin to establish a reputation for excellence. Recruitment soon takes on a life of its own!

Lori Ebbighausen is the Project Coordinator and Jennifer Batson is the Youth Program Coordinator for the Youth/Adult Participation Project of the Nassau County Youth Board in Mineola, New York.

Parents as Partners in Youth Programming

THE BROOKLYN CHILDREN'S MUSEUM HAS A HISTORY OF CHALLENGING THE BARRIERS THAT TYPICALLY EXIST BETWEEN MUSEUMS AND COMMUNITIES, through innovative exhibitions and high quality programming that is relevant, accessible, and engaging to its diverse audiences. The Children's Museum is also unique in that it opens its doors to neighborhood children unaccompanied by an adult with a program called Museum Team. Through Museum Team, the Children's Museum provides not only the place for inner city youth to learn about the wide world around them, from the sciences and their environment to culture and the arts, but also provides mechanisms for youth to learn about how they learn and interact within that world.

BY **BRENDA COWAN**

They needed assurance that the program was not only responsive to the needs of their children, but also was a long-term effort.

Museum Team is an award-winning, multi-tiered, after school, community outreach program for youth ages seven to 18. Museum Team provides ongoing educational programming, career readiness, volunteer, and employment opportunities for young people. It seeks to enhance their self-esteem and achievement through cultural awareness, enlightenment, and responsibility. The number of Museum Team participants has steadily risen throughout its ten-year history, and is currently around 1,200. The youngest Museum Team members, "Kids Crew," are between the ages of seven and 10 and comprise the largest group; approximately 1,000 youth are registered, and throughout the year approximately 200 of them consistently participate in our ongoing activities.

Museum Team participants can visit any day that the Museum is open, as often as they like, and many come to the Museum every day as a rule. For many, it is an integral part of their life; a safe haven, a place where their friends are, a place with supportive adults and always something to do. Many youth come in with great enthusiasm and high ambitions. They have families that are very supportive of their activity in the Museum, and who themselves participate in the Museum's many community programs and functions. Museum Team has provided a vital conduit for parents and families to become engaged in the institution's many different programs designed for adult involvement, including the Black Family Forum, which addresses issues of interest to the community, and Free Friday Family Fun, a summertime series of evening events geared towards whole family participation.

For many of the families that actively participate in Museum programming and whose youngsters participate in Museum Team, the Children's Museum is a familiar resource, an arena for enjoyment, education, and opportunity. For some Museum Team families, however, museums aren't familiar places, and the Children's Museum is a setting that poses some issues and potential conflicts.

Crown Heights, next to the Bedford Stuyvesant areas in Brooklyn, has a large immigrant population, primarily from the Caribbean, West Indies, and Africa, as well as a large group of Lubavitch Jews. Crown Heights has a history of racial tensions and high unemployment, from 12 to 17 percent. Of the 90,000 people in the community, about 20,000 are school-age children. Crown Heights public schools regularly score among the lowest in New York City, and though the area has a high percentage of youth, it has the lowest number of youth service organizations in the city.

In this environment of racial tension and too few opportunities, the great diversity of cultures in the Museum staff and the Museum Team participants make some parents apprehensive about their child's involvement. The unfamiliarity of some families with museums in general has aggravated these issues. Although this inclusiveness is a strong asset to the mission and educational philosophy of the Brooklyn Children's Museum, it is almost a threat to some parents for whom museum-going is not a common activity or who don't distinguish the Museum from other recreational facilities in the immediate area.

The Bedford Stuyvesant/Crown Heights communities have struggled with high numbers of single parent households and youth in foster care situations. Many families live in economically disadvantaged situations and in high crime areas. There are limited places available for recreation; a nearby park, a recreation center, and the sidewalks tend to be the places where children can play, and these areas are not always safe options. For some families, visits to the Children's Museum are the first to any museum. These issues have greatly contributed to the initial difficulty in engaging parents in their children's involvement with the Museum Team program. Although the youth were actively involved, many parents would respond to attempts at reaching out only when their child was in trouble or when it seemed that there were conflicts of interest regarding the functions of the program.

GETTING PARENTS INVOLVED As the Museum's youth program was evolving, cultivating parental involvement was difficult. How could we provide mechanisms that support whole family involvement on a consistent basis? How do we reach out to those parents who lack the time or ability to physically visit? How do we get our parents excited about the sometimes subtle achievements of their child's participation in the program? How do we nurture parental involvement in our program in an inclusive way that doesn't discount the unique and holistic approach towards learning that the program embraces? These were some of the hard questions we faced.

Parents not only had to be provided with specific opportunities and reasons to come in and see and participate, but they needed to be welcomed in a way that made them comfortable. Our parents needed to understand the nature of the activities that their children were doing in the Museum, and the short- and long-term benefits that could be reaped by participating consistently. They needed assurance that the program was not only responsive to the needs of their children, but also was a long-term effort.

With a program like Museum Team, parental involvement is essential. You cannot provide thoughtful educational services in an intense, ongoing program for youth without being involved with the family in some capacity. Parents need to understand what their children are doing in the program if they are going to support their involvement, if only to understand what the basic rules of participation are so that the function of the program is clear. Just as a school setting has specific codes of behavior and parameters for involvement, so does the Museum Team program, and many of the issues related to increasing and nurturing parental involvement arose out of situations where the level of youth involvement and nature of the setting were unclear. Parents who were unavailable, unreachable, or unwilling to discuss or observe their child's participation in the program tended to fail to understand the profound successes or great difficulties that their child was experiencing. Unfortunately, some parents made themselves available to us only when their youngsters were having great difficulty operating within the Museum successfully and had to be sent home or excused from the program altogether. This was not typically a pleasant first exchange.

Staff at the Brooklyn Children's Museum have developed informal relationships with the elementary school next door and a middle school several blocks away. Most of our participants attend one of these two schools and will often share report cards and daily school experiences with program staff. In an effort to strengthen our ties with the schools, we have implemented an after-school tutorial program that invites active involvement from parents and teachers of participating youth. The tutorial program attempts to measure a youth's progress through ongoing parent and teacher assessments, as well as through student test scores and report cards. Initial contact with the elementary school principal enabled us to create the beginnings of a formal relationship. Her support for our tutorial program enabled us to approach teachers and served to legitimize the program to the parents.

During a period of time while the Brooklyn Children's Museum was closed for renovations, we took the Kids Crew program to various locations throughout the community including the elementary school, the library, a family service center, and a local church. Not only did this make the program more visible and linked with community affairs, but it validated our efforts to provide consistent services for youth in the eyes of the parents. Most of our participants live within 10 blocks of the Museum and walk to our program, to school, and to other social settings such as the park.

Being successful in a museum environment requires very different coping mechanisms than being successful at school or in the park. To operate within the Museum Team program, youngsters need to exercise a fair amount of self control and self reliance. Youth have access to all program and exhibition areas during public hours, and staff members are not always available to guide or supervise every interaction. This independence is certainly part of the appeal to participants, but it can be difficult for youth who are in the process of learning to communicate effectively, make decisions easily, or solve small disagreements with their peers.

Many participants find the transition an easy one, and reap the benefits of engaging in an interesting, fun, and educational program. Those youth who are slow to draw upon museum-appropriate social skills, however, struggle to interact with youth and adults they don't know, and have problems figuring out how to participate in the workshops despite their good intentions or best attempts. In order to participate in the Museum Team program consistently, youth must have the ability to "shift codes" between social contexts, from home to school to park to Museum, and be able to learn the different, sometimes subtle ways of operating, communicating, and being accepted within each. Museum Team members who are "out of sync" with the program become discouraged with their lack of connection within the Museum environment. This often compounds the problem, making them "act out" or misbehave in an attempt to get extra attention and help. Too often, the misbehavior that alerts staff to the fact that a young person is having trouble is extreme enough to cause his or her dismissal from the program.

When a parent is aware of the nature of the program and the code of conduct of the Museum, these situations can be addressed in a cooperative and thoughtful manner. When a parent is not actively involved with or aware of their child's participation and finds them at home when they were expected to be at the Museum, parents can become concerned, skeptical, or even quite angry. Even in cases where parents are involved with their child's participation, interests or approaches regarding how they expect their child to behave have aggravated their child's attempts at engaging in the program successfully. For example, a youth I'll call Angelo was having a hard time coping with other Museum Team participants. "Angelo is getting judo lessons for a reason," his mother had told me. "He's not going to be bullied by other kids. At the Museum, though, I expect him to follow the rules. He should listen to the instructors."

When Angelo didn't have the undivided attention of a staff member at all times, he would use those judo lessons on the nearest Kids Crew member. So despite the parent's attempt at helping her child participate successfully, her understanding of the nature of the Museum environment and the difficulty of making a behavioral transition from one place to another made her child's participation very difficult.

PARENTS BECOME ASSETS Our relationships with parents have served to help us understand the various cultures and lifestyles from which our youth are coming. This is critical to creating programs and materials that are relevant and accessible. This was the case with Angelo's judo lessons. Once we understood the framework of behavior that was expected of him, we were able to more clearly understand his personal value system and how to help him better adapt to the Museum environment. Angelo's difficulty with adjusting from the community setting to the Museum could then be specifically addressed in ways that were more thoughtful and supportive, such as using our social-learning games called Kids Crew Checkouts.

There are many parents who are perpetually looking for ways in which to become more involved with their children and their activities. Parents are the key link in our tutorial program. They help us to identify specific areas of strength and weakness in individual students, and through written assessments and ongoing dialogue, we are able to work together in creating individualized strategies for learning. Even parents who have little free time attend our special awards ceremonies and receptions for children's exhibitions.

Parents have also helped us with various special projects, such as focus groups on planning exhibitions and program planning discussions. One parent, who comes to all her children's

Our relationships with parents have served to help us understand the various cultures and lifestyles from which our youth are coming.

events, now consistently attends the Black Family Forum events. She has become a big asset to the Museum. Another parent, foster mother to four Museum Team participants, attends the events regularly. She has now become involved with a 12-session film making Artist-in Residence program. Although designed for youth, her personal interest and enjoyment of the program have created an exciting dynamic of intergenerational learning.

Other parents who lack the time or ability to attend events call to talk with the program staff about their children's involvement or to suggest topics of interest to their children. All of these levels of involvement contribute to a stronger understanding of student needs and strengthen the quality of our educational services.

PREPARATION AND FOLLOW-THROUGH ARE ESSENTIAL Too often, youth programs either fall prey to city budget cuts, or are designed as specially funded "projects," not necessarily fully supported by the institutions in which they take place. Both situations can leave youth abruptly cut off from important relationships and searching for a new place to go. Early on we recognized the need to gain the trust of our parents and ensure them that the program is fully embraced by the mission of the institution and is sustainable. Throughout the past several years, the Museum Team program was able to foster this trust through many avenues:

Consistency If we say that we are going to do something we follow through, whether conducting an event, a trip, or a program, or supporting their children in a crisis situation.

Involvement We call home in the event of a problem or sensitive situation, in an effort to have the parent participate in creating a solution.

Crisis Management Although we are not a social service agency, due to the long-term relationships that are developed and the special care that is given to being responsive to the needs of youth, staff members are trained in crisis management. (We are also working towards training our teenage participants in peer mediation and crisis management.)

Personal Contact We call home and send letters to announce success stories as well as concerns, walk or drive children home after a special evening event, and make a visit to the home in the event of a highly sensitive or difficult situation.

Referrals We provide useful, up-to-date resources and contacts available for youth and their parents who need counseling or family services, in addition to our educational and career readiness resources.

Family Events In addition to the Museum's regularly scheduled family programs, we invite parents and families to special Museum Team awards ceremonies, receptions, exhibitions, and performances.

Family Trips We create special trips for entire family participation at little or no cost, creating situations for multi-generational activity and informal interaction with staff.

Personal Support We are responsive to personal requests for help with incidental things such as accessing resources or using the telephone.

Youth Advocacy We provide forums, such as a Youth Council, for children to speak their minds in a fashion that is productive.

The Kids Crew Checkouts The Checkouts are a series of Museum-based games that can be taken home. They instruct youth in social-learning skills, including a game designed specifically for a child and their adult care giver to play together. These create a concrete linkage between home and the Museum.

Community Outreach We provide programs in other neighborhood facilities including a local church, recreation center, family services center, and library, making the program and its staff more familiar and linked up with vital community resources.

There have been and probably will always be instances where youth act out for any number of reasons, and put the program in great jeopardy. In one instance, a young teen falsely accused another of rape. Our training with crises intervention and consistent parental involvement enabled us to identify the young person's call for attention and direct her to the resources that would give her the support that she needed in thoughtful cooperation with her parent. Our preparedness and contact with the parent enabled us to put a difficult situation into perspective and analyze the hidden needs. Our prior contact with the young person's parent gave us the basis of a relationship of trust that was needed in order to initiate a thoughtful discussion about this dangerous accusation. Not only were we able to help the young person, but we were able to save our youth program from scandal!

Youth programming does not happen in isolation; programs must be fully integrated into the mission and methodology of your institution, and they must be in consideration of and supported by the youth's families and community if they are to be successful. The lesson that we have learned is one of investment. You must be prepared to "walk the talk" if you plan to engage children and their families in long-term programming. It is an ongoing process that needs constant tending, and should be not only a mechanism that is put in place as the program is created initially, but should also be an ongoing attitude, shaped by the institution and embraced by the community.

Brenda Cowan is the Museum Education Specialist at Vincent Ciulla Design, where she does exhibition content development, evaluation, research, and audience advocacy. She was Coordinator of Youth Programs for Museum Team at The Brooklyn Children's Museum from 1992–1996, where she worked closely with youth and their families.

Student Preparation—The First Step to Effective Learning

NESTLED IN THE COMFORTABLE LOS ANGELES URBAN ENCLAVE LOS FELIZ, THE SPRAWLING CAMPUS OF MARSHALL HIGH SCHOOL OFFERS VIEWS OF THE PASADENA MOUNTAINS, tree-lined streets, and relatively little violence for a neighborhood close to the heart of the city. Formerly one of the Los Angeles Unified School District's flagship academic schools, Marshall's 4,200 students now have a graduation rate of only 37.5 percent. They have scored in the bottom percentiles in almost every section of the California Test of Basic Skills for the last five years. Gang affiliation among both male and female students is growing, and there is a waiting list to get into IMPACT, the school's drug and alcohol abuse counseling program. Even so, our top students have helped Marshall regain attention by capturing the National Academic Decathlon in 1987 and again in 1995, and our advanced placement students head to the nation's leading universities.

BY **STEVE ZIMMER**

...I have found student preparation meetings to be the place where the tone for a project is set.

Most Marshall students come on city buses from Echo Park, Atwater Village, East Hollywood, Virgil-Melrose, and other neighborhoods the newspapers describe as "gritty" or "impacted." More literally, our students come to Marshall from all over the world. One third of the students are recent immigrants enrolled in English as a Second Language (ESL) programs. More than 85 percent speak a language other than English at home. Some 45 different first languages are spoken each day on the Marshall campus. The cultural richness that student diversity brings to Marshall does not always translate into academic success or ethnic harmony. Despite an almost U.N.-like veneer, ethnic tensions run deep, for example, between Latino, Armenian, and Asian students. Students rarely have friendships or dates across carefully drawn race, class, and ethnicity lines. Occasionally, the general lack of communication spills over into violence with fights that further polarize the school.

In the midst of this environment, Marshall is engaged in several experimental programs geared towards enhancing the educational environment and opportunities for all students. Central in this effort is the Marshall Public Service Program. It seeks to engage all of Marshall's students in the issues that affect our community and actively involve them as participants in projects that address solutions. Our vision is that through participation and action, students will begin to see themselves as individuals who can and must make a difference in our neighborhood and in our school. The centerpiece of our Public Service Program is a 20-hour public service project that is required of all Marshall students before they can receive their high school diploma.

The 1995–96 school year marks the first year we are enforcing this requirement. As coordinator of the Public Service Program, I am given two hours each school day to facilitate most of our student's first community involvement projects. Eight months into the program, we have experienced the highs and lows, the growing pains, and the growing joys that any emerging project endures. The singular issue that has marked our successes and failures in this inaugural year is student preparation. It has made many of our projects work or fail. It has solidified or disintegrated so many of our partnerships. It has validated or called into question so many student experiences.

Because I am a teacher by nature and passion, I define service-learning simply as a good teaching strategy. As we know, however, no good teaching strategy is simple. Good service-learning or public service projects are a set of carefully coordinated plans executed with smooth transitions and followed through with clear assessments. Student preparation is the combination of a detailed lesson plan and the student motivation required to make that lesson plan work.

In teaching, the lack of a lesson plan dooms even the most gifted teacher to the sacrificial process of "winging it." Failure to interest students condemns even the most brilliant of lesson plans to be met with blank eyes and gaping yawns. The effects of such failures "in the field" on projects with ill-prepared or uninterested students can be even more dramatic. The examples range from the humorous, like the student who showed up for a neighborhood clean up in high heels and a long, flowing dress; to the disturbing, like the student translator who chose to interject her own judgments in a sensitive discipline conference between a parent and a counselor; to the disruptive, like the elementary Teacher's Assistant (TA) who told the principal what she could do with her dress code after she informed him that he was in violation of the school's policy; to the dangerous, like the student who chose to challenge a group of gang members who taunted him while he painted over their graffiti.

I failed to inform and emotionally prepare each of these students for the situations, conditions, and process they might encounter during their public service project. The young woman at the community clean up had no sense of what her project would entail. The translator wasn't presented guidelines for her role in the conference. The elementary TA had no idea the school in which he was placed operated under a dress code. The student painting over graffiti was unaware of the proper conduct in situations with gang members. In their resultant experiences, these students and the many students like them were no different from the student group who starts a biology lab without the proper instruction or a student who tries to write an essay without first understanding the topic.

Service-learning or public service projects, however, are fundamentally different from classroom projects because usually there is no classroom. In fact, in many cases there is no teacher to guide or supervise the project or placement once it begins. These differences present unique challenges for schools trying to implement a quality service-learning program. At Marshall we are beginning to meet some of these challenges. Gradually, we are creating a matrix for student preparation that incorporates the diversity of our campus, our community, and the experiences we try to offer as part of the public service program. The learning process is a slow one but I think we're making progress.

Just as subject matter and process knowledge is essential to a good lesson plan, a coordinator or teacher must access extensive information about a public service project or placement site in order to facilitate effective student preparation. At Marshall this has involved understanding the mission, needs, expectations, and demographics of any individual or organization we build partnerships with for public service projects. For example, when planning a graffiti removal project with a neighborhood group, ascertaining whether community members who will join us on the project have experience working with students will inform my preparation information and strategies.

If the situation involves an extended placement at a particular site, it is important to gather even more information about the organization's procedures, services, experience, and supervision capabilities. The best placement situations have occurred when I have been able to establish a relationship with a supervisor at the site. It is even better to make pre-placement visits to the sites so that the student preparation process can take place with your experiential perspective. These connections add a concrete reality to the transmission of expectations and allow the coordinator to better match the needs of a placement site with the skills and interests of a student.

To ensure that students are prepared, you need some information about your students. At Marshall we are committed to equal access to all public service programs for all students. This is crucial if the public service program is to meet the long-term goal of building cooperation and communication among the diverse student groups at Marshall. Gang members, special education students, students from all grades and ethnic groups, and ESL students are encouraged to participate in the projects that most interest them. The success of informed student preparation is thus dependent on me or the project coordinator spending time with the students before the project itself. "Blind" projects, or projects for which you meet the students for the first time as they show up to the site, are often recipes for disaster. There are obvious rationales for meeting with students before a project. You would not, for example, want to send a gang member into rival or disputed territory for a neighborhood clean up. Nor would you want to place a bilingual Armenian ESL students at an elementary school which only has bilingual Spanish classes.

We are currently implementing a process through which a student who seeks an individual placement goes through an application process that consists of both a form and an interview so that the student and I can collaborate on a placement. For on-going small group projects I try to have "pre-service" time with the group before the project begins and a set meeting time each week when we can reflect on what happened. It is most difficult to get to know students who are participating in large "one-shot" or single day projects. Even for these projects I have made attendance at preparation meetings mandatory. In these cases I use required transportation waivers as a means through which to build at least some rapport and expectation before the actual project.

The preparation session for a project or placement does not follow hard and fast rules. I usually feel like a mix between a quality control manager and college basketball coach. In other words, in style I try to balance motivation with precautions and guidelines. In terms of approach, like any good lesson plan, the ideal student preparation sessions involve something for every kind of learner: handouts and other visuals, oral lecture, and some kind of demonstration. The best sessions are those that occur when a person from the partner organization actually comes in and works with you and the students in the preparation process.

No matter what your technique, there are seven basic questions that should be answered in every preparation session:

1. Where are we going/Where are we meeting?
2. When do we need to be there?
3. What are we going to do?
4. Who are we going to be doing it with?
5. Why are we doing this?
6. How are we going to do this?
7. Are they going to give us lunch?

No project can be successful without students understanding these basic concepts. Do not assume that if you wrote these things on a flyer or on the board, they are understood. Remember, in any good lesson plan, you check for understanding. If these questions are answered in a preparation process, most students will be able to engage in a project with clear objectives and expectations. By the way, if you think number seven is intended to be humorous, try dealing with 35 9th graders who thought the community organization was going to feed them after their morning of work.

Beyond these basic factors, I have found student preparation meetings to be the place where the tone for a project is set. In going over expectations, I try to go beyond the concrete for every project. Moreover, I try to instill in the students a sense that they are important, needed, and appreciated in this effort, whether it be cleaning an abandoned lot or helping with an eligible immigrant's citizenship application form. When the projects involve classes and are directly tied to the curriculum, these connections are fairly easy to draw. Even if it is a "one shot" project, I try to expand on the "why-are-we-doing-this" component of preparation, including a local or national context of the issue, a concrete sense of possible long-term positive implications of a single action, a sense of the incremental process of change, and the fact that they will be ambassadors of the school and school district in everything they do and say. Although each student's understanding of these issues will be personal and may therefore operate on one of many different levels, I have found that when I take the time to put the project in a context, the students come with a more established sense of purpose.

Like the most effective lesson plans, successful student preparation plans are flexible and can adjust to changes in the many variables.

There is one hard and fast rule I've discovered for the issue of student preparation. No matter how complete your efforts, it is inherently impossible to *completely* prepare students for a service-learning experience. Precisely because service-learning breaks down the four walls of the classroom, it sacrifices the artificial controls those walls establish. There is no way to anticipate the multiplicity of scenarios that could transpire during a project or placement. No one was more surprised than I when, during an L.A. River Clean Up Project, we stumbled across an unidentified plastic bag that definitely contained something that was very recently alive. How do you prepare for that? There are any number of situations more and less dramatic than this that are impossible to anticipate.

What is most important is determining what preparation components are essential and universal to all your projects, and then what unique circumstances in a particular project must be understood before students begin. The seven basic questions are a good checklist to start with but they won't work for everyone. Every school, every program, and every project will have its own unique variables and opportunities. Like the most effective lesson plans, successful student preparation plans are flexible and can adjust to changes in the many variables.

It is impossible to say at this point whether the public service program at Marshall will have a positive impact on the statistics I presented at the beginning of this article. We do know that since August 1995, Marshall students have painted over more than 15 miles worth of graffiti-covered walls. Our students have helped process more than 2,000 applications for immigrants to become U.S. citizens and have assisted more than 100 bilingual K–3 classes, allowing teachers in dozens of feeder schools to work on new and exciting projects. Our students have planted some 400 new trees. And the list goes on. But what is most important is looking into the eyes of students who realize through their projects that they are an important part of a community. That their work counts. To us it might just be a wall, an application, a vacant lot, a dirty river bank. For a student, it can be the beginning of a transformation. For a school, it can be the rebirth of hope.

STUDENT PREPARATION IN ACTION

The Elysian Valley neighborhood of Los Angeles is bordered by the Los Angeles River to the North, the 5 Freeway and Dodger Stadium to the South, the 2 Freeway to the West, and the 110 Freeway to the East. The rectangular box of streets between these boarders is home to over 12,000 people, primarily second-generation Mexican and Central Americans and recent Vietnamese immigrants. This area is more commonly known as Frogtown because of the frogs that remain in the neighborhoods after the flood waters of the river recede.

Formerly a middle class neighborhood of small single family homes, Elysian Valley has come to represent the epitome of Los Angeles urban blight. There is not a single grocery store, health care facility, or small business in the neighborhood. Many of the streets in the area do not have a drainage system and flood to the point of impasse during winter rains. The smoky sights and sounds of light industry intermingle with the sounds of children playing and the sing-song of the ice cream trucks. The multi-generational gang, Frogtown Locos (FTR), virtually controls the streets after sundown. Median family incomes as well as high school graduation rates have dropped consistently in recent years.

Despite these obstacles, a grassroots neighborhood organization called Elysian Valley United (EVU) has developed in the past year. With the goal of increasing resources for young people in the community, EVU has begun youth programming and community service projects on the weekends and GED classes at a local Recreation Center during the week. At the beginning of this last school year, EVU and the Marshall High School service-learning program started working together to attack one of the central symbols of Elysian Valley's decay: the Los Angeles River Walkway. Spanning the three mile circumference of Elysian Valley, the River Walk was originally created to be a jogging or walking path. In the past ten years, however, the River Walk had become a dumping ground for everything from hazardous waste to discarded household items to bags of used drug paraphernalia. The River Walk had also become overrun with gang and drug activity. There was hardly a wall along the walk that was not covered from top to bottom with graffiti.

Albert Vargas, Executive Director of Elysian Valley United, saw turning the River Walk around as a central component to leading the Elysian Valley neighborhood in the right direction. A lifelong resident of the neighborhood, Vargas watched the River Walk go from a family gathering place to a gang organizing and staging ground. "To me, the River Walk symbolizes the irony of the area," Vargas said. "Here you have this environmentally beautiful stretch of the river and most of the children in the neighborhood have never seen it because of their parents' fear of gang violence and drug dealing. This was an issue that just had to be addressed."

The Elysian Valley United/Marshall High School partnership to revitalize the River Walk has served as one of our best examples of a student preparation in action. Mapping out a collaborative strategy to revitalize the River Walk block by block, Albert and I first walked the area of the river that would be addressed. We blocked out year-long tasks that could be addressed by teams working together and identified specific target areas that would connote demonstrable changes. By meeting Albert at the River Walk site, I was able to see first hand the challenges and potential of the project. Coordinating with Albert from the beginning helped me to understand the vision of the project as it connected to the needs of the community. We set out a constructive design for a program that would have Marshall students working with EVU members along the River Walk every Saturday morning over the course of the next year. Participating students would also have the opportunity to join special programs to learn about the eco-system of the neighborhood as well as the history of the neighborhood.

After laying out a tentative design for the program, we set about building effective student outreach and preparation models. Central to this mission was making sure the students had a broader vision of the role of the River Walk revitalization in the neighborhood, and insuring that students were aware of the safety and environmental issues involved in the actual clean up projects. Albert and the River Walk Project Director Gloria Moya agreed to attend all the initial training and preparation sessions. This was essential to project preparation because, as neighborhood residents and activists, they were able to present a personal view of the project's long-term importance.

Before the initial training session, Albert, Gloria, and I went over the basic questions that should be covered in a preparation session. We tried to set realistic expectations for student interest and commitment during the first part of the project. We also carefully determined the logistical components of the project. First, we decided exactly *when and where* the students would meet in the morning. Second, we had a plan A (city recreation center van) and a plan B (off-duty neighborhood ice cream truck) for *student transportation* to and from the river site. Next, we took pictures of some of the worst areas of the River Walk so students would have a visual understanding of the importance of the project. We also set a tentative schedule of tasks designed to rotate by teams so that the more disgusting work (dumpage removal) and the desired work (painting over graffiti) would be shared equally. Finally, we set a lunch menu for the first four weeks of the project, so those students who made community service project decisions based on lunch fare could be informed shoppers.

Albert and Gloria came to the first orientation meeting with the students to present the project and show the pictures of the River Walk. Because they both grew up and lived in the neighborhood, their personal interest and connection to the project was immediately apparent. Our students meet a lot of community folks who are passionate about graffiti and public safety, but they seemed genuinely moved by Elysian Valley United's vision for the River Walk. Although there were only a handful of interested students at the first meeting, the effective preparation, clear goals, and tangible outcomes of the projects quickly built the River Walk revitalization project into one of Marshall's strongest programs.

The satisfaction of immediate progress, positive rotating divisions of labor, and good lunches helped to sustain student interest in the L.A. River Walk revitalization initiative. Grass and wild flowers blossomed immediately, in part because they had been covered with trash for so many years. There seemed to be an almost immediate increase in runners, bikers, dog walkers, and others using the River Walk area. Such progress helped to energize and expand our efforts.

Important adjustments, however, needed to be made as we wound our journey through Elysian Valley, weekend by weekend. Every weekend the taggers and gang members "rehit" the walls that we had covered over the day before. Subsequently, one team of workers would be assigned to "touch up" for the first two hours of a given Saturday. This also necessitated changes in the student preparation process that involved preparing the students for seeing their work painted over again each week. A focus of the training became the importance of consistent effort in the battle against graffiti and gearing students to look at the long-term impact of community involvement instead of concentrating their efforts on a particular wall. We also had to readjust our transportation system as the recreation center director did not always show up at 9:30 and the ice cream vendor started working morning shifts. By pooling resources in the student preparation process, we were able to arrange weekly caravans from Marshall to the river sight. Finally, as the confrontations with local gang members began to escalate, we needed to work with the LAPD Northeast Divisions to have patrols drive the River Walk area while the crews worked the revitalization project. Of course, anytime the LAPD will be present at a work site, it is important to include this in the student preparation model and give students the chance to air their feelings before police and students are side-by-side in the field.

We are now almost five months into the River Walk revitalization project. The tangible results for the Elysian Valley Neighborhood are growing. Children and families have reappeared on the River Walk, some even with binoculars to check out the wildlife that somehow perseveres despite the chemicals dumped into the water by factories each day. Garbage dumping at the River Walk has slowed somewhat making it less likely for hazardous chemicals and drug paraphernalia to be mixed with the weekly array of beer cans and discarded furniture. Gang dominance of the River Walk has definitely been challenged as there are markedly less hits each week on walls that we paint over. Significantly, reports of gun fire in the river area have decreased in recent weeks. There have even been reports of incidents of détente between the dog gangs that roam in the river's bed and local domestic pets who venture out onto the River Walk without a leash.

Perhaps most importantly, the River Walk revitalization project has attracted more programs to the Elysian Valley area. Youth Task Force L.A., a city-wide high school program sponsored by the Constitutional Rights Foundation and supported by AmeriCorps, held its annual youth service day in Elysian Valley bringing over 300 additional high school students to the River Walk area for a day of clean up and tree planting. The Urban Resources Partnership, together with the Santa Monica Mountains Conservancy, have chosen the Elysian Valley L.A. River area as one of their youth education sites for the 1996–97 school year. This project will train Marshall High students as mentors who will become "river guides" for Elysian Valley area elementary school children who will experience the wildlife of the L.A. River for the first time.

It is the development of such projects as these that point to a possible renewal for the Elysian Valley neighborhood. As Analuisa, a senior, says, "The river project is one of those projects where you can really see change happening because of our work. The first time I saw a family walking along the River Walk, I knew I had made a difference."

Steve Zimmer teaches English as a Second Language (ESL) at John Marshall High School in Los Angeles, California. He also serves as the co-coordinator for Marshall's Service-Learning Program. Steve was a Fellow in NSEE's Leadership Development Program, funded by the DeWitt Wallace-Reader's Digest Fund, and he is the founder and facilitator of On Campus, a coalition of Southern California educators dedicated to resisting Proposition 187 and other legislation that targets recent immigrant students.

How Do You Assess Service-Learning?

BY WORKING IN THE COMMUNITY, STUDENTS CAN OBSERVE THE IMPACT OF THEIR SERVICE, SEE THEMSELVES HAVING SUCCESS IN AN ADULT WORLD, AND BEGIN TO DEVELOP JOB READINESS SKILLS. They can also begin to discover for themselves that answers to social issues are not easy and that solutions take time, effort, and collaboration. This type of learning, however, is difficult to measure in the short term. One of the biggest challenges of a service-learning program is to develop a clear system to assess community-based learning.

BY **ANNE PURDY**

Making service-learning an integral part of the school community takes time, effort, commitment, and patience.

The first step in accomplishing this task is to determine what you want to measure or evaluate. Then, you can decide what systems or approaches you want to use. These standards must then be clearly understood by students, parents, teachers, and supervisors at community sites. Different situations require various types of measurements. A curriculum-driven program has different needs from those that are more focused on job internships and community service. A school-wide system has different demands than individual class-based projects. Those classes requiring a final letter grade may approach evaluation differently than a more flexible system such as pass/fail or portfolio approach. The most important purpose is ultimately to enhance student learning, which requires rigor and interaction with students during the assessment process.

I am the Coordinator of Community Service/Internships at Central Park East Secondary School (CPESS) in the East Harlem section of New York City. About 475 students attend CPESS, grades 8 through 12. In the first three years, they spend one half day each week at a community service placement, usually staying in the same placement for the entire school year. Students in grades 11 and 12 have a more in-depth internship, with the amount of time per week in the community varying. Staff members of the community placement and Community Service staff supervise students in their placements. We try to see each student as least twice during the semester. We keep written reports on these visits, which help us in the final evaluation we do on the student.

For the first five years of our program, at the end of each semester we would ask site supervisors to write a paragraph summarizing each student's behavior and learning at their site. We asked them to address competency, flexibility, punctuality, and attitude. The paragraphs varied in depth and description. We asked for practically no feedback from the students and did not often seek their reflections as to how they were doing. We did not require an exhibition or project giving evidence of what they had learned.

We realized that we were not getting enough depth in our evaluation, nor was it increasing and extending the learning as much as it might. Students were feeling good about their contributions in the community. In a study, graduates said they remembered their community service and were proud of it. But we wanted to ensure that there was as much rigor in the service component of our students' learning as in the other aspects of the curriculum.

We decided to improve the evaluation process in order to enhance learning and to enable them to become more aware of the value of their community contributions, while also giving them job exploration and readiness skills. We still had some major questions to answer, however. What was the student's place in all of this? We wanted as much student input as possible. What could we do to ensure that similar standards were used by a variety of supervisors? How could we enable supervisors to be a more integrated part of the program?

MEASURING RACHEL'S GROWTH In the 8th grade, Rachel's community placement was as an assistant in an early childhood classroom. Her responsibilities included planning a cooking project each week for the class and making "family" books with each child. She got off to a shaky start. Her initial written reflections often mentioned that she did not know how or when to talk to her supervisor, who always seemed to be busy with many young children.

Student preparation is absolutely essential for our program. We have developed a curriculum that includes discussion of child development and child-centered classrooms, office procedures, appropriate work environment behavior, negotiation issues, and research on social issues. Often we will role play various scenarios of possible service site situations and decide how best to handle each one. Site supervisors come to speak with the students, tell of the work of students at their sites, and respond to the students' questions. Additionally, older students talk to them about their experiences in the service-learning program.

Placements are described in terms of the on-site responsibilities. Each student picks three placements and writes a persuasive essay as to why he/she would like the first choice. Being aware of the job description enables the students to know from the beginning the types of tasks they will be expected to perform and therefore some of the criteria on which they will be evaluated. In consultation with their site supervisor, the students determine their goals for their placement time and discuss these with the CPESS Advisor and with our staff.

At CPESS, every student is a member of an Advisory group, which has no more than 13 students and a staff member. Much of the reflection and feedback on service-learning is processed through this group, which meets at least three times per week This group is where Rachel's reflections brought her problem to light. Her Advisor and I worked with Rachel to arrange specific times for her to meet with her supervisor to talk about her progress, her feelings, and her goals. This process turned the experience around for her. At the end of the semester, her supervisor gave Rachel "Distinguished" grades, and Rachel graded herself highly. She reported learning how active and inquiring young children are and how much patience one must have to work with them.

Such evaluations go into a student's community service portfolio. At CPESS, each student graduates entirely by defending portfolios before a graduation committee. One of the fourteen portfolios that each student must defend is "Community Service/Internship." In the early years of our program, we focused the portfolio on the 11th- and 12th-grade internships, especially the major exhibits the students had to do in those years. Now we include materials from all community learning experiences. It has taken us some time to sort through what we want to accomplish with this portfolio.

Adolescents are often marginalized within society, and our program was clearly providing an opportunity for students to connect with adults and experience success within an adult work environment. But we needed to agree upon some broad areas of learning and more specific qualities within each learning area that could be assessed. These would include job readiness skills and appropriate behaviors within the world of work. As the students give valuable service, they are also exploring various career areas and becoming more aware of the work environment. Gradually, the components of our Community Service Portfolio took shape. They now consist of student goals, self evaluations, supervisor evaluations, exhibition assignments, journal writings and reflections, and a current résumé.

The current student and supervisor evaluations cover attendance and punctuality, as well as attitude, learning process, and performance. The form has a continuum of "grades" from "Distinguished" to "Less Than Satisfactory," with space for additional information and comments, which we encourage. Under "attitude," we seek assessments for responsibility, enthusiasm and interest, appropriate appearance and dress, courtesy and cooperation, emotional maturity, good judgment, and ability to relate well to a variety of people. The "learning process" section assesses degree of initiative, whether the student assumes responsibility for her own learning, and if she asks appropriate questions. The "performance" section asks whether the student begins work promptly, appreciates suggestions, completes assigned tasks, exhibits competence, progressively requires less supervision, is a dependable worker, and follows directions carefully.

Since our overall program emphasizes a work readiness model, our assessment focuses on work skills, goals formulation, and task completion. However, some of our students formulate their own rubric using categories specific to their responsibilities and goals. I encourage this. This kind of flexibility within each program helps enhance the overall learning process.

We are still struggling with the standards of what is *excellent* and what is *satisfactory* work. Some students clearly do a magnificent job for a high school student. But since the supervisor is used to working with college students, the supervisor may think that the results are just "Satisfactory." On the other hand, a student may perform what I consider to be a poor job at the site and the supervisor marks every category with "Excellent."

Likewise, it is important for us that the students' self evaluations are realistic and clearly show evidence of why they should receive the grade they are advocating for themselves. Some students easily give themselves a distinguished grade with little to substantiate it. Others are very hard on themselves and do not realize how very well they've performed.

REFLECTION AND EXHIBITION In the 9th grade, Rachel worked in the Education Department of the

Studio Museum of Harlem, where she was trained to be a tour assistant and to help with some of the scheduling work of the office. Rachel was asked to help prepare a gallery guide for young children. Her exhibition assignment for her portfolio focused on this guide and on the unique history and mission of the Museum. Rachel mentioned that even though she lived in Harlem, she had never been to the Studio Museum, and as a result of her placement, she had been given passes to take her family members. She gave them a guided tour and was very proud of herself.

The Advisory System, which is a part of our school organization, is essential for facilitating and fostering learning. We prompt the Advisors to encourage journal writing and build reflections into the major exhibitions. Some Advisors are better about this than others. We've been more successful as the years go on, but we are still attempting to get consistent support from all the Advisors.

We have found that sometimes students will state in a journal entry or in dialogue that they are being asked to do very different tasks from those which they expected to be doing. This is generally discussed with the student either by their Advisor or one of our staff. Sometimes intervention is needed, and it ought to be done quickly.

During the 9th and 10th grades, students do an in-depth exhibition, which requires research and critical analysis on their service site each year. This year the students responded to the following questions:

- Research the history of your nonprofit placement organization. When and why did it begin?
- What is the organization's mission/philosophy?
- How "true" do you believe the organization is to its mission? Give specific examples.
- How is the organization funded?
- Describe the various types of service you provided at the organization.
- How are organizational decisions made? Is there a Board of Directors? If so, how is the Board chosen?
- Research the Board of Directors meeting minutes for the past year and the agency's annual financial report to determine what major issues are facing the organization and its goals and aspirations for the future.
- Share a critical incident during your time at the placement. Why was it significant, and what did you learn from it?
- If you were a part of the decision-making body, what changes would you advocate which would allow the organization to more fully realize its mission?
- Assess how you have changed as a result of your service experience.

To assess this exhibition, the Advisor uses a portfolio rubric that has been developed for the school. These criteria are used for all portfolios, including but not exclusive to community service. Thus students, faculty, and parents are familiar with the components of the rubric: viewpoint, connections, evidence, voice, and conventions. These criteria are used across the curriculum and are therefore within the culture of the school community—or at least it is our goal that they are! Our goal is to have the portfolio language and culture as part of every aspect of the student's school experience.

Since our overall program emphasizes a work readiness model, our assessment focuses on work skills, goals formulation, and task completion.

CPESS CURRICULUM RUBRIC TO ENHANCE HABITS OF MIND

VIEWPOINT	CONNECTIONS	EVIDENCE	VOICE	CONVENTIONS
Encompasses wide knowledge base but is focused. • Clearly identifies, addresses key question and idea; • Demonstrates an in-depth understanding of the issues; • Presents position persuasively and discusses other views when appropriate.	The whole is greater than the sum of its parts. • Explains significance of problems/issues; • Conjectures, predicts, and explains observations where appropriate; • Organized so that all parts support the whole; • Contains useful transitions; • Concludes in a satisfying way.	Credible/Convincing. • Generalizations and ideas supported by specific relevant and accurate information, which is developed in appropriate depth; • Contains discussion of strengths and weaknesses of evidence; • Cites appropriate resources; • Uses graphs, formulas, figures, and equations accurately.	Engaging • Lively, interesting use of language; • Awareness of reader (explains concepts so that they are understandable to the lay person); • Student uses own language.	Legible and intelligible. • Excellent appearance; • Correct format; • Varied sentence structure; • Good mechanics and standard notation; • Appropriate, broad vocabulary and word usage.

D I S T I N G U I S H E D

Paper is highly focused showing good depth of understanding and good breadth.	All parts support the whole and make connections beyond the scope of the paper.	Paper is very convincing.	Paper is very captivating.	Excellent use of conventions.
Paper is focused with depth and some breadth.	Most parts support the whole, resulting in a paper more significant than the information provided in the parts.	Paper may be lacking in some of the qualities above but retains credibility.	Appropriate language, style, and tone chosen.	Paper has a minimal number of errors which do not interfere with understanding.
Focus is inconsistent, making it difficult to evaluate the depth and breadth of understanding.	Connections of parts to the whole are sometimes made.	Paper includes some evidence relevant to the topic, but lacks enough of the above qualities to diminish credibility.	Shows some awareness of reader and attempts to inform, but language, style, or tone is confused.	Paper contains errors which minimally interfere with understanding.
Lacks focus and direction.	Not yet able to connect the parts to the whole.	Paper contains little specific evidence relevant to the topic.	Paper lacks awareness of reader and adopts no particular language, style, or tone.	Poor use of conventions interferes with understanding of the paper.

L E S S   T H A N   S A T I S F A C T O R Y

COMMENTS

Adapted from the Central Park East Secondary School Community Service/Internship Program.

FACTORS FOR SUCCESS In the 10th grade, Rachel served at the Public Advocate's Office. Here she learned how to assist people with phone inquires and discovered how to access data bases and resources. By the end of her placement time, she was even being given her very own cases to follow to completion and had begun to formulate an Adolescent Resource Guide. This guide is in her portfolio. Rachel is now in the 11th grade and is hoping to go into social work.

She had three very different types of placements. She received a grade of "Distinguished" every year. Each placement gave her a particular type of experience. She told me that when she was young she thought that she was going to be a teacher. However, her service opportunities broadened her experiences and she has decided upon another field.

Making service-learning an integral part of the school community takes time, effort, commitment, and patience. One school where I've consulted, for example, does not request any feedback from the supervisors. Students are given a "pass" grade with no comments merely for showing up at their placement each week. The school is having an attendance problem. I am advocating a much more in-depth and meaningful preparation and evaluative process. They need to decide how best to do it for themselves. Another school has not allocated the personnel to connect with and prepare the supervisors. Supervisors as much as students and parents need to be aware of the program's expectations and have someone with whom they can immediately connect if issues arise.

The potential for success in service-learning is great. The following factors have contributed to our success and might be helpful to you:

- clear expectations regarding the categories and behaviors which will be evaluated;
- total school support for the students doing service;
- advisors assisting the students with their reflections and portfolio projects;
- continued networking with the site supervisors on student activities, learning, and evaluation; and
- getting feedback from students and community supervisors on ways we can improve our program.

Anne Purdy is Coordinator of the Community Service/Internship Program at Central Park East Secondary School in East Harlem, New York. She also serves as a consultant on service-learning for the Coalition of Essential Schools. Anne was a Mentor in NSEE's Leadership Development Program, funded by the DeWitt Wallace-Reader's Digest Fund.

Recognition and Rewards—Stepping Stones for Good Citizenship

AS A TEACHING METHODOLOGY, SERVICE-LEARNING HAS FOUR KEY COMPONENTS. For persons familiar with this philosophy, the first three—preparation, service activity, and reflection—present obvious opportunities for learning, not only during the student years but also while living in the community after leaving school. The challenge for many practitioners of service-learning comes as they seek to honor the fourth component, celebration.

BY MARIANNA MCKEOWN

Celebrations involving recognitions and rewards motivate students to more service.

Some educators question the value of rewards to motivate student behavior and learning. These skeptics believe that external rewards for behavior doom the behavior to remain surface at best. They contend that using outward reward to motivate students makes the reward more important than the behaviors involved in the service-learning process. When the reward ceases, they argue, the behaviors stop as well. Others express concern that students will be satisfied with making and being rewarded for some progress, and will ignore the need to attain mastery of subject matter and or procedures.

These may be valid concerns if rewards and recognition are used as an add-on, as less than a fully integrated part of the service-learning process. But the concept of celebration goes far beyond the type of reward that stands apart from the action or achievement that has earned it. Celebration is an extension of the action, of the service project itself. In celebration, all parties join in a recognition of the intrinsic joy or good that results from the service rendered. Celebration should be viewed as an outward affirmation of an inward revelation. Celebration is the recognition not only of participants' successes but also of their vision, effort, and growth.

At Ridge View High School and Spring Valley High School in Columbia, South Carolina, we have found that external recognition and rewards can be a key ingredient to a larger goal. Celebrations involving recognitions and rewards motivate students to more service. "If I can get students to participate in service to others once, the power of that service can hook them on service for life," says Sherrill Martin, Vice Principal for Curriculum at Spring Valley. "Students may initially engage in service because someone offered an extrinsic reward or public recognition. But the feelings of personal accomplishment and of self-worth generated through the service will be internalized by the students and realized in later service," says Martin. The service will reappear later as the result of intrinsic motivation where the reward is found in the service itself.

EXTRINSIC MOTIVATION HAS VALUE For the last 10 years, Spring Valley High has sponsored a school-wide service effort. Called "Winter Days," it involves collecting canned goods for the Council on Aging, money for a day care center for children of the homeless, and toys for a children's program, and finding sponsors for foster children. Each year, the debate over the role of extrinsic motivation surfaces. Some teachers believe the students should be motivated to participate solely from intrinsic beliefs, while others believe that intrinsic motivation can be one of the lessons learned through the experience. An assembly is held to celebrate the Winter Days accomplishments, with the entire student body and community invited. Agencies send representatives who publicly thank the students for their caring and efforts.

At the assembly, anyone who has contributed in any way is asked to stand. Some students perform and others speak. These options provide recognition that respects students' different roles and comfort levels. The result is an almost tangible sense of pride and accomplishment. More than 95 percent of the students participate in Winter Days, and the assembly involves them all in some way.

When Winter Days began, it was strictly a co-curricular activity. Then some teachers began offering class credit as an extrinsic reward for participating, which helped to increase the amount of money and goods collected. When teachers began connecting the service to academic goals through service-learning, the amount collected really soared. The curricular connections made more teachers comfortable about giving credit for participation in Winter Days.

When Ridge View High opened recently, absorbing many students from the overcrowded Spring Valley High, students immediately wanted to create another Winter Days. Students who had attended Spring Valley started planning a similar project at Ridge View. Notably, they did not start their planning by asking how the participants would be rewarded. Instead, they assessed which projects students wanted to support and what projects the community needed. As one of their projects, they decided to assist Spring Valley to ensure that competition with that program would not be, consciously or unconsciously, a method of motivation or a source of recognition. The primary motivation for these students was the desire to serve.

"The most difficult part of leaving Spring Valley for me was leaving Winter Days," says Ashley, a sophomore. "There were people I knew, and others I met as the year began at the new school, who didn't want to lose being a part of the spirit of giving that Winter Days created."

The faculty at the new high school also supported the new service project, called "Winter Wishes." These teachers had found ways to integrate the service with an issue or with content that was part of their curriculum. "Service-learning has allowed me to tie service projects to specific topics," says Denise Pearman, a teacher at Ridge View High. "I have observed that students reward themselves. They feel rewarded by the sense of having done something good for someone else. 'When can we do more?' is the first thing I hear when a service-based project is over."

GUIDEPOSTS FOR RECOGNITION The Winter Days recognition process followed several guideposts that helped instill a greater sense of service among the students:

1. It matched the recognition to the achievement and to the people involved.
2. It was timely and specific to the project, held immediately after the three-week collection period and the day before the winter break began.
3. The students were involved in the celebration planning and implementation.
4. The learning that took place was recognized as well as the achievements of the collections.

Following these guideposts can help rewards and recognition become an integral part of the service-learning process, as a 9th-grade class project on hunger found. The class planned recognition and rewards with both their academic and service goals in mind. To celebrate their research, their school-wide education project, and their canned goods collection project, the students rewarded themselves with a field trip to a local university to participate in a symposium on hunger. Also, they celebrated with the winners of the canned good drives at the other high school and at the neighboring elementary school. The class provided free pizza for their peers at Ridge View High and made treats and goodie bags for the elementary winners. They traveled to the elementary school to host a party for the younger students. Thus, the celebration of the initial service project involved more service.

The class also developed rewards that fit the achievement. Having asked participants to help feed others, the sponsoring class fed the participants, while also presenting a program to increase awareness among their peers about the issue of hunger. Also, the class further increased their own awareness by attending the symposium.

The recognition used was appropriate for the targeted participants. A pizza is a favorite among teenagers, but students generally understand that more is involved in this recognition than a piece of their favorite food. The pizza did not overshadow the service required to earn it. Similarly, at the elementary school, the contact with the high school students was more important than the goodie bags themselves. In both cases, the tangible rewards were secondary to the intangible rewards of self-satisfaction, camaraderie, and a sense of personal responsibility and accomplishment. This created a sense of celebration among all the participants.

The celebration was also timely and specific. There was daily recognition of classes that were participating, and the tangible rewards were delivered immediately after the canned goods were delivered to the project recipients. The students themselves helped plan the recognitions and rewards, including getting to go to the symposium and to the elementary school.

Celebrations need to recognize and appreciate what participants *learn*, as well as what they *achieve*. If done appropriately, the result is an even greater emphasis on learning. In traditional evaluation, a student does not have to get a score of 100 to have felt some pride in learning. Similarly, recognition and reward for service-learning activities should celebrate the growth and learning that have occurred, even when the students have not achieved 100 percent of a project goal.

In an effort to collect food for the Habitat for Humanity volunteers working on a "Blitz Build" in Columbia, members of one service-learning class conducted a drive for fruit to donate. Though they fell short of their goal, the recognition of their efforts by the Habitat volunteers and by the classroom teacher encouraged members of the class to become involved in other volunteer efforts. After evaluating the methods used to promote and conduct the fruit drive, students were able to devise an improved system for future drives of this type.

CELEBRATION BUILDS CITIZEN SPIRIT Building good citizens is one of the goals of service-learning. In an effort to recognize and reward community leaders, we present plaques, pin medals on uniforms, and erect monuments for public service. In the traditional classroom, teachers motivate students to master content areas by focusing on the rewards of grades, scholarships to college, and eventually, good jobs. While this recognition of hard work is well deserved, for society to benefit from excellence in the curriculum, the student needs to make the connection between the classroom and the world beyond. A stand-alone reward will not encourage the student to apply the knowledge and skills learned to the health of society. Service-learning, with its emphasis on celebration, is one strategy to help students apply learning and explore the possibilities in citizenship.

Through service, a good citizen contributes to feelings of mutual good will—the feeling that the entire group somehow shares the vision, the motivation, and the success of the server. This shared experience represents the purest form of celebration. It may in turn lead to service by those people who have been touched in some way by the good citizen's efforts or by the recognition of those efforts.

An interdisciplinary project at Ridge View High illustrates how students have connected with the world beyond. The celebration stage of this project has the potential for creating a greater sense of intergenerational community, of shared citizenship among young and old, and in suburban and rural areas. From art, dance, advanced theater, and talented and gifted classes, the students are creating a multimedia production/performance based on the oral histories of citizens from a nearby rural community. The service project takes the curriculum into the real world and establishes links among citizens that might not otherwise have come together. The production is open to the public and will recognize the citizens interviewed during the research phase of the project.

In the first month, the students rewarded the citizens interviewed with an appreciation of hearing their life stories, through thank-you notes and other gestures. In return, these citizens have rendered service of their own, giving freely of their time and memories. The intergenerational nature of the project has given students new insights about the value of the ordinary citizen, who lives a life worthy of reward but one not often publicly celebrated.

"The students had conducted research through primary and secondary sources," says Patty Drews, one of the project teachers. "They had acquired new skills such as interviewing and videotaping and had learned to organize people, equipment, information, and time. All of the planning came together in the service component. It added a human dimension to the work that motivated the students to see the project through to the end. The personal interaction and the practical application of learning demanded by the service project will ensure that the performance, which will include the recognition of the students, will be truly a celebration."

Service-learning, with its emphasis on celebration, is one strategy to help students apply learning and explore the possibilities in citizenship.

Recognition can be as simple as a pat on the back or as complex as a community-wide fair. Types of reward and recognition fit along a continuum, ranging from formal rewards such as letters for letter jackets for documented service hours, to systematic recognition that is part of an ongoing project design, such as posting photos of students at their service sites and including news of service regularly in newsletters. Outside guests or political figures can come and thank students. Formal celebrations and parties can be planned and held, like the Winter Days assembly. Performing service for others can also be part of a meaningful celebration, as the 9th-grade class demonstrated with its hunger project.

Regardless of the approach to celebration, students need to understand that neither the reward nor the recognition is the goal of service-learning—not for learning and not for service. When designed in conjunction with educational goals such as learning content, when applied to real work situations, and when helping to develop responsible citizens, recognition and reward can be motivational and celebratory. Celebration is a completion. When designed and applied appropriately, outward reward and recognition can result in introspection and the internalization of concepts. While celebration certainly completes a project, it also has the power to move the participants to a life of intrinsically rewarding service.

REFERENCES AND SUGGESTIONS FOR FURTHER READING
Silcox, Harry C. *Motivational Elements in Service-Learning: Meaningfulness, Recognition, Celebration and Reflection.* Philadelphia: Brighton Press, 1995.

Marianna McKeown is Student Activities Director at Ridge View High School in Columbia, South Carolina. She was a Fellow in NSEE's Leadership Development Program, funded by the DeWitt Wallace-Reader's Digest Fund.

Renewal

issue 7

In addition to their myriad responsibilities and concerns, service-learning practitioners must focus on their own personal and professional needs in order to sustain their interest, energy, and creativity. Service-learning provides opportunities for educators to renew their commitment to effective and innovative teaching and learning.

ELIZABETH GIBBS discusses the importance of forming networks with other professionals working with service-learning.

MARILYNN CUNNINGHAM describes peer consulting, a method for sharing expertise with other practitioners.

LOUISE GIUGLIANO AND **JEAN DI SABATINO** explain a unique model for professional development.

ELIZABETH FUGAZZI closes the section with a look at reflection and celebration for service-learning practitioners.

renewal

Networking—A Path for Teacher Renewal

THE LAST DECADE HAS PROVEN TO BE A TIME OF CONTINUAL CHANGE. LITTLE REMAINS CONSTANT INCLUDING THE AREA OF PROFESSIONAL CAREER CHOICES. Many professionals seek career changes two or three or many more times over their lifetime. However, one career area that seems to be less affected by this trend is education. One can walk into a traditional American high school and witness teachers who have been teaching 20 and 30 years, still using the same methods as when they first started. While the need for professional renewal is apparent in all professions, it is especially true for teachers and administrators. Teachers who are energetic and still interested in pursuing the best teaching methods available have a far more positive impact on students than those who have "burned out" and may just be waiting for retirement.

BY **ELIZABETH GIBBS**

For service-learning opportunities to be available to students, faculty members need to be willing to try new things. But most teachers do not take risks on their own. A teacher who is burned out, feeling isolated, or insecure will be the teacher least likely to take the risk of a service-learning approach. Service-learning itself can function as a means of personal renewal for teachers—if teachers can get involved in it in the first place. The key step is for teachers to network with others doing this work, to avoid isolation, and connect with their colleagues. High school teachers rarely have the chance to learn about their colleagues' work. Professional networking both within a school district and outside of it is very important in helping educators receive a broader perspective of the teaching profession.

Personal renewal is important for all teachers. Ideally, a school district will offer teachers a chance to step back from the daily demands of the classroom and re-evaluate their initial goals and motivations as a teacher. But this is not always possible. So it is important to offer other alternatives to leaving the classroom. Service-learning is one means that offers teachers an opportunity to connect with a larger world on a regular basis. But how can teachers link up with these networks, beginning in their own schools? And, how can such networking result in personal renewal?

Along with two other high school teachers, I was given the task to develop and implement a restructured high school curriculum as an alternative to the traditional high school in the Bloomfield Hills School District in Bloomfield Hills, Michigan. This project took more than a year. For the first time since I began teaching, I had the opportunity to view education from an outside perspective rather than from being intimately involved. The project motivated me to begin reviewing and researching academic projects and teaching methodologies as well as to visit

Service-learning is one means that offers teachers an opportunity to connect with a larger world on a regular basis.

other successful restructured high schools. It was part of my professional and personal renewal. I was meeting others in various school districts and learning about their work. I was involved experientially in my task of restructuring the high school. I was modeling what many consider to be at the forefront of good teaching and learning—experiential education.

BROADER OPPORTUNITIES Every teacher in the district did not have the opportunity I had. But the school district did decide to institutionalize service-learning in our schools. That offered the potential for renewal to many more teachers. It is not possible for teachers to spend substantial amounts of time away from their classes. Not only is it costly in terms of supplying substitutes but it can also be disruptive to the students learning. So it is important to offer alternatives to leaving the classroom.

A good first step to broaden teachers' exposure to service-learning is to involve teachers in opportunities to dialogue about service-learning experiences. Some school districts have built in time within their school calendar to accommodate the need for networking and sharing. Some schools may begin later in the day, perhaps two or three hours a day every other Wednesday, for example, to allow teaching staff professional growth experiences. These are good times to introduce the concepts of service-learning or experiential learning. In addition, the faculty could spend time in a service setting that would allow them to experience first hand what service-learning is about.

Another possibility for bringing teachers together for learning about their colleagues' work in service-learning is during lunch. Typically, most high schools are departmentalized even during lunch hours. Teachers do not have the chance to find out about projects and curriculum ideas outside of their own discipline. As a site for NSEE's Pilot Project, supported by The Hitachi Foundation, to strengthen and sustain high school service-learning programs, our district was able to set up a format during lunch for teachers of various disciplines to share their ideas regarding service-learning. We called these our "Learning Circles" rather than an advisory committee for service-learning. A survey went out to help identify teachers who were interested in participating in the Learning Circle as well as those who just wanted to find out more information about service-learning. Support for this kind of network may be needed from your district's administration. In our case, some teachers may have needed a substitute teacher for one lunch period since we chose to meet during the entire lunch block, which was two 40-minute periods. This networking and dialogue opportunity for staff was a great example of teachers deciding for themselves what they needed in order to continue to grow both personally and professionally.

From the Learning Circle experiences, we found out what else our teaching staff needed to continue this professional growth process. It soon became apparent that the staff needed opportunities to learn more about service-learning and experiential education beyond the confines of their lunch hour. With the monetary help from Learn and Serve state grants, we sent interested teachers to state and national conferences in service-learning. In addition, we brought in service-learning consultants for several one-day workshops with our Learning Circle participants. This helped to re-energize many of our teachers who had a difficult time with new methodologies. By seeing other professionals also engaged in educational methods such as service-learning, the teachers were not isolated in their cause and began to see the world around them.

While these grants have provided many special opportunities for us, educators do not need to rely on special funding to organize formal or informal networks with other professionals. In schools or districts where there are few people involved in service-learning, teachers can link up with others—from the arts, vocational education, career services, or any academic discipline—who are committed to or engaged in education reform, hands-on learning, or innovative teaching practice.

NETWORK OUTSIDE YOUR AREA One of the best professional experiences for me has been the involvement with NSEE's Leadership Development Program, funded by the DeWitt Wallace-Reader's Digest Fund. This program paired academic professionals together in a fellow-mentor relationship and provided leadership training over a two-year period. Programs like these are highly successful in encouraging educators to take on more leadership roles in their various communities and schools. It is important for professionals to share their expertise and training, but there are very few avenues that are provided in the academic world that encourage teachers, especially secondary educators, to do so. In addition to participating in leadership training programs like this, teachers need to have opportunities to present their service-learning experiences at various national and state conferences. The recognition and networking that is acquired by presenting at a national conference is a tremendous motivation for most educators and is seen as a good example of professional renewal.

In addition to providing more opportunities for professionals to present at national service-learning and experiential education conferences, educators need to get involved with publishing in academic journals. There is a definite need for publications and research in the area of service-learning and experiential education. The recognition and respect that an educator receives from such an experience will provide the needed motivation to keep researching the best teaching practices available. Take advantage of the venues for writing and publishing on K–12 service-learning. This takes *time,* but allows you, the educator, to reflect on your work, practice synthesizing and communicating your experience, and achieve some recognition for yourself and your program.

Through regional or national organizations, teachers can form professional networks with others outside of their schools or districts. For example, several graduates of NSEE's Leadership Development Program, along with other service-learning educators, formed the Service and Experiential Learning Network (SELNET) as part of the Association for Supervision and Curriculum Development (ASCD). SELNET debuted at the ASCD national conference in March 1995, and now publishes a newsletter, sponsors meetings, and conducts workshops at ASCD and other conferences.

As educators, we have a responsibility to bring to our audience the best and most relevant teaching methods known in education. Service-learning provides students with one of the most

It is not a new concept, that students learn best and retain the most if engaged in school experientially.

meaningful and engaging academic experiences in schools today. It also provides teachers with the necessary information to bring this type of learning to the students. It is not a new concept, that students learn best and retain the most if engaged in school experientially. However, many academic veterans as well as the "new kids on the block" just need to be taught how to do it. The opportunity for professional growth and renewal is there. We just need to grab it!

> *Elizabeth Gibbs is Coordinator of Community Service in the Bloomfield Hills Public Schools in Michigan. She has been a Mentor in NSEE's Leadership Development Program and a Consultant with NSEE's National Initiative, funded by the DeWitt Wallace-Reader's Digest Fund. Beth was also a key liaison for NSEE's Pilot Project, supported by The Hitachi Foundation, to strengthen and sustain high school service-learning programs.*

Consulting with Peers—An Exchange for Mutual Renewal

EXPERIENTIAL LEARNING PROJECTS ARE DEMANDING TO ADMINISTER AND COORDINATE, WHETHER FOR INDIVIDUAL TEACHERS OR OVERALL PROGRAM ADMINISTRATORS. Students are engaged with the perspectives of the community as well as those of the classroom teachers and other students. The responsibility of the learning shifts to the student and is more student centered: the community site becomes the classroom, the student becomes her own instructor, and the community resources become the textbooks. While such projects highly motivate students, developing and implementing them requires an ongoing commitment to change.

BY **MARILYNN CUNNINGHAM**

As a change agent, it is a challenge to keep an adequate flow of personal energy to facilitate service-learning as an instructional strategy and at the same time withstand the scrutiny of the school personnel's traditional viewpoint. So who motivates the change agent to keep on keeping on?

After 12 years in such a situation, motivating myself, I needed personal renewal. I needed assistance from adult peers who knew what I was going through. I needed to renew the energy, enthusiasm, and creative thinking I took to my service-learning programs. I began to look outside my institution for a group of people with whom I had more in common. Otherwise, I was in threat of burn out. I discovered a process called "peer consulting," where two professionals engaged in service-learning work together so that the consulting process benefits them both. I was fortunate to participate in a structured peer consulting program, but you can use peer consulting in an informal way as well.

When I began to participate in this program, my first question was, "What is a peer consultant?" I knew of peer coaching, peer mentoring, and peer tutoring, but I had never heard of peer consulting. I learned that the two words describe the process pretty well: peers work together, with one in a consultant capacity. Many fields including education utilize consultants to help solve problems of all sorts. And many fields including education draw on various peer programs, where people of the same age, job status, or some other equal footing relate, usually with one peer teaching the other.

What is different about peer consulting, I have found, is that the peers remain in a position of equality, even though one is a consultant to the other. What makes this possible is the philosophical commitment of both parties to the service-learning process. The consultant goes into a situation to serve the peer as well as to learn more about her own life and work. The peer seeking the consultancy is serving by inviting a colleague into her everyday world, and in turn, learning from the consultant's reflections. There is a transfer of energy in both directions. With the equal status understood, the process

Both the peer and the consultant learn through serving each other.

tends to renew both people, generating new energy, ideas, and excitement for the "peer" as well as the "consultant."

GETTING CONNECTED When trying to be an agent of change within a traditional field such as education, there is a danger of getting isolated. I found peer consulting through my efforts at networking with others in experiential education, initially through NSEE. It supplied cutting-edge information to support my base of awareness. I could read NSEE's journal and know that I was not alone. Then I attended an NSEE national conference and discovered a network of people who offered an identification different from anything else I had ever encountered. Conversation, meaningful conversation, filled every nook and cranny of the conference site. The sessions included not only a base of knowledge on experiential learning, but also how this information could be applied.

The conference was exhilarating. We talked about concepts like the importance not only of *what* you *know* but what you *do* with what you know, including the impact of knowledge and service on the common good. The learning was multi-perspective, multi-dimensional, and multi-leveled. It charged my internal battery with enough energy to last a year. To help me sustain my personal struggle as a proponent for service-learning in the traditional instructional arena, support was just a telephone call away.

For several years, I attended the NSEE national conference as a part of my annual professional growth plan, which led to a strong relationship with a small group of other secondary educators who made the same commitment. We wanted more secondary school educators involved, so NSEE sought and received funding for this purpose from the DeWitt Wallace-Reader's Digest Fund. The grant provided for peer consulting. I was selected to participate in the program and learned the peer consultant model developed under this grant. Under our program, a broker agency, in this case NSEE, served as a middle man, linking a service-learning peer with a consultant. A middle man is not necessary but may be helpful in some cases.

Peer consulting reflects the service-learning concept. This is an opportunity for two or more people to gather together for the purpose of bringing about change in an existing situation. It offers an opportunity for a give-and-take relationship between two people who hold similar or equal positions in two separate organizations. This give-and-take relationship becomes dynamic when the depth of the engagement captures the essence of service-learning. Both the peer and the consultant learn through serving each other. To solidify the contract, the consultant is offered monetary income or gain from the broker or the professional organization receiving the service, and the peer is offered psychic income or gain from the consultant's outside view or expertise.

HOW PEER CONSULTING WORKS The process begins when the peer contacts a broker or a potential consultant to discuss the need for an outside opinion or expertise to help move an organization along. A broker agency can help determine the best match for the peer from a pool of consultants. After the purpose for the consultation is determined, the peer takes the leadership in the relationship by providing information to the consultant. This reflects good planning, whether a broker is involved or not. This provides the consultant with background materials so that the consultant can begin an analysis and synthesis. During this process, the two plan a visit. The visit offers the consultant an opportunity to observe and collect information, meet others at the site, and become involved with different viewpoints than the peer.

The peer is accountable to the institution and grounded within the organization seeking assistance. The peer is connected to everyday, practical realities, which are necessary for activities to be conducted in an efficient and effective manner. The consultant is not grounded within that organization and hence can be open to whatever she can visualize. While the peer presents the realities, the consultant observes with a mind for possibilities. Their interaction creates the process of peer consulting and by its very nature promotes change. Problems have a chance to be observed as opportunities.

Through the exchange of information on both an informal and formal level, the two develop a plan of action. It usually takes the form of a written recommendation to the peer and can be copied to the key stakeholders within the peer's organization. The recommendations can transform questions about "what is happening" to ideas of "what can be" and "how can we get there." The consultant returns to her workplace ready for her own challenging realities with a renewed frame of mind and spirit.

Peer consulting reflects good practices within the service-learning field. Both the peer and the consultant gain through the acts of giving, serving, and learning. Their relationship offers an opportunity for the inside view and the outside view to come together for the purpose of establishing stronger connections. The peer and the consultant have separate but equal roles. The success of peer consulting rests within their ability to relate. It is in the relationship that personal renewal evolves for the consultant and the peer. For that reason, I connect the basic concepts of my peer consulting experiences to the letters in the word RELATE, using it as an acronym for Real, Equal, Learn, Alert, Think, and Energize.

These six elements of the peer consulting process are guideposts for all models, whether a broker is involved or not. As true partnerships between schools and community agencies expand in the service-learning field, where agencies do more education and schools do more service, the peer consulting model, with service-learning as the underpinning philosophy, can help educators as well as professionals in other fields.

Real. The more I can experience the reality of a culture and climate of a school system, the more I can be of service. The most successful visits are when the processes and procedures represent the everyday exchange among people. When the visit is staged, my observations do not have the opportunity to be authentic. The more I am included in each event, the more I can gain trust and thus add credibility for my peer. In Massachusetts, my peer involved me in the set-up of rooms, organization of materials, errands at the central office, lunch with the teacher's union representative, and parts of teachers' work lives. In all, I consulted at this site four times.

My most memorable experience happened on my third visit. Contrary to our planning, the school was not in session. Students on their own time came to school to share their stories with me.

For a treat, they were offered lunch—their choice. I was honored to be invited. In my black suit and high heels, we ate chicken dinners set on the hood of a car. There, we had an open discussion of the promises and challenges of service-learning within their school. When a visit allows me to listen to the stories of students, parents, and teachers, I have the opportunity to gain trust, become involved, offer perspective, and be of service. When my view is real, my ideas are relevant. Then, I can serve my peer in a more practical way. The "how to" makes sense.

Equal. Both the peer and the consultant have much in common. We exchange our shared information and experiences from a common perspective, and it forms a bond or bridge over which we can extend our helping hands. This bond is built on common levels of status and privilege within our respective organizations, as well as our shared value systems. We both agree and understand the strength of the learning gained through the act of serving the needs of others. We concur on the need to preserve service-learning within the organization as a credible instructional strategy. I enjoy staying in the home of my peer when I conduct a visitation. This offers more time to reflect and build a relationship around our commonalities. I can ask questions about my observations and check out to what extent my perspective is in touch with reality.

Even in the most real situations, as a person experiencing what my peer experiences, I see with an eye that notices opportunities instead of problems.

Learn. New learning promotes creativity and new levels of awareness. For this reason, on a visit, I leave my organization and past behind and become open to the experiences and realities of my peer. I connect to this new awareness much like an artist connects to her art. I unite myself with my peer's organization as if it were my work. I plan, produce, and see my peer's work as if it were my own. This unity creates a transformational learning. Immersed like this, I experience, reflect, and connect to create new learning or new awareness based on prior knowledge or experience. While returning home, I take time to separate from the visitation. The follow-up reports and letters offer the formal opportunity to reflect and document the new learning.

Alert. While consulting, I assume the ability to respond to my peer within the context of her organization. I find it important to be mentally responsive through multiple ways. I am alert to the written word. Before a visitation, I read data and descriptions of the culture and climate of the organization and the community within which it exists. I listen to the perspective of my peer. When I visit, I am engaged. However, I am outside my experience and observing all the time with a keen eye. In this alert state, I make notes that serve as a reality check before recommending action.

During a peer consultation in Kentucky, two peers and I met in advance to plan my visit. Rather than travel to six different schools, we decided to have one representative team from each school come to the volunteer center for a training. Using their Learn and Serve grant applications as a planning tool, our goal was to lead the group through the planning steps, one at a time. I began the session with the theory behind experiential learning, connecting it to service-learning and the steps on the forms. When the teams started on the first step, they became engaged. The room was buzzing with activity. I became alert to the fact that they were moving ahead to the next steps. Immediately, I adapted my format. Rather than continue ahead with the planned agenda, I circulated about the room and offered consultation as requested. They were an empowered group. Each small group moved at its own pace and with its own energy. I simply facilitated.

Think. The process of analysis and synthesis is important. I find it essential in my report to communicate the analysis with the big ideas divided into manageable parts. After breaking down the large concepts and experiences into pieces, they can be put together into a unique vision. This serves as a recommendation. When pulling the essential parts together, it is important to recognize the simplest ideas first, then build a connection to the most complex ideas. This moves the awareness to another level in a careful and thoughtful way. The report can serve as a tool for organizational growth and change.

A peer consultation in Ohio last summer illustrates how a report can help promote organizational change. The school system, under my peer's influence, had included in its five-year plan for all ninth graders to have a service-learning opportunity. She arranged for me to meet with the key stakeholders to discuss the implementation of this strategy. Unfortunately, her direct supervisor, who oversees curriculum and instruction, was unable to attend. This underscored the importance of a careful analysis in a follow-up report written to my peer and copied to her colleagues. I organized the report around four concepts: Define the school system's vision for service-learning, describe your expertise with service-learning, describe the best fit of your expertise and the school system's strategic plan, and finally, recommend steps for you and your director to begin. This offered a simple, but uncompromising format for my peer and her director to use as a point of reference.

Energize. Management of energy is essential. Through all the RELATE processes of peer consulting, the Reality of the situation, the Equal foundation, the Learning focus, the Alert posture, and the Thoughtful follow-up, Energy is imparted with a lighthearted attitude. Negative experiences can be recycled into positive ones. Instead of being upset, angry, or disappointed, offer encouragement and hope. Even in the most real situations, as a person experiencing what my peer experiences, I see with an eye that notices opportunities instead of problems. Change in the middle can sometimes look like failure, and offering a different perspective can be a stabilizing force. Such attitudes form personal and professional renewal. In Ohio, my peer and I shared roles in the discussion with the key stakeholders. I facilitated and moved the conversation along. Although I was aware of some inconsistencies in perceptions, I was not concerned. I wanted everyone's opinion on the table. Throughout the hour of discussion, consensus was evident and I was able to repeat what I heard. When the assistant superintendent suggested I write down the group's consensus, I called on my peer's energy. For she, as the observer, remembered the details. Likewise, she needed my perspective for the consensus. Our exchange offered synergy. We were two, gathered together, to serve, learn, and renew.

Marilynn Cunningham is the Professional Development Specialist with the Fayette County Public Schools in Lexington, Kentucky. Previously, she was the district's Communications Coordinator of the Experience Based Career Education Program. Marilynn has been a Mentor in NSEE's Leadership Development Program and a Consultant with NSEE's National Initiative, funded by the DeWitt Wallace-Reader's Digest Fund.

Constructivist Professional Development

A SCHOOL ON THE WEST COAST CALLS TO REQUEST A DAY OF CONSULTING ON SERVICE-LEARNING. We talk several times with administrators and teachers to get the best possible understanding of the school and its needs. With the school representatives, we decide to focus the day around the topic, "How can service-learning be integrated into the curriculum?"

BY **LOUISE GIUGLIANO** AND **JEAN DI SABATINO**

...one cannot predict the exact route that will be taken to reach desired outcomes.

The workshop is being held in a room that is long from left to right and not particularly deep. The participants head for the two ends, leaving only those seated in the middle third in a position to be engaged. Within an hour, side conversations start and irritation seeps to the surface. The tension we had sensed from the beginning is emerging. We take a moment and in a quick conversation decide that we cannot ignore this tension, recognizing that the group's "sub-text" will become the focus for this professional development day.

If we fail to address what is really on their minds, they may experience a day that is irrelevant to them at this time. Therefore we will *construct*, with the group, a means of addressing the undercurrents that are preventing them from moving toward future goals. In essence this will provide the opportunity for:

- collectively deciding on the *issues* that are most pressing—i.e. the work to be done,
- identifying *common ground* from which issues will be addressed, and
- delineating the *enablers* that will provide a means for the work to be done.

The needs of the participants, shown by the tension in the room and the apparent low expectations, are dictating the content of the day. Only after this process-oriented work do we feel confident that the content related to service-learning will have a foundation from which to spring. Through use of metaphor and other diagnostic processes, the participants are able to identify the troubling undercurrent. There is a lack of trust around how critical decisions are made. This is eroding a collaborative spirit, splintering the group toward a "we-they" and "leader-follower" dynamic.

To avoid such dichotomies, we lead the group through a process called "histo-mapping." They delineate the major events, trends, and decisions that contributed to the development of the school. This helps the group discover for themselves the priorities and assumptions around which curricular decisions have been made. With our guidance, the participants then reframe their questions to generate answers rather than accusations. For example, the question "Who makes curriculum decisions?," which involves finger pointing, becomes "How are curricular decisions made?" In participant-led small group discussions, they outline their own future investigations and professional development around the issues of curriculum and service-learning.

As the end of a productive day draws near and with some assurances of how they will proceed in the future, a teacher asks, "So how *is* service-learning integrated into the curriculum?" The group is now ready to engage with the fundamental principles of service-learning, snapshots of what integrated service-learning looks like, and suggestions of various tools with which to work. The teachers discuss how service-learning will fit with the other work they are committed to and how they will proceed. They want tools and not packaged plans where "one size fits all"—and eventually fits no one.

The one-day workshop highlights some of the strengths of what is called "constructivist professional development." In this approach to adult development, the facilitator poses questions and guides the group's work, as in the tradition of the Socratic teacher. The group members engage in the central work, which is *processing* and *producing* through *collective inquiry*. Through this work, clear outcomes evolve but without pre-defined structure. That is, one cannot predict the exact route that will be taken to reach desired outcomes.

FACILITATOR ROLE As facilitators of this process, we acknowledge the professional capabilities of a group to achieve outcomes they have set for themselves. *Our role is to guide them through the process.* As professional developers, we have moved beyond the traditional formats of "staff training" which views adult learners as technicians in need of knowing how to perform discrete tasks. We do not see ourselves as experts charged with imparting information to the unknowing. Nor do we believe that if we teach folks to know what we know then schools will be better places. Instead, we are committed to the notion that individual practitioners have the "intellectual prowess" to inquire, to reflect, to create and to solve problems, and to decide what is best teaching and learning practice. What is often missing, however, is the capacity to do this collectively and regularly. Therefore, the work we do with practitioners is singularly focused on building the capacity within their community to collectively inquire, create, and reflect.

Deborah Schifter, a teacher and professional development consultant, describes the conventional format of professional development as one in which "people (students) acquire concepts by receiving information from other people (teachers) who know more... if students listen to what their teachers say, they will learn what their teachers know." Self-discovery, on the other hand, through questions and probes, is the approach of the constructivist facilitator. The facilitator's task is to pose questions which will lead people through possible uncertainty or puzzlement to the construction of important concepts and to different ways of thinking—not merely different ways of doing.

Along with guiding and probing, modeling best practice is essential in a constructivist professional development session. You do what you want them to do. Their experience with active engagement and taking responsibility for their own learning is not only rewarding but is exactly what they want for their students. The other important and generative piece of the facilitator's responsibility is to diagnose continuously, monitoring the work and the group's progress. Using these techniques the facilitator helps to build a group's capacity to operate in a healthy and productive manner—a style that will continue long after the facilitator is gone.

COLLECTIVE INQUIRY DEFINES WORK Helping a group to be clear about their desired outcomes reveals the range of content needed for a workshop. From this, the facilitator develops a framework and not an agenda. A structured agenda is not by its nature a constructivist tool. We work without knowing the exact route we will take. We come with a range of content and processes, but the route is determined by the personality, strengths, and desires of the group.

To find out what they want from the session, we do a lot of probing beforehand. How will this session fit with the bigger picture? What is the bigger picture? While a considerable amount of probing is done before the session to target the work as closely as possible to their needs, diagnosing will go on continuously. From the moment the session begins, even introductions are set up to diagnose. Decisions are made right from the start about their level of knowledge, the openness of the group to the work planned, and other prevailing needs.

We must honor the process as well as the content of learning to be equal partners with the learners by becoming learners ourselves.

A climate of collective inquiry and joint problem solving is essential. The balance between allowing individuals to strive for their personal best must not supersede the communal discovery and learning. The constructivist activity is one which is embedded in and enabled by contexts of social interaction. Within the constructivist framework, the interaction between participants is more valuable than the interaction between participants and facilitator.

For example, a principal at an East coast school requests a week-long summer institute to integrate service-learning into curriculum. Through extensive interviews, we establish five outcomes around which we plan a framework for the week. At the workshop, the teachers take their own pulse to see where things are at this point in time. They collectively identify frustration with communication and with the issue of planning time. Moreover, they do not have a schedule for the opening of school, which is just a few weeks away. This has prevented the group from being able to focus on the desired outcomes.

We had anticipated that teaching teams would be able to develop an interdisciplinary curriculum, but we discover that they are not functioning enough in their teams to do this at this time. Collectively, the group comes to the decision that while there is this new work to be done, there is neither the team capacity nor the school culture to do it yet. Therefore, issues of school culture and of the school as a learning organization with a capacity to change and an ability to operate from introspection, mutual critique, and teamwork become the presenting curriculum for the first days of the institute. We proceed, taking them where they are rather than where we had planned for them to be.

While there were specific skills to hone at the week-long institute, we strived to provide opportunities for the staff to think differently about service, school development, and their roles. We had hoped that the staff would be able to develop a common knowledge base of service-learning as a strategy for teaching, learning, and school development. While the outcomes seemed content-bound, we were clear that we would not deliver the content as technicians.

BUILDING CAPACITY To build capacity ensures a group's own future ability to manage, implement, and assess their progress. It means being reflective about their goals, a practice which needs to be ongoing and internalized by the group. It includes exposure to new tools, content, and skills to design and assess their work so that it is continually moving forward. Practice in problem solving, analyzing, and developing new insights through working together is at the heart of building capacity to be a community that learns together. This translates ultimately to a group engaged in the art of discovery, of making meaning, of gaining the artful skills that support renewal.

With renewal as our driving force, we need to know what this group knows and what they can do now. What are they bringing with them? The East coast school, as one would expect, had a knowledgeable, if uneven, background in curriculum development processes. But they knew little of service-learning. Is service-learning content or tool? Is it civic education or a means to all education? In traditional professional development formats, these questions are answered by the workshop leader. Within constructivist professional development, the facilitator asks such questions.

At the week-long institute, we facilitated the group's working through these questions. We used examples of other schools' work, information about best practices as defined by the Alliance for Service-Learning in Education Reform, and the outcomes they had as part of their educational program. The staff worked through their frustrations and stayed with the work of the institute despite obstacles in their path. The force that seemed to carry them through all of this was that they worked well when they were given the opportunity to take charge of their own professional development.

In constructivist professional development, there are no models, no formulas, no simple answers to complicated questions. There is a way to organize one's thinking, which is then brought to a specific context. An exploration of what is needed and wanted in this place, at this time, is determined in concert with the group. As constructivists, we ask no less of ourselves than we ask of educators embroiled in the process of reforming educational practices. We must honor the process as well as the content of learning to be equal partners with the learners by becoming learners ourselves.

REFERENCES AND SUGGESTIONS FOR FURTHER READING
Schifter, Deborah. "A Constructivist Perspective on Teaching and Learning Mathematics." *Phi Delta Kappan* (March 1996): 492.

Louise Giugliano is a national educational consultant based in Narberth, Pennsylvania, and a member of the National Faculty of the Coalition of Essential Schools. She was a key liaison for NSEE's Pilot Project, funded by The Hitachi Foundation, to strengthen and sustain high school service-learning programs, and she has been a Consultant with NSEE's National Initiative, funded by the DeWitt Wallace-Reader's Digest Fund.

Jean di Sabatino is State Coordinator for the Pennsylvania RE:Learning/Coalition of Essential Schools Initiative in Harrisburg. Her work within the Pennsylvania Department of Education has included design of innovative professional development structures.

Professional Renewal Through Reflection and Celebration

I WANT TO SHARE WITH YOU A PERSONAL STORY. I feel that it characterizes the underlying principles upon which renewal through celebration and refection are based.

BY **ELIZABETH FUGAZZI**

...we grow both when we are at the center of a celebration and when we are merely a member of the audience.

As a young and eager business education graduate, I embraced the challenge and opportunity to teach. I felt blessed when I was hired immediately out of college in 1970 by the Fayette County School System in Lexington, Kentucky, to teach at Lafayette High School. I jumped in with both feet, teaching a variety of business and English courses over the next 14 years. In my original interview, I remember that when I was asked "Can you teach Business Law?" my response was "Give me the course outline and I can teach anything!" My optimism could easily be equated to that of a new kindergartner!

But by the fall of 1986 I had begun saying things like "I only have 16 more years until I can retire" and doing things like writing in the corner of each page of my daily lesson plans the number of days left in the school year—as though I were serving a prison sentence. My daily life was taking its toll: the realities of teaching; coordinating a program that involved recruiting, placing, and monitoring about 50 seniors working for credit in community businesses; sponsoring the National Honor Society; being involved in community service organizations; and being a wife and mother. I felt exhausted all the time, lost weight, and that fall, was under a doctor's care for ulcers. I was really feeling the stress of my professional and personal life, and I was struggling to keep from being completely burned out.

I realized that something had to change. I had already completed my Masters in Education and a course in "Leadership Lexington," but I still felt that something was missing. The event that began an entire chain reaction of change in my professional career happened when teacher records were computerized and it surfaced that I had been teaching a business law course that both my students and I loved for 14 years, but I was not certified to do so because my Business Education Certificate was limited to secretarial courses. The University of Kentucky, where I had earned my degrees, had already changed its program of studies, and my graduate work was too old to apply toward the needed certification. My principal's solution was to delete the course from the curriculum. I was absolutely crushed—and angry.

About that same time, I was being recruited by an outstanding educational publisher to become their Kentucky Sales Representative. I accepted the position, thinking that I had found the answer to reducing my frustrations and stress. I resigned my tenured position and left the classroom the same year that the Challenger exploded with Christa McAuliffe on board. Her words, "I touch the future; I teach," were posted in the teachers' workroom. My colleagues gave me a going-away party in that room immediately before marching as a faculty in our caps and gowns onto the football field for commencement exercises. Only then did the reality of my leaving hit me. It didn't take me long to realize what frustrated me was not exclusive to the high school.

My time outside of the classroom helped me grow more personally and professionally than at any other time in my life, including my college years. Within two years, I had gotten over my hurt and indignation over losing my favorite class, had gone back to college to broaden my teaching credentials, and had reactivated my application to try and become a part of the Fayette County School System again. Those three events—the Challenger explosion, the going-away party, the graduation ceremony—gave me great cause for reflection. I realized that my heart was in the classroom. That "ah-hah" experience occurred as a result of my personal and professional renewal.

I realized that teaching is service to others, that teachers with the right attitude plus excellent skills can create a vision for themselves and for others. I had been spending so much energy worrying about my own situation that I had forgotten that the mission of teachers is to help others help themselves. As much as it sounds like a cliche, I re-discovered that teaching is, in fact, a very honorable profession that truly touches all our futures. I began trying to sort out and make meaning out of my experiences in the hopes that I could return to Lafayette, where I had literally "grown up," with the new goal of being a better teacher than ever before.

BUILD RENEWAL INTO LIFE I never did get back to Lafayette. I wound up teaching marketing at another high school and then moving into Experience Based Career Education with the Fayette County Public Schools, where I have been able to draw upon my own personal experiences to help others get past their "hurts." Guiding other teachers through professional development workshops on personal and professional renewal has helped me with my ongoing renewal.

We all have "wounds." We can either turn them to our advantage and make them our strengths or we can focus on them and become bitter. I found that when I was able to focus on helping others, I didn't think so much about my own problems. And that is where service-learning comes into the picture. As a teacher, many times I have tried to help a student who I perceived as "needy," only to discover later that I was the one who was in need and the student helped me instead! This "reverse service," or community service, focuses us on serving others but also makes possible our own renewals. Only when we are concerned with serving others can we rise to a higher level of effectiveness. As long as we are concerned only with helping ourselves, we do everything less well. In other words, those who need us may very well be the ones we need the most.

To guide our students so that they choose to help others, knowing their only reward will be personal satisfaction gained by contributing to the world in which we all live, is an honorable, professional, renewing thing to do. It usually is the teacher/sponsor who "plants the seed" that empowers the members of school clubs and organizations to have meaningful service projects. And the possibilities for service-learning are limited only by the thinking of the teachers who sponsor the groups and the members who carry out the projects. For teachers to be able to provide such guidance to students, we need to constantly renew ourselves. Two fundamental aspects of service-learning can help us build renewal into our daily lives—celebration and reflection.

CELEBRATION School celebrations serve a very important role in the renewal process. Teachers who seem happy and renewed are usually the ones who sponsor the school organizations or attend the school ball games, plays, pep rallies, and academic meets. School traditions that serve as a renewing celebration are baccalaureate and commencement for high school graduates. What pride we as teachers feel when we witness the formal celebration of our students' successes. It is important to remember that we grow both when we are at the center of a celebration and when we are merely a member of the audience. And when we connect and talk with others, we all gain energy.

When we win an award or special honor, such recognitions can sometimes be renewing, but not in the same way as a daily celebration process. Making celebration part of our routine requires drawing on principles of service-learning. By facilitating growth and learning among students, we can celebrate as they mature into caring adults. But we need regular ways to do this. An important way to feel renewed by students' growth is to connect with our peers and not remain isolated. The synergy created by these connections is a very powerful source of renewal. These conversations and connections need to be both formal and informal. If we can think out loud and talk with others about plans, activities, accomplishments, and challenges, the sharing process brings everyone along.

These conversations and connections need to be on three levels for most teachers: with our students, with other professionals within a school or department, and with administrators. It is important to note that conversations with students must be appropriate for a teacher-student relationship; the reflection should be centered around the student, not the teacher. Such conversations or "conferences" can help the teacher feel renewed through the sharing of the students' successes.

We are incorporating the idea of formal celebration here in the Fayette County School System. Once a month, students and teachers are the main focus of the Board of Education meeting. The Board Members see student performances or hear about students' accomplishments and give them formal recognition for their successes. The entire community can share in the celebration because the local school system's educational television channel broadcasts these meetings live over the cable access.

Taking time to enjoy and celebrate our small successes with others helps us feel refreshed and renewed. Teachers on the elementary level send home certificates, stamp "happy faces" on children's hands, and put stars on charts in their classrooms as ways to celebrate successes. Somewhere along the line, however, many high school teachers forget to include celebration as a regular part of their classroom activities. As high schools move toward restructuring, culminating performance-based events can become a wonderful way for teachers to gain energy and feel renewed as they help celebrate their students' successes just before they graduate.

REFLECTION Just as students need to incorporate regular reflection into service-learning education, teachers also need this reflection process. As we have concrete experiences, we can be more fulfilled if we take time to reflect. David Kolb, a leader in experiential education, has developed a construct that shows how "learning is the making of meaning." In other words, we can use the reflection process to make some meaning of our experiences, which renew us, helping us to see challenges as opportunities rather than problems.

When we slow down enough to think about the feelings connected to a specific experience, we can then extract meaning from the feelings. We can understand the meaning of the experience in terms of concepts. Then we can use or build on the concepts to find out what meaning can be made of the experience. The concepts can prepare us for future concrete experiences upon which we can again reflect.

We can all feel the sense of renewal so critical to our professional growth and development if we have the opportunity to reflect, especially in the learning cycle construct developed by Kolb. The first step in this cycle is to recall a positive professional experience. You can do this in a workshop setting, with a leader drawing on guided imagery and other techniques, as well as in personal journals or daily or weekly structured settings with colleagues. After recalling the positive professional experience, the second step is to reflect on that experience. Third, share the experiences with your colleagues. And, fourth, identify the characteristics that made that experience meaningful, so that you can recreate its positive impact.

This four-step process allows veteran teachers to regain their enthusiasm by first approaching renewal from within themselves and then spreading the same concepts to their entire learning organization. Shared reflection is the key to teachers' understanding more about themselves and their students. This energizes a teacher to create classes where students have fun; they are engaged in learning because the teacher is personally and professionally renewed. The Kolb Learning Cycle conceptualizes learning as a circular process.

Shared reflection is the key to teachers' understanding more about themselves and their students.

LEARNING IS THE MAKING OF MEANING

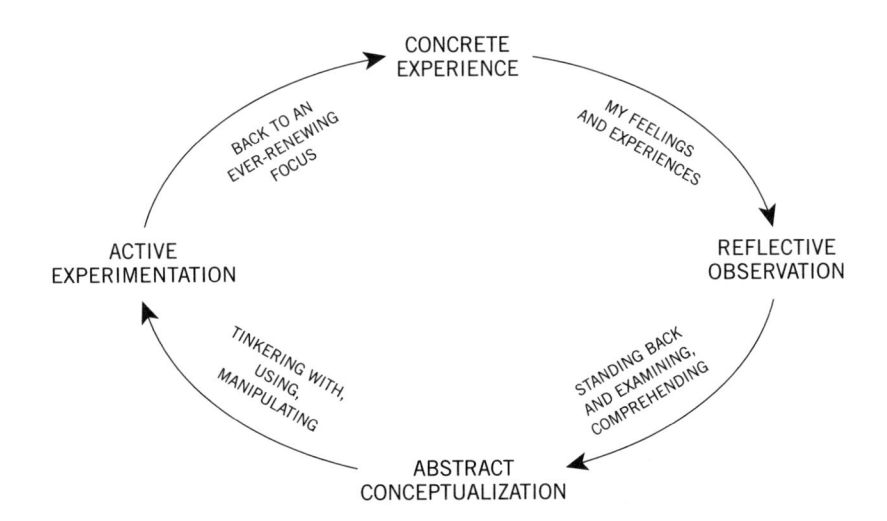

Adapted from Kolb, David A. *Experiential Learning: Experience as the Source of Learning and Development.* Englewood Cliffs, NJ: Prentice-Hall, 1984.

HOLISTIC RENEWAL Renewal through celebration and reflection, to be most effective for teachers and others, needs to affect our entire lives. The renewal will be short lived if we isolate it to specific work experiences and live with chaos or unsatisfied feelings in other dimensions of life. In the *Seven Habits of Highly Effective People*, Stephen Covey frames this holistic renewal in terms of maintaining a "liberal arts" approach to life, balancing four major aspects: physical, spiritual, mental, and social or emotional.

The physical dimension includes getting enough rest, engaging in regular exercise, following good nutrition, and finding ways to relax. Many books discuss the importance of physical health. The spiritual dimension is the very center of our commitment to our own personal value system. People examine their motives and value systems in very different ways—some through meditation or prayer, others through music or reading or giving themselves up to the harmony and rhythm of nature. Reading, writing, organizing, planning, involving ourselves in professional organizations, serving on school committees—all provide mental renewal opportunities. And finally, the social/emotional dimension of renewal occurs when we gain the synergy of connecting with others.

I remember being appointed part of a Philosophy Committee one year at Lafayette High School as part of the Southern Association of Schools evaluation process. The committee met regularly after school to discuss Lafayette's philosophy or mission statement. What I especially remember, though, was that the committee did not disband after the accreditation process ended. The members of the group continued to call themselves "The Philosophy Committee," and we still meet on a regular basis. It was a renewal process that we have continued to draw on, long past its initial purpose.

It is important for us to as educators to realize that balance must come from within each of us. In other words, we must be proactive in our search for renewal as we exercise "all four dimensions of our nature, regularly and consistently in a wise and balanced way" (Covey 302). Further, we must model for our students this balanced life so that they can learn how to become life-long learners who are self-motivated.

TIPS TO HELP WITH PERSONAL AND PROFESSIONAL RENEWAL

1. Cultivate a circle of personal and professional friends and colleagues during the good times. Share your celebrations with them; be their audience so that they can share their victories. Don't wait until things are going wrong.

2. Recognize when things are going right, and celebrate in little ways. Remembering those times will help you get through the tough times.

3. Never give up. Remember that anything that doesn't kill you will make you stronger.

4. Learn to embrace change. To lead and empower oneself, change is necessary even when it hurts. That's why people talk about "growing pains"!

5. Focus your energies on those things you can influence. Live life one day at a time, celebrating the goodness of each day.

6. Teach with a "coaching philosophy." Remember to play to the strengths of each student.

7. Take time to reflect so that you can make meaning out of your experiences and recreate more positive professional experiences.

8. Maintain a balance in your life among the physical, spiritual, mental, and social dimensions.

REFERENCES AND SUGGESTIONS FOR FURTHER READING

Covey, Stephen R. *The Seven Habits of Highly Effective People.* New York: Fireside, 1989.

Hunt, David E. *Beginning with Ourselves.* Cambridge, MA: Brookline Books, Inc., 1987.

Kolb, David. A. *Experiential Learning: Experience as the Source of Learning and Development.* Englewood Cliffs, NJ: Prentice-Hall, 1984.

Manning, George, and Kent Curtis. *Stress without Distress.* Cincinnati, OH: South-Western Publishing Company, 1988.

Maxcy, Spencer J. *Educational Leadership: A Critical Pragmatic Perspective.* New York: Bergin & Garvey, 1993.

Elizabeth Fugazzi is the Community Resource Developer in the Experience Based Career Education Program of the Fayette County Public Schools in Lexington, Kentucky. She was a Mentor in NSEE's Leadership Development Program, funded by the DeWitt Wallace-Reader's Digest Fund.

Epilogue

Community Partnerships in Service-Based Experiential Learning

THE STORIES IN THIS BOOK CLEARLY SHOW THAT ELEMENTARY, MIDDLE, AND HIGH SCHOOLS ARE FOCUSING ENERGY ON ARRANGING COMMUNITY SERVICE OPPORTUNITIES FOR STUDENTS IN WAYS THAT CREATE EXPERIENTIAL LEARNING CHALLENGES. These stories demonstrate that young people can and do learn well in community settings. However, most of the emphasis is on students and their growth.

BY **ROBERT L. SIGMON**

The voices of the citizens who receive the students and the community organizations who often broker the relationships are rather muted here. For service and learning enterprises to thrive in an atmosphere of mutuality and trust among all the partners in these experiences, there is room for raising some questions, offering a tool for sustaining relationships, and suggesting some reframing of emphases.

The work of linking learning with being in service with others through sustained community partnerships can sometimes be illuminated by our personal stories, and so a story:

Following my undergraduate college experience, I found myself invited to live with and work alongside children from outcaste families in Pakistan. My jobs were to be an English teacher, coach, and residential boarding manager for the 125 boys who came to the school at the sixth-grade level. There I came face to face with realities that had not been part of my elementary, high school, and college education. The misfortunes that many children and their families suffered were numerous and often devastating. The injustices of the economic and political systems were cruelly unfair to the people who took me in and cared for me for almost three years.

What I slowly discovered was that I, along with well intentioned Pakistanis, could extend a helping hand 24 hours a day, seven days a week, 52 weeks a year, and the overall impact on the conditions which were so oppressive would not even be touched. Reflection on these misfortunes and injustices nudged me into thinking about systems influence, social justice issues, and common sense cultural meanings, much beyond the one-to-one "charity"-oriented service perspective which informed my initial work.

I slowly discovered that the people I was supposedly "serving" were in fact "serving" me. They taught me Urdu and some Punjabi; exposed me to another faith (Islam); showed me the consequences of domination by Euro-centric impulses over several centuries; challenged me regularly about "preaching brotherhood" as they showed me pictures of dogs jumping on and water hoses firing on African American citizens in my native country, the United States of America.

My schooling experiences had not prepared me for this type of learning. But other experiences had. Working on a self-sufficient farm in North Carolina with my grandparents, working as a teenager in numerous for-pay jobs, having leadership roles in a small

We have seen that all human beings want to contribute and want to learn....

Methodist church, and working with my carpenter Dad as he did his work making and repairing wood things were more useful orientations for the work I was asked to do in Pakistan than all my school-based experiences.

These meanings were slow to evolve for me. Returning from Pakistan, I worked with the American Friends Service Committee in a service-based learning program with young people in the Southeast during the Civil Rights Movement. Here in my own country, I saw the misfortunes, the injustices, the oppressive nature of systems on people. And again, the very people we were working with became our teachers in what it means to be human, to be a part of community, to be in relationships of mutual trust and care, and to be part of systems which either enable or oppress.

In talking with many of my peers over the past 30 years about what has led them into working with communities and students in a variety of community service-based experiential learning programs, I have heard stories similar to mine. They tell me that they were exposed to misfortune and injustice, saw its human horror, and were moved to try to do something about it. They have also spoken of being "over schooled," that is, told what to study, how to study it, and how well they studied it. And yet they also knew that their self-initiated experiential learning had been powerfully influential in their careers and lives.

Each time I have had a conversation with passionate folks working in community service-based experiential learning, a similar story line emerged: We have seen that all human beings want to contribute and want to learn, and when we link these two fundamental drives, we have the framework for creative and compassionate work and learning, or what some of us refer to now as "service-learning."

A MODEL FOR PARTNERSHIPS Partnership building and sustaining have become more active words in the experiential education "movement" in recent years. The concept of "partnership" involves each of the major players being clear with the other players about what it is that they seek, and what their conditions are for working together to meet their intended outcomes. Partnership also means that each person in the arrangement is teacher and learner, contributor and contributed to. The "Anatomy of a Service-Learning Partnership" chart (developed by Jennie Niles and me) is suggested as one tool for addressing this concept and realizing the potential when there is mutuality and respect across the boundaries. There are four major players in this model, and six relationships.

Two of the players are institutional and two are individual. One institutional agent is usually a business, a public agency, a nonprofit organization, or a community-based organization. This agent helps to define tasks that students address in communities. The other institutional player is a school that is seeking to broaden its range of learning opportunities through tasks with citizens and organizations in the community. The creative work of building and sustaining relationships across the widely differing goals of these two entities requires major attention and leadership. This is one of two primary relationships (A).

The second primary relationship (B) is between citizens in a community and students. Students want to learn and to contribute something within the framework defined by the citizens. Citizens invite in the students, to teach them and to get their assistance.

The other four relationships follow the perimeter of the Anatomy chart: (1) Citizens with community agencies or organizations; (2) Community organizations with students; (3) Students with their schools, particularly the faculty; and (4) the schools and faculty with their fellow citizens in communities.

ANATOMY OF A SERVICE-LEARNING PARTNERSHIP

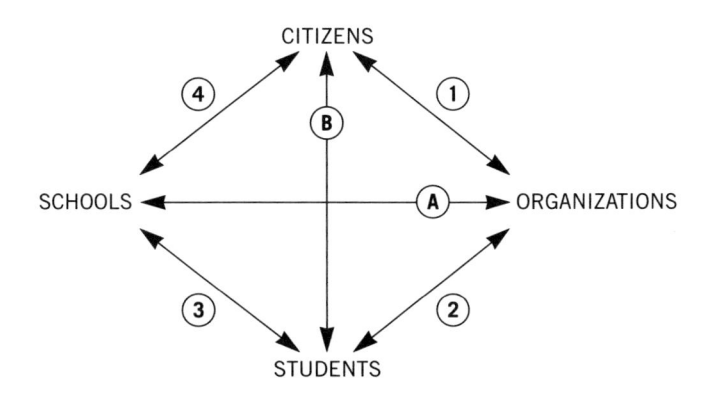

Each of the parties is in a position to be teacher and learner, to contribute and be contributed to. This assertion is rooted in the value of mutuality, of reciprocity. As each participant sees herself/himself as learner/teacher and contributed to/contributor, the conditions for a dynamic and mutually enhancing experience for all is created.

Try using this Anatomy to determine where the strengths are in the six sets of relationships within the programs you arrange. Look also for where the relationships can be more open and engaging. In using this chart with others recently, people gained new awareness about some of the dominating and patronizing assumptions in many community-based service and learning programs.

No matter how hard we try, the inherent power and control factors will be at work, leading to distorted communication in these relationships. Faculty, when involved with academically related service-based learning, have enormous power over students as a result of having to assign grades and make sure that the academic dimension is addressed. Students know this and hold back some of their questioning and insights. Likewise, agency leaders have influence over citizens who are dependent on their resources. "Services" can be withdrawn or limited if the "client" is not cooperative. Students can be dominating forces with those they want to serve and learn from when they appear before people with an attitude of "I am blessed and therefore I must help you." Within community organizations, there are many very skilled and talented community leaders who can play a dominant, sometimes manipulating, controlling card to match or better any card the faculty, the agency leaders, or students play.

In my experience, there is a 100 percent chance that these forms of domination and power imbalances will lead to distorted communication in service-learning programs, and thus dilute the potential learnings of all the participants. A first step in addressing this problem is for all the parties to acknowledge the potential of domination and power imbalances. The next step is for all the parties to work together, with the Anatomy model as a starting point. By using it, they can ask themselves and each other a series of questions to help clarify the nature of the partnership.

As each voice speaks, the other voices listen respectfully without judging. Clarifications can be addressed. At some point, ground rules for further dialogue can emerge, which call for all parties to be able to speak their own truth through their stories, put out any proposition or interpretation, or challenge any assertion, but to do it in a civil and respectful manner. In my work with this model and this inevitable problem, I have found that a provocative way to stimulate this process is to ask: *Who among the partners? Is seeking what? As defined by whom? Via what pattern of relationships?*

SHIFT IN MIND SET In my experience, the prescriptive steps just listed are ideals. Rarely do we achieve a level of undistorted communication and openness across the boundaries of the six relationships in a service-learning experience. This does not suggest, however, that we should not proceed. An awareness is one level of understanding. Once into a set of relationships in a linked service and learning experience with partners shown in the Anatomy Chart, we have the conditions set so we each can explore fundamental mind sets or "common sense cultural meanings" shaping our work.

In service-learning, two contests over common sense cultural meanings or mind sets are central to our work. These involve "service" and "learning."

Within our American culture, service systems have primarily been set up and defined in ways that tend to keep many of those served in a dependency relationship to those systems and persons who do the serving. John McKnight and John Kretzmann, authors of *Building Community from the Inside Out*, explain that the primary public resources for caring for those without means to care for themselves most often go to the providers. Many service providers speak of "providing service to those with needs." Within service-learning, a different meaning is emerging. The aim of a service activity is to engage with someone so that the service is one of mutuality, each serving the other, so that each can be more autonomous and more able to care for self and care for others. Providers in this frame of mind talk about "being in service with" rather than "providing service to." Building new common sense cultural meanings at this level is hard work, for "mutuality" and "being in service with" are not yet dominant values in service delivery practice and systems.

Or take "learning and teaching." Teaching is often seen as the practice of passing on the accumulated knowledge of the past and designing situations to help learners develop critical-thinking capacities through lectures, simulations, library reading, and exams. Learners in this mode are seen as passive, expecting to be told what to learn, how to learn, when to learn, and whether or not they have learned. In service-learning activities, teaching becomes much more

We can learn to serve and be served by our work in the world, wherever it may be.

facilitative in the sense of helping arrange external community-based environments for learning, and then creating opportunities for reflection on these experiences. Within the national debate over whether knowledge has social utility or knowledge is for knowledge's sake, the voices for reframing the common sense cultural meaning of teaching in terms of facilitation are gaining more and more visibility and credibility.

So, when we link service and learning in a partnership context of individuals and institutions with widely varying motivations and methods of working, we are stepping into a fertile, yet uncertain, arena.

A friend who is a teacher put the traditional mind set to me this way recently. "Bob, you are creating dangerous situations when you link service and learning the way you do. Don't you know that when you ask students to serve well and also be served by their interactions that you are asking them to do something very strange to them? Don't you know that when you ask students to be active participants in their own learning, to be self-initiating learners, that you are asking them to do something they have very little practice at doing while in school? Do you not know that many of the agencies serving the public are not supportive of your view of mutuality, that these agencies need the needs of folk they are serving so they can stay in business?"

Given a bent to listen, I heard this volley and sat back for the next round. She kept going strong.

"As a teacher, you have the audacity to ask me to share my students with folks in the community, go out and make connections with them, even expect these citizens to teach my students, and expect me to connect my academic discipline to what the students are experiencing. You've got some nerve, my friend. But most troubling to me is the fact that you send these kids out, green and naive and with few skills, to groups and individuals that have more than enough trouble already on their hands. Many of them do not have time or energy to be taking care of our students like this."

"Been there, heard that before," I said to myself as the past 30 years of being with students, faculty, community folk, and community organizations unfolded quickly in my memory like a newsreel. A reframed mind set or common sense cultural meaning comes out in a different voice for me, for I have seen powerful learning and creative service when service and learning are linked, rooted in the belief that everyone wants to contribute and everyone wants to learn.

We can accomplish our aims quite well, thank you, when we choose to work in partnership with one another, linking the groups identified in the Anatomy of a Service-Learning Partnership. With thoughtful planning in which all parties participate actively in defining what they seek and what they can offer, sound programs responding to my friend's concerns can be created. We can learn to serve and be served by our work in the world, wherever it may be. We can learn to be self-initiating learners. We can work diligently to overcome dominance and oppression as we name and deal with the distorted communication that emerges in response to the controlling of a few over the many. We can learn to express ourselves, listen to others, and find common ground in our differences that eventually facilitate the sustaining of just and viable communities.

The principles of mutuality and partnership suggested here are fundamental underpinnings to living and working in ways where more just relationships emerge and each person has opportunities to contribute and learn. There is no one standard for this work of linking service and learning. Nor should we expect one. We each are challenged to make our own calls and definitions about how we see it taking place in our situation. That is what is so distinctive about this movement. Most service-based learning practitioners willingly share their ideas and materials. National organizations, such as the National Society for Experiential Education, provide forums for this sharing. New insights come from all the parties regularly. Connections are made with larger movements, like the current "outreach" movement in higher education and "school success outcomes" in secondary education. The current networking via the Internet among hundreds of practitioners gives more actual practice to look at and think about.

The challenge and opportunity before each of us is to figure out what we can do within the framework we have available to create the conditions for people to contribute (serve) and grow (learn) over their lifetimes so that more just relationships and thriving communities become a reality in our culture.

REFERENCES AND SUGGESTIONS FOR FURTHER READING
McKnight, John, and John Kretzmann, *Building Communities from the Inside Out: A Path Toward Finding and Mobilizing a Community's Assets.* Evanston, IL: Center for Urban Affairs and Policy Research, Neighborhood Innovations Network, Northwestern University, 1993. Distributed by ACTA Publications, 4848 N. Clark Street, Chicago, IL 60640.

I am grateful to Paul Castelloe for assistance with reframing "common sense cultural meanings"; to Nancy Nickman for her phrase "being in service with"; to Jane Kendall for her phrasing that we all want "to contribute and grow"; to Jennie Niles for her assistance with the "Anatomy" chart; and to Gita Gulati-Partee and Bill Finger for their constructive editing of this epilogue.

> *Robert Sigmon is President of Learning Design Initiatives, a private consulting and training practice. His areas of expertise include service-based experiential learning, community partnerships, servant leadership, and self-directed learning. Bob is a founding and life-long member of NSEE.*

Appendices

Services and Publications of the National Society for Experiential Education

The National Society for Experiential Education is a nonprofit membership association and national resource center that promotes the use of learning through experience for:
- academic development
- civic and social responsibility
- career exploration
- cross-cultural awareness
- leadership development
- ethical development

NSEE's mission is to foster the effective use of experience as an integral part of education, in order to empower learners and promote the common good. Founded in 1971, NSEE assists schools, colleges, universities, and organizations in the field of experiential education, which includes:
- service-learning
- internships
- field studies
- study abroad programs
- cooperative education
- leadership development programs
- practicum experiences
- active learning in the classroom

NSEE publishes the *NSEE Quarterly*, resource papers, monographs, and books, including:
- *Combining Service and Learning: A Resource Book for Community and Public Service*
- *Service-Learning Reader: Reflections and Perspectives on Service*
- *Research Agenda for Combining Service and Learning in the 1990s*
- *The National Directory of Internships*
- *The Experienced Hand: A Student Manual for Making the Most of an Internship*
- *The Internship as Partnership: A Handbook for Campus-Based Coordinators & Advisors*
- *The Internship as Partnership: A Handbook for Host Agencies & Site Supervisors*
- *Strengthening Experiential Education within Your Institution*
- *Legal Issues in Experiential Education*
- *Origins and Implications of the AmeriCorps National Service Program*
- and other publications covering issues of Practice and Application, Rationale and Theory, and Research

NSEE's National Resource Center for Experiential and Service Learning provides information and referrals on the design and administration of experiential education programs, policy issues, research, and more. NSEE sponsors national and regional conferences and offers consulting services for those wishing to strengthen experiential education within their institution.

Benefits of NSEE membership include:

- a subscription to the *NSEE Quarterly*—to keep you informed on innovations in the field

- substantial discounts on publications, annual conference registration, consulting, and NSEE Resource Center materials—to give you the tools you need for improved practice

- opportunities to join Special Interest Groups and Networks—to connect you with colleagues across the country

- opportunities to participate in special projects—to test new experiential learning approaches

- full voting privileges as well as eligibility for election or appointment to the NSEE Board of Directors—to exercise leadership in the organization and the field

For more information or to become a member, contact NSEE:
3509 Haworth Drive
Suite 207
Raleigh, NC 27609
919/787-3263
919/787-3381 fax
nsee@datasolv.com
http://www.tripod.com/nsee

Other Resource Organizations for K–12 Experiential Education

American Youth Policy Forum (AYPF)
1001 Connecticut Avenue, NW, Suite 719
Washington, DC 20036
202-775-9731   202-775-9733 fax

The American Youth Policy Forum is a nonprofit professional development organization serving the needs of United States congressional staff and senior executive branch policy aides. AYPF provides voluntary, non-credit programs on education, employment training, and other youth development topics, and supplements these with field trips to innovative educational programs around the country.

Association for Experiential Education (AEE)
2305 Canyon Boulevard, Suite 100
Boulder, CO 80302-5651
303-440-8844   303-440-9581 fax
aeemikal@nile.com
aeepia@nile.com

The Association for Experiential Education is a nonprofit, international, professional organization with roots in adventure education, committed to the development, practice, and evaluation of experiential learning in all settings.

Service Learning/Experiential Learning Network of the
Association for Supervision and Curriculum Development (ASCD)
1250 North Pitt Street
Alexandria, VA 22314-1453
703-549-9110   703-299-8631 fax
http://www.ascd.org

The Association for Supervision and Curriculum Development is a diverse, international community of educators, forging covenants in teaching and learning for the success of all learners. The Service Learning/Experiential Learning Network is an informative, dynamic, and participative organization sponsored by ASCD. Its primary focus is to provide a forum through meetings and newsletters to share working models and ideas for effective learning.

Close-Up Foundation
44 Canal Center Plaza
Alexandria, VA 22314
800-336-5479 x350

Since its founding in 1970, the Close-Up Foundation has grown to become the largest citizenship organization in the United States. The nonprofit, nonpartisan Foundation encourages responsible and informed participation in the democratic process through educational programs, publications, and television programming for students, teachers, and senior citizens.

Coalition of Essential Schools
Brown University
Box 1969
Providence, RI 02912
401-863-3384

The Coalition of Essential Schools was established at Brown University in 1984 as a high school-university partnership. Faculties in more than 200 member schools in 37 states and one Canadian province are committed to rethinking their schools' priorities and redesigning their pedagogies, curricula, and structures.

Community Service Learning Center
333 Bridge Street, Suite 8
Springfield, MA 01103
413-734-6857   413-747-5368 fax

The Community Service Learning Center is a nonprofit organization that provides training and technical assistance for the development of community service-learning in K–12 schools and communities throughout New England.

NOTES

Constitutional Rights Foundation (CRF)
601 South Kingsley Drive
Los Angeles, CA 90005
213-487-5590   213-386-0459 fax

The Constitutional Rights Foundation offers staff development to educational organizations and schools interested in CRF's law-related education and civic participation/service-learning programs.

Corporation for National Service
1201 New York Avenue
Washington, DC 2525
202-606-5000   202-606-5271 fax

The Corporation for National Service is a federal agency that provides a broad range of opportunities for all Americans to serve their communities. Corporation programs include: AmeriCorps, a national service program that allows people to earn help paying for college through a year of service; the National Senior Service Corps, which involves people ages 55 and over in service that relates to their professional and personal interests; and Learn and Serve America, which involves students in service to their communities as part of their school experience.

Council for Religion in Independent Schools
4405 East-West Highway, #506
Bethesda, MD 20814-4536
301-657-0912   301-657-0915 fax

The Council for Religion in Independent Schools is an association of schools which serves its members by providing professional resources for moral and religious education. The Council promotes sound religious instruction and supports the ethical and spiritual development of young people with publications, curricular materials, consultations, workshops, and conferences for teachers, students, administrators, and parents.

Council of Chief State School Officers
379 Hall of the States
400 North Capitol Street, NW
Washington, DC 20001-1511
202-393-8161   202-393-1228 fax

The Council of Chief State School Officers is a nationwide nonprofit organization comprised of the 57 public officials who head the departments of elementary and secondary education in the 50 states, the District of Columbia, five extra-state jurisdictions, and the Department of Defense Dependents Schools.

Jobs for the Future (JFF)
One Bowdoin Square
Boston, MA 02114
617-742-5995   617-742-5767 fax
jff@jff.org

Jobs for the Future is a national nonprofit organization that conducts research, provides technical assistance, and proposes policy innovation on the inter-related issues of work and learning. JFF's goal is to encourage policies and practices that prepare all citizens for effective transitions between learning and work.

The Lincoln Filene Center
Tufts University
Medford, MA 02155
617-627-3453
http://www.tufts.edu/as/lfc

The Lincoln Filene Center provides training, technical assistance, and research in nonprofit management, citizenship, popular education, youth development, and community service-learning (K–16). The Center works to strengthen and develop individuals, institutions, and communities committed to a vision of society characterized by justice, equal access to resources, life-long learning, self-determination, and stewardship toward each other and the planet.

Maryland Student Service Alliance
Maryland Department of Education
200 West Baltimore Street
Baltimore, MD 21201-2295
410-767-0358   410-333-2379 fax

The Maryland Student Service Alliance is dedicated to the institution of high quality service-learning in Maryland's public school systems.

National Association for Partners in Education (NAPE)
209 Madison Street, Suite 401
Alexandria, VA 22314
703-836-4880   703-836-6941 fax

The National Association for Partners in Education provides leadership and assistance to partnership directors, educators, businesses, parents, citizens, government officials, and community-based organizations in developing collaboratives that support systematic change in education. The IDEALS project works on developing partnerships between schools, communities, and businesses in order to support the integration of service-learning as a strategy for education reform.

National Center on Education and the Economy
700 11th Street, NW, Suite 750
Washington, DC 20001
202-783-3668   202-783-3672 fax

The National Center on Education and the Economy is a nonprofit organization that engages in policy analysis and development, institutional design, technical assistance, and professional development in the arenas of student performance assessment, school-to-work transition, occupational skill standards, school and school system restructuring, and the adaptation of the private sector's most successful management and organization techniques to the needs of the education and training sector.

National Helpers Network, Inc.
245 Fifth Avenue, Suite 1705
New York, NY 10016-8728
212-679-2482 or 800-646-4623
212-679-7461 fax

The National Helpers Network, Inc., works to make service-learning a possibility for every young person. The Helpers Network assists schools and agencies in meeting the developmental needs of young adolescents through training, program development, research, advocacy, and information sharing.

The National School-to-Work Learning & Information Center
400 Virginia Avenue, Room 210
Washington, DC 20024
800-251-7236   202-401-6211 fax
stw-lc@ed.gov
http://www.stw.ed.gov

The National School-to-Work Learning & Information Center provides information, assistance, and training to build School-to-Work opportunities in the United States. The Center utilizes the latest information technology to increase the capacity of professionals, and to develop and implement School-to-Work systems across the nation. Its services are available to state and local School-to-Work offices, employers, schools, labor organizations, parents, students, and the general public.

NOTES

National Service-Learning Clearinghouse
R-290 VoTech Education Building
1954 Buford Avenue
University of Minnesota
St. Paul, MN 55108
800-808-SERV   612-625-6276 fax

The Clearinghouse's mission is to provide leadership, knowledge, and technical assistance to support and sustain service-learning programs within six primary audiences: Learn and Serve America grantees and sub-grantees, K–12 teachers and administrators, community-based organizations, teacher education programs, state and local officials, and the general public.

National Youth Employment Coalition
1001 Connecticut Avenue, NW, Suite 719
Washington, DC 20036
202-659-1064   202-775-9733 fax

The National Youth Employment Coalition was founded in 1979 as a nonprofit organization to increase the employment, education, and training opportunities for America's youth.

National Youth Leadership Council (NYLC)
1910 West County Road B
St. Paul, MN 55113
612-631-3672   612-631-2955 fax
nylcusa@aol.com

The mission of the National Youth Leadership Council is to engage young people through innovation in learning, service, leadership, and public policy. NYLC sponsors a national service-learning conference and provides technical assistance, publications, consulting services, and training institutes for K–12 educators, youth workers, policy makers, and community members.

Project Service Leadership
12703 NW 20th Avenue
Vancouver, WA 98685
360-576-5070   360-576-5068 fax

Project Service Leadership assists Pacific Northwest school districts to integrate service-learning into their curriculum. Project Service Leadership provides technical assistance, publishes resource books and a quarterly newsletter, and offers institutes for teachers.

Public/Private Ventures (P/PV)
2005 Market Street
Philadelphia, PA 19103
215-557-4400   215-557-4469 fax

Public/Private Ventures is a national nonprofit organization that seeks to improve youth policies and programs. P/PV designs, tests, and studies initiatives that increase supports and access to opportunity for teenagers in low-income communities, and provides training and technical assistance to practitioners and programs in the youth field.

Quest International
1984 Coffman Road
P.O. Box 4850
Newark, OH 43055
800-446-2700

Quest International provides the Lions-Quest Programs for educational institutions. These comprehensive K–12 programs develop essential personal, social, and character-building skills, incorporating character education and life skills, drug/violence prevention, civic values and citizenship, and learning through community service.

NOTES

NOTES

Service Learning 2000 Center
50 Embarcadero Road
Palo Alto, CA 94301
415-322-7271   415-328-8024 fax
SL2000@forsythe.stanford.edu

The Service Learning 2000 Center, a program of the Stanford Educational Collaborative of the Stanford University School of Education, provides program support, resources, and research necessary to help build quality service-learning throughout California. The Center's partners are Constitutional Rights Foundation, Haas Center for Public Service at Stanford, and the Volunteers Center of California.